Fat
Chance

Julie Hadden

Fat Chance

*Losing the Weight,
Gaining My Worth*

foreword by JILLIAN MICHAELS

Guideposts
New York, New York

Fat Chance

ISBN-13: 978-0-8249-4788-0

Published by Guideposts
16 East 34th Street
New York, New York 10016
www.guideposts.com

Distributed by Ideals Publications, a division of Guideposts
2636 Elm Hill Pike, Suite 120
Nashville, Tennessee 37214

This book has been carefully researched, and all efforts have been made to ensure the accuracy of its information as of the date published. The information contained in this book should not be considered a substitute for the advice of a qualified medical professional, who should always be consulted before beginning any new diet, exercise or other health program.

All of the procedures, poses and postures used in the exercises should be carefully studied and clearly understood before being attempted. The recipes in this book are to be followed exactly as written. The publisher cannot assume responsibility for your specific health or allergy needs. A health professional should advise you on whether the recipes and/or exercises are safe for you and your family.

A continuation of the copyright page's acknowledgments is on page 255.

Library of Congress Cataloging-in-Publication Data

Hadden, Julie.
  Fat chance : losing the weight, gaining my worth / by Julie Hadden.
    p. cm.
  ISBN 978-0-8249-4788-0
  1. Weight loss. 2. Weight loss—Psychological aspects. 3. Weight loss—Religious aspects.
I. Title.
  RM222.2.H217 2009
  613.2'5—dc22

                                          2009021927

Cover design by Mingovits Design
Cover and interior photographs by Kelly La Duke
Interior design by Laura Klynstra
Typeset by Nancy Tardi

Printed and bound in the United States of America
10 9 8 7 6 5 4 3 2 1

For Michael.

*Although my size changed many times, your love for me did not.
You're the greatest God-given gift I will ever receive.*

CONTENTS

ACKNOWLEDGMENTS

BIRTH NEVER HAPPENS without pain. But whether it involved my children, my thinner self or this book, the pain has *always* proven itself worthwhile. Thank you, first and foremost, to my family and friends—two groups that now are hard for me to tell apart. I didn't truly realize how important you were until I had to live for four months without you. Because of you, I officially have received more phone calls conveying words of encouragement, more hot meals on especially crazy days and more dinky articles cut out of the *Putnam County Courier* with my name highlighted and clipped to notes bearing sentiments like, "We're so proud of you!" than a girl could possibly know what to do with. Especially Mom, Gigi, Jenny, Great MaMa, Betty and Dad, thank you for standing in the gap for me—supporting me, encouraging me, praying for me and caring for my child—while I was away, chasing a dream. In a world where people so easily can become consumed with themselves, it's refreshing to know that good souls like you have my back.

Noah and Jaxon, you remain my primary source of inspiration for sticking with the changes I started two years ago. I count it an honor to be your mom and pray that you enjoy the happy, healthy life I've discovered—for many years to come.

I could talk about Jillian Michaels for days on end, but when it comes to summing up her value to me in a small block of text, there simply are no words. How do you thank someone who believes in you when nobody else will, who invests in you when you aren't even investing in yourself and who celebrates the most microscopic progress as though you've already met your goal? Thank you seems so inadequate, Jillian. But thank you is all I've got.

Rachelle Gardner saw my book proposal fly across her desk and was gracious enough to catch it midair. I still don't know how that proposal made it to you, Rachelle, but I do know that God's grace was involved. You are a terrific literary agent, creative champion and friend. Thank you for channeling your interest and energies my way.

There's no greater gift for a first-time author than to be introduced to a collaborator who genuinely cares about the finished product as much as you do, and Ashley Wiersma was exactly that gift. Thanks, Ash, for persisting in this process with me, for loving me as you learned my story and for believing that this book really could help change a few lives. A girl couldn't ask for a better alter ego than you.

To the NBC, Reveille and 3 Ball Productions families, thank you for giving me the opportunity of a lifetime on one of the greatest shows our generation knows. Mark Koops, J. D. Roth and Dave Broom—the inventiveness and approachability you three possess are a rare and beautiful combination. I count it pure joy to be in your orbit.

It has been a privilege to publish with the team at Guideposts. Linda Cunningham and Rebecca Maker, thank you for finding value in my story and for encouraging me to share it.

Season 4 black-team members, I owe you a debt of gratitude I will never be able to repay. Together we were cast and then outcast and then able to do what nobody thought could be done. Bill and Jim, the brothers I never had; Jez, my soul-twin, separated at birth; Isabeau, my bossy little sister; and Hollie, the one I *still* talk to until long into the night— you five friends are family whom I love with no holds barred.

Lastly, I feel grateful to my God. I was singing a praise song one day and realized that the lyrics perfectly capture what I want to say to him about this agonizingly wonderful book-writing debut.

To my everlasting Father, whose light will shine when all else fades,
never ending, Your glory goes beyond all fame,
and the cry of my heart is to bring You praise
from the inside out

Choose to Bet on You

BY JILLIAN MICHAELS

I 'VE BEEN AN adrenaline junkie my entire adult life, and one of my favorite rush-inducing pleasures is racing motorcycles. I'm no pro, but I do follow the pros. And a guy who caught my attention more than a decade ago is Valentino Rossi, one of the most successful racers of all time.

Nearly one hundred race-wins before the age of thirty—the guy was incredible, but so was his bike. And after he claimed back-to-back Grand Prix championships a few years ago, skeptics began to wonder how much of Rossi's success was due to sheer talent and how much was due to the ride. So, in a move that surprised fans and critics alike, he switched bikes. Rossi let his contract with Honda expire and signed with rival manufacturer Yamaha, maker of an undeniably inferior machine.

Talk about going all-in on a highly unlikely bet.

When Julie Hadden showed up on *The Biggest Loser*, I was unimpressed, to say the least. She was smaller than the other contestants. She cried all the time. And she lost a grand total of two pounds her first week on the show. *I'll just give this poor girl a few helpful hints*, I thought, *and put her back on a plane headed home.*

But as if reading my mind, Julie did something that probably shocked us both: She actually began to prevail.

People often ask me what it takes to make it through an abrasive, aggressive, confrontational experience like *The Biggest Loser*, and my answer's always the same: courage—and a lot of it. If you want to change your life, you have to first be brave enough to face the truth of who you are, brave enough to look deep inside, to take responsibility for what you find there, to stop behaving like the victim you believe yourself to be and to learn to use your faculties for something *other* than absolute self-destruction.

As I trained Julie those first few times, I saw the courage of a champion peeking through. She did not whine, she did not complain, she did not stop and she did not quit. As stronger contestants unraveled, it was Julie who kept pushing through.

Some judge of character I am, right?

Early into the season, after an especially tortuous workout one morning, I pulled aside a very sweaty Julie, looked intently into her eyes and told her the story of Valentino Rossi. "It wasn't about the bike," I explained. "His victories came because *he* was well-made. And although anybody in a right mind would tell me to bet on the bigger, stronger guys on this campus, I'm choosing to bet on *you*, Julie. You're my Yamaha."

For four months straight, Julie endured the worst that my beatings could offer a girl and emerged a woman who knew her own strength. What was flabby became firm. What was slow became fast. What was timid became brave. And *nothing* could hold her back now.

The two years following his very bold move, Valentino Rossi would capture back-to-back Grand Prix titles—and do it, unbelievably, on a Yamaha. After his victory lap on Valencia's course in Spain, Rossi swung himself off his bike, fell to his knees and planted a kiss on the track. Funny how I witnessed a similar reaction from a thirty-something stay-at-home mom while she was netting a victory of her own. Several weeks before the finale, overcome by the joy that accompanies finding courage she didn't know she had, Julie Hadden fell to her knees and kissed the scale that in the end would declare her a full 45 percent thinner than she'd been.

Back at the finale, as she sobbed her way toward an ear-to-ear smile,

I shook my head in absolute admiration of the "too-small, too-weak" girl who'd proven her critics dead wrong. It was a picture of courage personified that I'll remember for a long, long time.

I'm a firm believer in the idea that you can build courage in the same way you build physical strength. While most fat people can't curl twenty-pound weights their first day in the gym, a few weeks into their regimen, you wouldn't believe how their capabilities have changed. In the same way, even those who are utterly paralyzed by panic and fear will one day emerge victorious and strong, if they suck it up and do the work that transformation demands.

The process played out for me starting in my early teens. I was in desperate need of a catalyst and a motivator, of an educator and an encourager, when I got all of that and much more. A martial-arts instructor stepped into my life, and despite my hefty weight, my cavernous wounds and my wavering self-esteem, he bet on me to win. It was a vote of confidence that propelled me into the soul-level passion for fitness I've been thriving on ever since.

If you're in need of an advocate who will cheer you on toward change, I've got just the one for you. Let Julie—and her compelling book, *Fat Chance*—inspire you and change you and draw out your courage. You are worth the life you long to live. You are capable of bringing it to pass. And the time has come for you to finally bet on *you* to win.

Fat
Chance

Part One

Moment of Recognition:

Something's Got to Give

CHAPTER 1

From "Why Me?" to "Why Not Me?"

YOU KNOW YOU'RE FAT when you wake up one morning and find that your gargantuan breasts have somehow merged with your double chin to form a mountain of flesh that is completely blocking your line of sight to the alarm clock. That oh-so-suffocating day dawned for me in March 2007, just thirty days before I hoped to be cast for Season 4 of the reality TV show, *The Biggest Loser.* "For the *love!* This is ridiculous," I thought as I struggled to part the great divide and find the time.

My mind raced as I took in the neon numbers staring back at me. "Ten o'clock? Noah is going to be *so* late for school." But as suddenly as it had appeared, my panic dissipated into peace as the familiar smell of cinnamon rolls wafted underneath the closed bedroom door. *Ah, Saturday.* My husband Mike had let me sleep in, bless his soul.

For quite some time I hadn't been sleeping well, but the previous night had broken all records for insomnia; I was restless every single hour. I'd been struggling with the general aches and pains associated with being obese, but the little stuff of being overweight was now becoming big stuff—simple things like breathing were becoming increasingly difficult. And I assumed that if I made the show, at some point I'd need to breathe.

As I lay flat on my back that morning and tried in vain to catch my breath, I looked down at my puffed-up hands and wiggled my fingers—ten little sausages in their casings. The rest of me was no better off. My arms, my hips, my legs, my feet—every part of me felt stretched to its limit, tender and achy and numb. It was an all-over hurt I was experiencing, like the hurt after a car wreck. *Truly*, I thought, as if realizing it for the very first time, *something has got to give.*

For a split second, I thought back to the documentaries I'd seen on TV where emergency workers who were trying to remove severely overweight people from their bedrooms had to cut a giant hole in a wall and pluck them out with a cherry picker or hoist them up with the same contraption that is used to lift a whale. I cut my eyes toward the bedroom window and exhaled a sigh of relief when I saw no EMTs standing outside.

I rolled over to my side, my big belly gurgling as it shifted and flopped down onto the mattress as though it were a separate entity entirely and thought, "Seriously. I am *big*!" It should have concerned me that despite these all-too-real reminders that my size had gotten out of control, I continued to fantasize about those cinnamon rolls. But still I made my way to the kitchen, an addict in search of her fix.

FAT-CAMP DREAMS AND TWINKIE WISHES

Having a cinnamon-roll addiction doesn't exactly contribute to a figure that's svelte. I'd ballooned to more than two hundred pounds by the time I auditioned for *The Biggest Loser*, but interestingly, at five-feet-two-inches tall I remained the smallest person in the running for the cast that season. The irony wasn't lost on me, the one who always had been the Large Marge in the room.

Despite my excitement at the prospect of being on national TV, auditioning wasn't my idea. In the summer of 2006, my girlfriend Melissa found out that producers from *The Biggest Loser* were hosting an open casting call in our hometown of Jacksonville, Florida. Shortly thereafter, my cell phone rang, and I spotted Melissa's number on the screen. "Julie!" she exclaimed as soon as I picked up. "You're *not* going to believe who's in town!"

After indulging a few of my unsuccessful guesses, she enthusiastically spat out the answer: "*The Biggest Loser*! They're doing an open casting call!"

"*Really?*" I cheered.

"Yes!" said skinny, never-has-struggled-with-her-weight Melissa. "And ... well, I think you'd be ... *great* ... on that show."

"Girl, are you calling me fat?" I accused playfully.

In a tiny voice that matched her tiny self: "Well . . ."

I first started watching *The Biggest Loser* during Season 2, and while I could relate to the contestants, I didn't see myself *or* them as "morbidly obese," to quote the show's announcer. I focused so much on what their "after" state would look like that I guess the "before" reality somehow faded away. These people were polished and pretty pursuers of a completely new life, and I couldn't help but cheer them on.

That season, I resonated most with Suzy Preston—a wisecracker whose witty remarks and animated expressions had me captivated from the start. She had short, blonde hair like me and at five-feet-four with ninety-five pounds to lose, we seemed to share similar dimensions. I'd watch Suzy and the other contestants compete in challenges, fight through temptations, work out every now and then and think, "That's something I could actually do!" Much like a high school swimmer watching Michael Phelps go for gold in the Olympics, I saw the people on the screen living my dream and wanted more than anything to join them.

> I loved watching *The Biggest Loser.* I'd stop by the grocery store each week, pick up a new snack, and curl up on the couch to watch every episode. During challenges, I'd look at my husband Mike and say, "I could do *that.*"
>
> Yeah, right, Miss Big Talker who's sitting on her big ol' butt.

Since childhood, that "dream" had been to go to fat camp. My chubbiest friend at the time, Tammie, and I even made a pact that if either of us ever won the lottery, we'd take the other one to fat camp. Of course, we *also* agreed that we'd probably be the most rebellious campers the camp had ever seen. We'd be the ones plotting ways to break into the snack shack late at night and eat our way through boxes of Snickers and Twinkies, figuring when you're as rich as we'd be, you could eat whatever you want.

Tammie had struggled with her weight as long as I had, and both of us knew that the only way we were going to drop a hundred pounds each was if we signed up for a massive kick in the pants. These days, people look to gastric-bypass surgery or a Lap-Band insertion. Back then, assuming you didn't care to have your jaw wired shut, fat camp was the do-or-die choice. But honestly, what's more fun than camp? With that rhetorical question in mind, I gathered up my purse, my courage and my assumptions about life on *The Biggest Loser*, and I headed for the casting call.

MAKING THE CUT

I asked half a dozen friends and family members to come with me to my *The Biggest Loser* audition, but every one of them declined. They loved the show and supported my desire to try out, but given the fact that 250,000 people were auditioning for it, they thought my efforts were a colossal waste of time. To be fair, the odds *were* staggering, and being cast on a nationwide reality show just doesn't happen to people "we" know. Plus, there was the fact that I wasn't exactly famous for my track record of completing the things I set out to do. I always had wonderful intentions, but somehow, someone or something seemed to distract me from accomplishing the goal. And so I would go to the casting call alone, me, the one who doesn't even go to the *bathroom* by herself.

I also asked every overweight person I knew to go to the audition with me, but each person said no. "Have you *seen* what they make contestants do?" they all asked. I wasn't sure if they were referring to the challenges or to the Spandex weigh-in attire, but either way, they wanted *nothing* to do with that show.

As I entered the atrium of our local mall, I realized that my friends and family might have been right. The main floor was flooded with hundreds of prospective contestants, some with neon poster-board "Pick Me!" signs in hand, some with colorful Afro wigs, one in a full-body sumo-wrestler costume. Handprinted signs pointed me toward the line where I would stand for hours, left to my insecure thoughts about how I stacked up next to the far more interesting people all around me. *Fat chance*—it's what I remember thinking about the likelihood that I'd actually make the cut, lose the weight, change my life for good.

A casting assistant from the show ushered us into a meeting room six at a time. As soon as my group entered and sat down, a tall, thin, official-looking man with thick, gelled-back hair that made him look exactly like John Stamos during his *Full House* days glanced at us and said, "Tell us about yourselves, one by one." He looked at the woman sitting at the other end of the line from me. "We'll start with you, and keep it brief. Ten minutes and the bell will ring, which will signal your group to leave."

I did the math and concluded that even if the other five people talked fast, I wasn't going to have much time to share my story. What's more, I realized in that moment that I didn't even have a story to share.

The first woman piped up with a slow, steady twang. "Well," she said, "I'm fat because I drive an ice-cream truck for a living."

The hurricane victim made it all the way through the casting process and wound up being a contestant on the same season as I did. Told you she'd be stiff competition!

John Stamos chuckled and then asked several follow-up questions about life on an ice-cream truck before moving on to the next person, who had lost everything in the wake of Hurricane Katrina. An ice-cream-truck driver and a hurricane victim? How was I supposed to compete with that?

The third person was a beautiful young woman who explained that she was getting married soon and wanted to lose weight before her wedding day. She was so desperate for change in her life that evidently she even was willing to postpone her wedding date for a shot on the show. The other two had equally compelling and heartrending tales to tell, and as the conversation made its way down the line everything around me blurred out of focus as a full-on panic attack set in. "I'm Julie," I practiced silently. *Now, what do I say after that?*

Finally that gelled-haired head swiveled my way, and I knew it was my turn to speak. Before I even said my name, I leaned forward, craned my neck toward the other end of the row, and with a dose of recognition and a thicker-than-usual twang said, "I *knew* you looked familiar! I was the fat lady chasing your ice-cream truck yesterday! You shoulda slowed that thing down . . . I was hungry!"

Waves of laughter filled the room as I sat back against my chair and let my shoulders fall. When the impromptu moment eventually passed, I said simply and with a genuine smile, "Kidding aside, I'm Julie Hadden— a stay-at-home mom here in Jacksonville." And with that, the bell rang.

⌒〜∧〜⌒

I dialed Mike's cell phone number the moment I exited the room. "You're already done?" he asked. The shock in his voice was undeniable.

"Yeah," I admitted. "I'm glad I did it, but it's pretty much over." Of course this news came as no surprise to Mike. With each syllable I spoke, I was validating his pipe dream suspicions. We agreed to meet at the food court to grab lunch and chat about the day. Partway through our meal I noticed the casting people walking by. They grinned at me, glanced down at my greasy oversized slice of pizza, and probably fully understood why I needed to audition for their show. "So, it's really over?" Mike asked, after they'd passed. "You're done, just like that?"

I explained that I'd overheard someone in my group of six ask one of the show's representatives what would happen next. "We'll contact you if we're interested," came the reply.

The next day, after church, lunch and a long and lovely nap—made possible by my wise husband's thinking to turn off the phone ringers—my life completely and dramatically changed. It was almost eleven o'clock at night when Mike remembered to turn on the ringers again, and soon after, he noticed that we had six voice mail messages waiting. "Julie!" he shouted moments later. "*The Biggest Loser* people have called six times and want you to audition again. If you don't contact them by eleven, they're going to give away your spot!"

I bounced up and down and squealed like a giddy schoolgirl. And then I took a deep breath and called them back.

FINDING A STORY TO SHARE

The casting director's request was a no-brainer. "We'd like to interview you again," he said, "but the date we have in mind falls on the Fourth of July. Can you make it?"

Was he serious? It could have been Christmas and I would have gone.

July Fourth arrived, and as I entered the appointed hotel room I noticed a single video camera positioned to my right. Despite the small crowd of onlookers, I immediately felt put at ease—both in my surroundings and in my own skin. Amazing what the prospect of real life-change can do for a person.

Minutes into my discussion with my interviewer, I slipped off my shoes, folded my legs up under me on the couch, shrugged my hands to chin-level as if surrendering all hopes of self-preservation and said, "Ask me anything you want."

We got through questions about how my weight affected my sex life, what my friends would think about my being on a reality TV show and what aspects of my body I most disliked. At that point, I pulled off the cardigan portion of my sweater-set and tugged on a flabby underarm. "Well, this, for starters," I said. Uncharacteristically, I then stood up, twisted into an about-face and jiggled my well-endowed butt. "And I don't need to clarify why *this* is a problem."

Just before I left the room, I was handed a piece of paper by the casting assistant. "Julie, I want you to make a video that shows your struggle in everyday life," she explained. "Send it to this address, and make sure you write, 'Attention: Christmas Package,' on the envelope in big bold print, okay?"

I knew then that I might have more than a fat chance.

Who knows how much time elapsed, but eventually, after I had complied with the original request for a video, I received another phone call from someone requesting a second one. "Show us a few more of the realities that you face," came the instruction.

My patient husband trailed me with a video camera for two days straight, capturing real life as a large woman. One scene showed me trying to make Noah's top-bunk bed by standing on the bottom bunk; as soon as I shift my weight to tuck in the sheet, the entire bed almost falls apart. Another scene features me folding clothes. First you see Noah's tiny tighty-whities and then me holding up a pair of what I affectionately referred to as my big-girl panties. Still another shot is of me attempting in vain to squeeze my oversized self into an old size-eight pageant dress that had been hiding in the recesses of my closet. Despite the sobering realities depicted in those images, I like to think my lighthearted, buoyant self shone through.

At some point that fall, I received word from an NBC representative that the show had gone into hiatus. "And we don't know when it will resume," he admitted.

Months and months went by, which really proved challenging for someone who typically spent her days fretting about how to lose weight. How was I supposed to get motivated about losing weight now that my fat-camp dream, a la *The Biggest Loser*, might just come true? Regardless what NBC said, I still had great hopes that I'd be cast. Soon enough I'd have all the help I needed—for now, I figured, I'd live it up.

My hopes crested when I finally heard from the show's lawyer. Evidently, I needed to submit to an extensive background check, which to me meant that I really was in the running to be selected as a cast member. My hunches were right, and sometime in April 2007, I was informed that I had made it to the final audition and would need to fly to Los Angeles to be pitted against thirty-five others who were vying for spots on the show.

The naysayers in my life were stunned.

Coming from Florida, I was the last person to arrive in LA. In short order, I was escorted to meetings with more interviewers, a psychologist, a medical doctor and a nutritionist, as well as told to complete what must have been a five-hundred-question survey that probed my family history, my relational intelligence and my reasons for being fat. At last, I was taken to a prep session for what I was told would be my "final interview."

I entered a large meeting room at the hotel and remember thinking that I had never seen so many beautiful fat people in my entire life. I immediately took note of my would-be-teammate Isabeau, although I didn't yet know her name. *Will they cast two girls with platinum-blonde hair?* I wondered skeptically.

We were asked to have a seat, and then the show's executive producer, J. D. Roth, said, "We want to hear your story in this interview. We don't want you to be especially happy or sad or contrive *anything* that's not true of you. We simply want to understand why you're here."

With that we were dismissed to our hotel rooms and told that within the next three-hour block, we'd be called down for our interview.

The entire elevator ride to my floor, I cried. After making my way into my room, I let the door slip shut behind me, I fell onto the bed, I dialed Mike's cell phone, and as soon as he picked up, I cried some more. "I don't have a story!" I sobbed. "I have to go down there and tell my story, and I *still* don't have a story to tell!"

My gracious and loving husband spoke whatever words I needed to hear just then, and by the time I emerged for my interview, I felt competent and capable and strong.

S potlights shone on a single red velvet chair, positioned in the center of the interviewing room. Surrounding it was an arc of forty chairs or so, dimly lit and possessed by faces I could not see. *Intimidating*—it's the only word that came to mind.

As I took the seat that obviously was intended for me, I chuckled nervously and said, "Whew! I'm sweating like a Twinkie at a Weight Watchers meeting."

A nameless, faceless voice piped up from the back. "Are you nervous, Julie?"

"Like a long-tailed cat in a room full of rockers!" I shot back.

Laughing, another voice cheered, "Give us another one!"

But I couldn't fulfill the request. "Sorry," I said with a shrug and a smile. "That's all I've got."

The lighthearted exchange calmed my spirits and settled me for what was to come. At some point, someone said, "So, tell us about you."

I wasted no time in telling the truth. "The first thing you should know is that you absolutely sent me over the edge this morning, with the whole we-want-to-know-your-story plea. I cried all the way to my room!"

"Why?" several people said in unison.

"Because I don't *have* a story. Or at least that's what I thought. But the more I considered it, the more I realized that I *do* have a story to tell. And it's the same story so many wives and mothers would tell you, if they were sitting here instead of me. I love my family, and it's with the best of intentions that I invest everything I have in them. But at the end of the day there's nothing left for me. I am my own last priority."

I paused to collect my thoughts and then continued. "I'm tired of being this way. I'm tired of looking like I'm headed to a funeral every day, with all the black I wear. I'm tired of waiting until nightfall, when no one's around to see me, to play outside with my son. I'm tired of worrying about whether I'll live to see my son grow up, or whether I'll sit by my husband in a rocking chair when we're eighty, or whether I'll even make it to forty years of age. I'm *tired of being fat*."

The room was strangely quiet as I spoke, and when I finished, silent tears rolled down my cheeks. I should have been curious about what my interviewers were thinking, but I was not. I had spoken straight from the heart and could only hope that it was enough.

In the end, of course, it was.

SAVIOR ON A STEEL HORSE

Making the shift from being a viewer of *The Biggest Loser* to being a contestant on the show proved far more challenging than what I had expected. At eleven o'clock at night following the final round of interviews, eighteen of us received a knock on our hotel door and instructions to meet downstairs in one of the on-site ballrooms. Once seated, J. D. Roth congratulated us on successfully completing such a rigorous casting process and informed us that, officially, we comprised the cast of *The Biggest Loser, Season 4.* In response, some laughed, some cried and still others cheered.

"But let me tell you what you're in for," J.D. cautioned. And with that the stories began to unfold. As he talked about how incredibly difficult the next four months would be for us—physically, mentally, emotionally—I felt my stomach start to churn. What had I gotten myself into? I knew only time would tell.

My castmates and I had exactly one hour to pack up our things, place phone calls to loved ones and turn over cell phones and laptops to production assistants' hands. When Mike answered the phone, I heard his groggy, "Hello?" and remembered that it was 3:00 AM his time. With equal parts shock and awe, I said, "I did it! I made the show!"

In that moment, the same husband who thought it would take divine intervention for me to land a spot on reality TV believed in miracles once more. I sat on the floor of my hotel room and cried precious tears as he conveyed how proud of me he was. "When do I get to see you again?" he finally asked.

"I don't know!" I replied. And as the words came out, I realized that I really *didn't* know when I'd see him again. Or when I'd see my six-year-old, Noah. Or when I'd be back home. "I have no idea what all of this means. Really. I don't know where I'm going, I don't know what I'll be doing, I don't know when we'll be able to talk again."

A wave of trepidation washed over me, but I knew that I had to go. "Take care of my baby, and tell him I love him. And Mike? I love you so much too."

I wouldn't be allowed to communicate with my family for more than two full months after I found out I'd made the show. All Mike knew was that I was living in California, and that I was trying to lose some weight.

O ne of the early twists of Season 4 was that six of the eighteen original contestants were sent home the very first day. Or so we had been told. We had all been taken to a desert, where we raced each other down a mile-long sand dune in an attempt to reach trainers Bob Harper and Kim Lyons, who had parachuted to the bottom of the hill. The two contestants to reach Bob and Kim first would be deemed team captains and given the distinction of selecting their own team members. Bob would then train his six blue-team members. Kim would train her red-team six. And those of us who were left unchosen on the sand lot would simply be sent home.

It came as no surprise to me that the smallest of the eighteen—yours truly—was left without a team. In that moment my greatest fear was being realized. What I was most afraid of had nothing to do with adopting a new diet, enduring a grueling workout routine or even facing America in nothing but Spandex and a sports bra as I broadcasted the weight I had been lying about for years. What I was *most* afraid of was making it all the way to the show and then being sent home before I'd lost a single pound.

Despite a lifetime of serial rejection, somehow this rejection seemed the worst one of them all.

After the red and blue teams were driven away by bus, the remaining six of us walked toward the café where we'd be picked up and carted off to the airport. But just as we neared the entrance, a motorcycle could be heard approaching from the distance. I stopped in my tracks, took in the size and shape of the person on the bike and said to my teammates, "Please let that be Jillian."

Jillian Michaels, a *machine* of a personal trainer, might as well have been riding on a white horse, for the sense of rescue we all felt. She pulled off her helmet, let her hair cascade down and with the spunk that only Jillian can manifest, said, "You just *wish* you were going home, dudes! You're my new black team!"

At the sight of my weight-loss savior named Jillian, my hopes for change were resurrected. I bent at the waist, clutched my knees with both hands, and wailed like an inconsolable baby.

Even though it seemed like Jillian rode up immediately after the bus pulled away with the red and blue team members aboard, in reality, the six of us outcasts sat around for more than an hour before she arrived, lamenting the fact that we were obviously headed home.

HERMOSA HORRORS

The black team really was a secret from the other players and trainers, but after we finally made our appearance, we learned that some of the contestants had suspected a third team. Evidently, the culprit was the kitchen floor. In a house that boasted red and blue comforters in the teams' bedrooms, red and blue towels in the teams' bathrooms, and red and blue rugs in the entryway, the kitchen featured red, blue and *black* tiles. Observant types figured that something was up.

Since the existence of the black team was supposed to be a secret for the first part of the season, we had to stay in hiding until our grand entrance into *The Biggest Loser* house. So, for two weeks, our workouts were held in Hermosa, a town a hundred miles from campus.

Jillian Michaels' objective on day one every season is to separate the wheat from the chaff. All she wants to know is who is serious and who is not. Who will persevere and who will not. Who can handle the fire and who will utterly melt. At one point during our first workout, I heard a teammate whine, "Jillian, I'm gonna throw up!" The response I overheard gave me a little window into my trainer's soul. "Then puke and keep on moving!"

Jillian had a special disdain for those who threatened to quit. "You wanna quit? Then quit!" she'd shout right in their face. "It'll be one less person I have to deal with!"

For two and a half hours, our newly formed black team exercised. I'm not sure what I expected going into that session, but I know it was not what occurred. I thought that since my teammates and I were so fat, she'd go easy on us. After all, what can a bunch of overweight couch potatoes do the very first time they work out? I envisioned a nice tour of our surroundings, some time to relax and get to know each other, maybe an afternoon snack.

Clearly, I was mistaken.

The fierce and feisty trainer I had grown to love from the safety of my living room couch certainly was not the same person screaming at me—with viciousness to spare—to hold my big self in plank position for thirty more seconds. Jillian Michaels was *far* meaner in person than I imagined her to be, and I had a feeling I was in for a very long afternoon.

We convened on a large patch of desert sand dressed in team-honoring all-black attire. That would have been fine, had it not been ninety-six steamy degrees outside. To the tune of Jillian's rants and raves—"Why weren't you chosen by the other teams? Tell me why you weren't chosen!" and "Go faster! *Now!*"—we were told to flip five-foot-diameter tractor tires for a hundred yards, and then to flip them right back. We were forced to wind-sprint forward and back-pedal back, commando-crawl our way through six inches of blazing-hot sand, hoist twenty-five-pound sand bags above our heads while doing jumping jacks and lug those same bags up a massive hill using rappelling ropes. When the end of the torture came, my muscles were yelping and I wanted to die—a fate I was sure would feel better than this.

Several times that afternoon, I was so overheated that I thought I might faint. While standing on a hill between drills at one point, Jillian walked directly toward me with a water bottle in hand, unscrewed the top, splashed half the water up into my face and turned around to walk off. I remember gasping for breath underneath the ice-cold sensation and realizing only afterward that by reawakening my senses she'd saved my hide.

As I look back now, it occurs to me that an entire camera crew was on-site every moment of our impossible first workout. And while one might think that vanity and pride would cause a person to perform with a little more poise while cameras are rolling, I was so engulfed by physical pain that I couldn't have cared less who was there. I liken it to when you deliver a baby; during those critical moments of pushing, do you really care if anyone is watching? The physical rigors of your situation cause you to focus in laserlike fashion on nothing but getting that child born, and in the desert that day, the baby I was birthing was named "Living through Jillian's Workout without Weeping, Fainting or Sudden Death."

THE DAY I GOT KICKED OUT

In addition to working out in the desert, Jillian made accommodations for our team to exercise in a nearby gym. She knew that if the six of us were to stand a chance of competing against the red and blue teams upon entering

Every time my teammates and I worked out in the Hermosa gym, we felt like bona fide stars. Amazing how much attention you receive when you're flanked by Jillian Michaels!

The Biggest Loser house, we needed real workouts on real equipment in a real fitness setting that only a gym could provide.

Without exception every black-team member had endured one form of reconstructive surgery or another. Well, except Isabeau, I guess. Jim, Bill, Jez and I had knee surgery, and six months prior to the show Hollie had ankle surgery. No wonder we were the "unchosen" ones: We were all but broken-down!

About a week into our desert-then-gym-then-gym-then-desert routine, I got a taste of Jillian's wrath, this time aimed directly at me.

Since I'd had two knee surgeries and been sedentary for years, the incessant workouts had taken quite a toll on my knees. Still, I did everything that Jillian told me to do and worked as hard as I possibly could. One afternoon a teammate and I were running on side-by-side treadmills at the gym, when Jillian approached me and said with a scowl, "Get out."

I hit the emergency stop button on the treadmill, wiped off my face with my towel and craned my ear toward Jillian. Surely I had misunderstood her.

"What?" I asked.

"Get out!"

My head was spinning. I hadn't been slacking off. I was doing exactly what she told me to do. Why was I being kicked out of the gym?

"Jillian, I'm doing . . ."

"Out," she said. "Now."

Being the smallest person on the team, I knew that I needed every minute in the gym that I could get, to avoid being the first one voted out.

"But *why*?" I pleaded.

Jillian looked at me with disdain. "Why are you even *here*?" she asked.

"I want to lose weight!" I cried.

"Get out," came the reply, as she turned on her heels and strolled away.

I reached for my water bottle and made my way toward the exit as my entire slack-jawed team looked on.

I paused momentarily and met Jillian's gaze. "When can I come back?" I whispered.

She stormed toward me. "This whole 'I'm the smallest . . . I'm the weakest link' deal of yours is nothing more than a *cover*. I want to know what you're *really* made of, why you're *really* here. Until you quit saying, 'Why me?' and instead start saying, 'Why *not* me,' I want you gone."

A production assistant took me back to the hotel where my team was staying. I staggered up the flights of stairs to my third-floor room, cursing the absence of an elevator with every step. Tossing my water bottle on the floor as I entered the room, I grabbed my Bible from the nightstand and plopped down on the edge of my bed. "What in the *world* . . ." I said to no one in particular. Completely demoralized, I sighed as I untied my shoelaces and began to pull off my right shoe. Immediately, a stream of sand poured out onto the floor. I eyed the sand, the dirt and the grime, and all I could think about was how sick I was of the desert, of exercise, of this entire experience.

I emptied my shoe until the sand quit flowing and then brushed off the sole with my hand. My palm was caked with crusty sand, and as I stared at it through a cloud of tears, God brought to mind a passage of Scripture I've always loved. Psalm 139:17–18 says, "How precious to me are your thoughts, O God! How vast is the sum of them! Were I to count them, they would outnumber the grains of sand." I couldn't even count the grains on one *inch* of my hand, let alone my whole palm. To think about every grain of sand on every beach and in every desert in the world? It made my head spin.

Years prior I had read that there are roughly seventeen thousand grains in every teaspoon of sand. What came to mind as I sat slumped over on a scratchy comforter on top of a squeaky bed in a dark room of a budget motel was that if God's thoughts toward me were so gracious and numerous, then he obviously saw me differently than I saw myself. It would be the first of many spiritual lessons I'd learn while on the show.

"Why *am* I here?" I said out loud, echoing Jillian's demands. Since my first audition at the open casting call in Jacksonville, I had considered myself the smallest, most unlikely person to be cast on a show like *The Biggest Loser*. I had considered myself the weakest link. But why?

The answer came to me in waves, as if whispered from God himself.

I had spent so much of my life being held back because my weight was excessive. Now I felt like I was being held back because I was too light. Would I ever be "just right"? I was told by the cast and crew alike that I was funny and fun-loving, that I'd be the last one to cause any trouble for anyone, that I was a "great girl." But nobody thought I could actually win; I didn't have enough weight to lose, and on a big-people show, the biggest people take home the prize.

Somewhere along the way, I had turned over my belief to their doubts. But thanks to some divine insight from a very loving God, that would all change the next day.

THE LIFE I WAS MADE TO LIVE

The following morning, although uninvited, I showed up at the gym with the rest of my teammates. Jillian's reception was more than a little cold. "Hey," she chirped toward me, her arms crossed against her chest, her head cocked and looking totally self-assured. "Why are you here?"

With fresh resolve, I squared my shoulders and said, "I'm here because I *deserve* to be here. And I'm here because I'm determined to live the life that I was made by God to live. I can work hard, Jillian. I can *do* this." All at once, I felt "just right."

As if in slow motion, Jillian eyed me up and down. I stared right back, hoping she couldn't see my fast-thumping heart through my jumbo-sized sports bra. As I took in her face, I could have sworn I saw the beginnings of a grin. The edges of her lips twitched upward ever so slightly as a single word made its way out of her mouth: "Excellent."

With that, my teammates and I worked out.

Being forced by Jillian to explore why I really wanted to lose weight was a beautiful gift from God. Not only did it pave the way for a deep and abiding friendship with the hard-core trainer I'd eventually come to love, but also it solidified early on my desire to achieve both a new waistline and a new life.

Despite all of the blood, sweat and tears—and there had been plenty of each already—I reasoned that if persevering in my *The Biggest Loser* experience could right the wrongs of thirty-five years of settling for less than the life God had in store for me, then persevere I would. And perhaps even win the whole thing too. After all, *someone* had to take home the title, right?

I figured, Why not me?

Determine the Source of Your Strength

Most obese people I know have dangerously low self-esteem. That certainly was the case with me. I had bought the lie that said that my value as a human being rose and fell in direct proportion to the number that showed up on the scale. When my weight went down, my value went up. When my weight went up, well . . . you get the idea.

Immediately after I was cast on *The Biggest Loser*, I wondered what I had gotten myself into. Within a couple of weeks' time, I wasn't so sure I wanted to work out six hours a day. I wasn't so sure I wanted to live with a bunch of overweight, cutthroat strangers. I wasn't so sure I wanted to serve as the poster girl for weight loss. I was a no-name with no special story who suddenly had been thrust into the limelight, and something about that situation felt very intimidating to me.

"I'm not cut out for this, God!" I'd protest in vain. "Surely you picked the wrong girl!"

I felt fearful and incapable and doubtful and weak, but God knew he'd made no mistake.

One of my favorite Bible characters has always been Moses—a guy who was also handpicked for a role that he didn't quite see himself playing. I'm not sure how things really went down the day that Moses was told of his task, but I like to think a temper-tantrum was involved, complete with a fair amount of pouting and stomping of feet: "I can't string two sentences together without stut-stut-stuttering myself into oblivion, and you want me to go convince some big-shot leader to set an entire nation free? Come on, God. Get real."

Moses thought that God had picked the wrong guy for the job. But God knew he'd made no mistake.

If I learned one thing during all my childish displays of fear and doubt along the way, it's that it's okay to be weak. Because in my weakness, God's strength is best revealed.

Clearly, I'm no Moses. But whether you're asked to win over a tyrannical leader like Pharoah or face Jillian Michaels in the gym, it helps if you know ahead of time the unfailing source of your strength.

CHAPTER 2

What Fat Stole from Me

THIS MORNING UNFOLDED like most weekday mornings do since being back from *The Biggest Loser.* I pulled on exercise clothes, shoveled apple slices into my mouth and headed to a local park to meet my trainer Margie for a seventy-five-minute workout.

If Jillian Michaels taught me the value of exercise, Margie Marshall now forces me to live out that value on a near-daily basis. I adore Margie, and I also despise her—a paradox that is fully warranted, given the torture chamber her cheery classes always prove to be. Take this morning's workout, for example.

> If a workout is an hour long, I think of it like a TV show. Water breaks become commercial breaks, and I know that after five of them, I'm done.

Amazingly, I arrived at the park on time, and ahead of two other women who are under Margie's tutelage as well. Eventually there were five of us gathered there, eagerly anticipating the tricks our beloved trainer had up her sleeve for the day. We began with five minutes of running around an adjacent set of soccer fields, followed by multiple one-minute rotations of exercises including push-ups, sprints, plyometric jumps, mountain-climbers, jumping rope and planking ourselves atop a basketball. I was huffing and puffing by the end of that section, but absurdly, I was still having fun.

> Camaraderie during workouts is always a good thing, if only to talk about your trainer behind her back. Misery loves company, especially when that misery involves wind sprints.

20

Toward the end of our time together, Margie asked us to run suicides. She'd dotted dozens of tennis balls along the field, twenty or thirty yards apart, and had us compete with each other to see who could race to the first ball and bring it back to the bucket the fastest, and then race to the second ball and bring that one back too—on and on in this way, until every ball had been retrieved.

It doesn't take expensive equipment to get a good workout. A water bottle makes a great hand weight. You and a friend can play tug-of-war with a spare T-shirt. Hula hooping, as my son Noah and I discovered, can make for one of the most effective—and most competitive!—workouts around.

The agony finally came to an end, and I knew that if I never again saw another tennis ball in my life, I'd be perfectly content. As that thought made its way through my mind, I glanced sideways to find Margie launching those evil yellow spheres as far as her arm could throw them, one hundred of them in all. "Okay, ladies!" she cheered, with the annoying enthusiasm of someone who *wasn't* about to have to run all over creation like a headless chicken. "As soon as you bring me all of the balls you see out there, class is officially dismissed!"

With both hands on my hips, I eyed the giant Easter-egg hunt before me and said through grinding, gritted teeth, "You have *got* to be kidding."

In fact, she was not.

I don't know why it still surprises me when Margie pulls one of her frequent ultracruel and hyperactive stunts. She'd always been a bit crazy, even before I started to train with her. But "crazy" is what I was instructed by Jillian to find. "When you get home," Jillian had said during my final days at *The Biggest Loser* campus, "I don't want you to find some narcissistic diva to train you. I want you to find someone who is passionate about you and who is *crazy* about working out."

Margie, of course, fit that bill.

I had known of Margie through a mutual friend before I even auditioned for the show, and word on the street was that she was so serious about physical fitness that she couldn't find even one friend who would work out with her. "They'd throw up every time they went to the gym with me," Margie later explained, as if perplexed by their distaste for abuse. "Finally they just refused to go."

> As horrible as it seems to work out so hard that you throw up, it's actually your body's normal way of releasing toxins that are holding it back.

When I returned to Florida from *The Biggest Loser* campus, Margie contacted me and said that she would love to help me maintain my newfound figure and that perhaps we should work out together. I could tell in one conversation flat that she was the trainer for me.

That was a full year ago, I thought, as I forced my legs to race back and forth across the Easter-egg-dotted field. In a flash of insight, it occurred to me how different the previous twelve months had been compared to the thirty-five years leading up to them. Little more than a year ago, I couldn't have brought in a sack of groceries without enduring severe heart palpitations and stress. Now I was sprinting across a soccer field with a (semi) smile on my face.

Revelations like those are hitting me frequently these days, and they always pack an unexpected punch. They bring to mind the person I used to be, not the woman I am today. In my mind's eye I see her—the overweight, underwhelming version of me—with the same fine-

> Even if you never learn to love exercise, you do learn to love how you feel afterward. Pride in your accomplishment, increased strength, additional endurance—what's not to love about that!

tuned clarity of a burglary victim who can remember every nuance of her ransacked house. I wore her skin and shame for so much of my life that I find it's a daily battle to let her die—to let go of her self-doubt and fear—and let the new me be beautifully born.

THE ROBBING OF MY CHILDHOOD

Earlier this week, I drove the few miles to the park where Margie and I meet. The air was thick and cloudy, and partway through our workout, it started to rain. Margie is unfazed by bad weather, but I for one hate being wet. I considered dashing to my car to grab another layer, but the only available garment would have been the extra-small jacket I keep stashed in the trunk for Noah, who seems to lose everything he touches and seems *always* to be cold. It would help a little, I supposed, but the sleeves would be way too short. Quickly, I moved to other options, which is when it hit me: I could borrow something of Margie's.

Holy cow.

I could actually borrow something from Margie—*Margie,* who has a flawless figure and no visible fat. I could borrow something from *that* woman. I could *fit into something* that Margie can wear. The revelation brought tears to my eyes and a distant memory back to mind.

When I was a fresh-faced kindergartener, the other five-year-olds and I spent an hour every day in recess. I remember like it was yesterday playing outside one afternoon when it started to rain. Young, blonde, beautiful-in-every-way Mrs. Robertson raced toward the playground under the protective covering of an umbrella and ushered us kids through the doors that led back into Arlington Heights Elementary School, where we were instructed to select dry alternatives to our school clothes from the lost-and-found box.

If my memory serves me well, and if the few pictures I still possess tell the truth, I wasn't exactly obese at the tender age of five. But when every other girl your age is twiggy and wispy, somehow you gather that a shapely bottom and tree-trunk legs don't contribute to a "look" that will work.

Grudgingly I tugged at a pair of pumpkin-hued shorts until they broke loose of the weight of the other clothes in that dreaded lost-and-found box, held them up in front of my young face and eyed them with intense suspicion. Would they slip over my already ladylike thighs? Would their snap-closure come together to confine my proudly plump tummy? Or would they be the source of ridicule all the rest of my kindergarten days? I knew then that I wasn't at all like the person I was supposed to be.

I just *thought* too-small orange shorts would be my life's worst fashion nightmare. In reality, wearing nothing but a skin-tight tank top and shorts on a giant scale before a national audience would top the list. Please tell me it doesn't get worse than that!

When I was little there were two options for children's clothing: "regular" or "slim." How sad that there is such pervasive childhood obesity today that clothing companies now actually manufacture plus-size clothes for kids.

It was the start of a laundry list of what "fat" would steal from me.

Childhood years are supposed to be innocent, carefree and fun. And yet these certainly are not the themes that I'd say marked the first decade and a half of my life. Just before I started kindergarten, my parents' wildly flawed marriage dissolved into divorce. I don't remember them ever being married. I don't remember them ever living under the same roof. All I remember is the day that my dad left. My father had borrowed his buddy's green El Camino and had backed up the car to the front door of our house, right onto the grass. I stood there watching as he loaded the car, emerging from the house with arms full of possessions each time. When he had finished reclaiming his belongings, he turned toward me and asked, "Jules, who would you like to go with?" Instinctively, I inched toward my mother, who looked down at my confused countenance and whispered, "Sweetie, if you pick me, I'll give you a roll of Life Savers."

My dad, overhearing Mom's offer, eyed me and said, "Honey, you come with me, and I'll give you all the Life Savers you want."

Although Dad moved out that day, things wouldn't really explode between them until a few years later, when a series of custody battles rocked the first few months of my third-grade year. They played me against each other, and when that didn't work, they included my grandparents in the fight. I must have been a fairly resilient kid because despite the wobbly world in which I lived, I somehow maintained a fair degree of steadiness and even chose to develop a sense of humor about things. Little did I know how much I would rely on it through the years. "If I can get people to laugh *with* me," I thought, "then maybe they won't laugh *at* me."

In addition to handing me the shards of my undeniably broken family, the third grade also provided my first official realization that I was fat. For the entire school year, I obsessed about cresting one hundred pounds. A girl who had been in my class ever since the pumpkin-shorts fiasco three years prior was visibly, morbidly obese, and *she*, I had found out, weighed just over one hundred pounds. I compared myself to her daily, wondering if I was as fat as that.

I realize now that despite the dysfunction always inherent in divorce, at least I was lucky enough to be "wanted" by both my mom and my dad. Mom's persistent care went deep with me during my growing-up years, and truly, some of my best childhood memories are of the many weeknights spent on "dates" with my dad. McDonald's for dinner followed by movies like *Herbie* at the theater—it was a little girl's dream come true. Sure, I craved an intact family. But I remain grateful for the bits and pieces of bliss I knew.

Finally I made it to the fourth grade, but unfortunately my inner anguish made it there too. In the evenings before bedtime, the nine-year-old version of me would squat over the too-hot water of my bath and, having nothing better to do while I waited for the water to cool, I would fixate on my chubby thighs and puffy, peaking breasts that were developing *well* in advance of my peers'.

> My hunch that I was already fat at age eight was validated by my mom's enrolling me in a Weight Watchers program partway through my third-grade year. Not fond memories, to say the least.

A healthy sense of self—self-worth, self-confidence, self-esteem— had been taken from me in a flash. Another victory I had unwittingly handed to that terrible thief who answered to the name "Fat."

L ater, junior high brought with it a torment all its own. By that time I had ballooned to the point that I remember being afraid of not fitting into the yellow phys ed uniforms that were issued at the start of each grade. If the school *did* make one my size, I just knew it would come only by special order, and with an "XXXL" sneeringly printed on the tag. Still, that had to be better than the alternative: outsizing even their special-order offerings and being forced to drag my rail-thin mother to the local large-person clothing store to buy a plain yellow tee-shirt that we'd pay to have embroidered with the school's name. The obvious distinction of that attire would clearly have been the end of me.

It was during those same days that a boy in my eighth-grade class —I'll call him Jimmy, because his name *was* Jimmy—bestowed upon me my latest nickname. Chicago Bears defensive lineman William "The Refrigerator" Perry was receiving a lot of press as a fan favorite at the time, and Jimmy thought it would be funny to dub me "The Freezer." Sort of The Fridge's equally enormous sidekick, I guess. Every single day I entered the class I shared with Jimmy, I heard him mockingly shout, "Hey, Freezer!"

> Ironically, Jimmy would wind up asking me out during my somewhat-thinner college years. In reply, I think my exact words were: "As *if!*"

There was no comeback swift enough, no rebuttal fitting enough to match the depth of his crushing words. And so the funny fat girl would slip into her seat, silenced and rebuffed once more.

I didn't deal with Jimmy much after that, but I have bumped into a few other schoolmates over the past several years. When we were kids, I was the devastated recipient of their disdain. "Why are you so fat?" one had asked me. "What gives?" another probed. "Your *parents* aren't that fat." And then there was the girl who shooed me from her lunchroom table with four words that made her position abundantly clear: "Fat girls not allowed."

Interestingly, after my experience on *The Biggest Loser*, several of them tried to befriend me. I have a feeling they'd stand by their story that we were great friends in school, that of course they'd never done anything to harm me. But something in me simply stayed away, probably that same something that felt scraped out all those years ago, when cutting comments etched their way onto my soul.

———

For many kids, high school days are the glory days, the last great hoorah, the lovely, melodic tune that sings them right into adulthood. But for me, those days were just the constant refrain of an all-too depressing dirge.

To make matters worse, I spent that time living in a humid, oceanside community in Florida, which meant that every birthday party was yet one more reason to convene at the pool or the beach. If only granny-style skirted one-piece bathing suits and oversize men's T-shirts had been in vogue for a sixteen-year-old! Not only did I not *own* a bikini, but had I ever chosen to show up in one, I felt sure everyone in the immediate vicinity would have cleared out in a heartbeat as my pasty-white lumps of flesh and I rolled and strolled our way by. Why hand over more ammunition, I figured, when I'd already been shot down so many times?

It was for that same reason that I never, ever ate lunch at school. Instead, I would use my buck-forty's worth of lunch money to purchase a doughnut or two before class started, and use the remaining thirty-five cents on a midday milkshake I'd sip all alone. Of course, I'd return home from school and devour everything in sight, but at least in my mind I hadn't given people an obvious explanation as to why I was "that unbelievably fat."

> I saw a survey that the TV show 20/20 did one time, where they asked kids to look at photographs of two people and select the more attractive person. In every instance they chose the thinner one, even when the heavier person was drop-dead gorgeous.

I wanted to be thinner. I really did. Actually, I wanted to be "skinny"—that one word summed up my complete definition of all that it meant to be likeable, healthy and cool. But I was handed that goal from others in my life. "You could get any boy you want," well-meaning family members would say, "if you'd just lose that weight." (Translation: You'll mean a lot more to this world when there's a *whole* lot less of you.)

Eventually, I did lose a few pounds. Needing a way to look acceptable for the prom I would never attend, I fad-dieted and deprived my way to a "me" two dress sizes down. Sadly, though, my also-fat friends and I would always fall back into the trap of using food as our comforter. Which is how I know that even at the bargain price of four boxes for a dollar, mac-and-cheese can't satiate a starving soul.

These days, I look back and realize that my upbringing wasn't *all* bad. There were youth-group trips and dances and Christmas parties. But when I catch sight of photos of those "fond memories" and see a big, fat cow in the frame, the fondness somehow fades a bit. What's

> I'd learn the hard way throughout my life that "event dieting" never works. As soon as the event has come and gone, so has your motivation for losing weight.

more, now that I have hindsight on my side, I see more clearly the reason I became fat in the first place. I'm sure that psychotherapists would have a heyday analyzing my background and linking every major event to the cause of my obesity, but in my heart of hearts, the only theme I know to be true throughout my childhood and beyond is this: I was fat because I did not believe that I was worth the effort it would take to be fit.

Sadly, it would take me until age thirty-five to adjust my views on that.

THE ROBBING OF MY WOMANHOOD

When I was in my early twenties, I got my five-foot-two frame all the way down to one hundred and forty pounds and tried my hand at pageants. Admittedly, it was a lark. I had thick legs, as you'll recall. And by this point, I also had quite a robust bust—some of which was natural and some of which was due to the extra padding I added in an effort to bring my wide hips into proportion. In fact, on the heels of one especially disappointing swimsuit competition, the strongest

> These days I'm learning not to allow myself to be defined by a number that shows up on the scale. If I were to go by the standard height/weight charts, I should weigh between 105 and 110 pounds. Yeah, right.

"affirmation" I received came from a female judge who said, "I see how those breasts balance out that backside, Hon, but my *word* . . ." This was uttered mere moments before I learned that while everyone else had received eights and nines in that part of the competition, I had been granted a three. Lovely.

The evening-gown portion was no better, really. I couldn't fit into traditional, beaded gowns, and so I opted instead to debut the A-line dress. This was before anyone knew about A-line dresses, so I got points for trendsetting. But that was about it.

"You could be Miss America! If only you'd lose some weight." "You have such a pretty face! It's just that you've got all that weight." "What a lovely dress! It covers your flaws nicely." I'd heard a version of the judges' comments throughout my entire life. Would "fat" be my reality forever?

⁓∧∧⁓

It will come as no surprise to you that I never wore a crown. (Although I *did* do quite well in the "interview" portion, thank you very much.) But I took home a prize of another kind from those odd, odd pageant days: my wonderful husband Mike.

Mike was perhaps the only person in that pageant audience who saw more in me than what meets the eye. We were friends for five years, and although I had a terrific crush on him, my self-defeating ways caused me to keep that under wraps. Instead, when he confided in me as his friend that he was interested in one of the other "pageant girls" we knew, I'd enthusiastically prod him to ask her out. "Oh, she's gorgeous!" I'd rave. "You should date her!"

At my recommendation, he usually did. And as each girl came into his life and then left, I died another death. When would it be my turn?

When longing finally turned into reality and reality eventually produced a stunning engagement ring, I experienced a euphoria I had never previously known. At our engagement party, a mutual friend nodded toward me and said to her date, "She looks like a Mike Hadden wife." I soared on her words for hours. I knew the incredible women Mike had dated. And I was elated to be the last one among them.

Although I wasn't thin when Mike and I got engaged, I was the thinnest I'd ever been. Still, something in me said I was fat. As soon as we got married, I allowed the self-fulfilling prophecy to run its course, gaining pounds, it seemed, by the hour.

Just as quickly as I put back on the weight, Mike put on the role of my enabler. I didn't weigh myself very often, but I always knew when I had gained a lot of weight because my clothes no longer would fit. My dismay over my returning obesity became a constant topic of conversation between Mike and me, and when he just couldn't take my moaning and groaning any longer, he would come home from work with a treat. Mike's treats were always the best, because he knew exactly what I liked. Nachos, southwestern eggrolls from Chili's, a blooming onion from Outback, gooey chocolate cake—these always did the trick.

Mike proposed marriage to me during the decorating of my Christmas tree. He handed me one particular ornament—a beautiful gold ball—to hang, but only after I'd opened it up to find a princess-cut diamond ring inside.

That is, until I gained even more weight and grew even more despondent about the situation I was in.

Eventually the cycle would veer into such dark places that I'd refuse to go out with Mike.

"I can't fit into anything I own!" I'd whine. The next day I'd walk into our bedroom to find eight new pairs of pants on the bed.

Mike's enabling behavior was not helpful, but it was clearly motivated by love. He craved a normal, happy wife and a normal, happy home. It devastates me now to know that because of me, he had neither. In his eternal defense, Mike never once told me that I looked fat, that I *was* fat or that I needed to lose weight. But he is a man. To have thought that my obesity had no effect on him would be lunacy. Throughout the course of our early married life, and out of respect for the highly visual part of a man's needs and wants, I would try to diet my way back into clothes that had once fit. But as soon as I made it to my goal weight and people acknowledged my progress, I'd congratulate myself with my good old friend: food. Soon enough, those pounds I had lost would find their way right back to me.

Being fat caused dysfunction in other areas of our marriage too. Like most newlywed couples, Mike and I enjoyed a great vitality—and frequency!—in our sex life. Day or night, tired or not, we looked forward to sharing intimacy with each other. In our first apartment, the closet doors of our master bedroom boasted full-length mirrors. And although this didn't bother me at first, as I grew in size, I also grew increasingly uncomfortable with catching glimpses of myself in those mirrors. The puckers on my large thighs, the rolls of flesh around my belly, the droopy skin along the back of my arms—I couldn't bear to see these things, and I insisted that Mike not see them either.

Eventually I swapped the freedom I'd enjoyed for a finicky list of demands. First, there would be no sex during daylight hours. Second, when there was sex at night, all lights must be turned off. Third, since I could no longer fit into my lingerie, all expectations for sexy attire must be squelched at once. Fourth, Mike must initiate all sexual encounters. After all, what if one day I gained the pound that finally thrust Mike over the edge and he was no longer interested in me in "that" way? I refused to risk rejection on that level.

Given the heightened insanity I catalyzed during that season of life, it's something of a miracle that Noah was conceived. But six months before my twenty-ninth birthday, Mike and I welcomed our first baby into the world.

Looking back, I'm stung by the reality of how my food addiction would affect Noah in his early childhood. Any reasonable person would be shocked to see a drug addict taking her child into the crack house with her. You and I would both look down on an alcoholic who loaded her child into the car just before taking a spin fully drunk. But somehow it was lost on me that I was doing the very same thing. I was enveloping Noah in my addiction, without any regard for his life. What I ate is what he ate. My sedentary life was his sedentary life. All of my bad choices were his bad choices, simply because he was my son. My six fast-food meals a week became his fast-food habit too. My couch-potato ways became his lethargy as well.

What kind of mother would do this? It's not the mom I wanted to be.

The last chapter of the book of Proverbs paints a beautiful portrait of what a wife and mother ought to look like. "A good woman is hard to find, and worth far more than diamonds," *The Message* paraphrase says. "Her husband trusts her without reserve, and never has reason to regret it. Never spiteful, she treats him generously all her life long. She shops around for the best yarns and cottons, and enjoys knitting and sewing. She's like a trading ship that sails to faraway places and brings back exotic surprises. She's up before dawn, preparing breakfast for her family and organizing her day. She looks over a field and buys it, then, with money she's put aside, plants a garden. First thing in the morning, she dresses for work, rolls up her sleeves, eager to get started. She senses the worth of her work, is in no hurry to call it quits for the day.

"She's skilled in the crafts of home and hearth, diligent in homemaking. She's quick to assist anyone in need, reaches out to help the poor. She doesn't worry about her family when it snows; their winter clothes are all mended and ready to wear.

"She makes her own clothing, and dresses in colorful linens and silks. Her husband is greatly respected when he deliberates with the city fathers. She designs gowns and sells them, brings the sweaters she knits to the dress shops. Her clothes are well-made and elegant, and she always faces tomorrow with a smile. When she speaks she has something worthwhile to say, and she always says it kindly. She keeps an eye on everyone in her household, and keeps them all busy and productive.

> I find it interesting that the Proverbs 31 woman dresses not only her family well; she also dresses *herself* well. She is on her own priority list, and not in the very last spot.

"Her children respect and bless her; her husband joins in with words of praise: 'Many women have done wonderful things, but you've outclassed them all!' Charm can mislead and beauty soon fades. The woman to be admired and praised is the woman who lives in the Fear-of-God. Give her everything she deserves! Festoon her life with praises!"[1]

Now, I don't know what *you* take away from those verses, but I'm thinking that any woman lauded in Scripture for making breakfast for her family was probably making more than a Krispy Kreme stop. Any woman who planted a vegetable garden probably had kids who actually knew what fresh broccoli tasted like. Any woman who was eager to roll up her sleeves and work in the morning . . . well, the old version of me wouldn't know *what* to make of that. Any woman who mended clothes obviously wasn't outgrowing her pants every six weeks. And any woman who always said "worthwhile" things clearly didn't bemoan her big butt.

Even as I read that passage again now, the stark contrast between the wife and mom I chose to be for so many years and the woman portrayed in these verses is almost too much to take in. How completely I craved the ambition, the motivation, the diligence of that woman!

I knew I had my husband's and son's unwavering love. How desperately I desired to gain their respect. Thankfully, God knew those deep, deep desires of my heart. And as I'd learn soon enough, he had paved the path to my becoming a woman just like the one I admired.

THE ROBBING OF MY PEACE

The loss—on so many levels—of my childhood and then of my womanhood carried with them a common thread. Weaving its way through all of those years was the devastating loss of my peace.

Most obese people I know are people-pleasers at heart. Truly, it is enough of a daily challenge to bear up under the weight of your own insecurity, shame and self-condemnation. The last thing you want to attach to all of that is the disappointment of others.

I practiced my people-pleasing ways early on in my life. When I was still a preteen, and in deference to my mother's health-fanatic ways, I would eat modest portions at dinner. What she didn't know, of course, was that her people-pleasing daughter would clear the table and then stuff herself silly with every morsel that remained, in between scrubbing glasses and plates.

Later, during my pageant stint, I would attempt to work out four or five hours a day with fellow contestants so that they would be pleased with my efforts toward weight loss. But upon leaving, I'd sabotage every ounce of progress made by stopping and purchasing a box of Little Debbie cakes that would be devoured well before I got home.

> These days I have friends who tell me they make their kids join the Clean Plate Club before they can be excused from the dinner table, and my reaction is always the same: "Quit that!"

Throughout my entire existence, it seems, I had two lives going. There was the me that others saw, and the me that was truly me. The end-result of my duplicity was inner turmoil that is tough to explain. What is not tough to explain is how God *intended* for life to be lived.

In Genesis, God says that he thought so highly of us that he created us in his own, perfect image. In the book of John, we learn that he has equipped us for lives lived to the fullest. Five chapters later, we are told that we're capable of a level of contentedness that can actually cause us to *leap*.[2]

Acceptance, abundance, joy—this was hardly the life I'd been living.

I'd be shopping at Target with Mike and would catch sight of a friend I hadn't seen in years, but instead of approaching to say hi, I'd hide behind the clothing rack until I was sure she was gone so that she wouldn't see how terrible I looked.

I'm an adventure-seeker by nature, but when a friend invited me to skydive with her, I shrunk back and declined for fear that the jumpsuit simply would not fit.

When Mike and I attended Noah's soccer games, I'd refuse to stand up and cheer because I knew that my arms and my midsection would keep jiggling long after the rest of me had stood still. Worse than that, I denied him the delight of swimming with his buddies because I couldn't bring myself to go to the neighborhood pool during "normal" hours. I'd wait until late afternoon and watch him swim all alone, while nobody was around to watch big, fat me.

Acceptance, abundance, and joy—knowing who you are in God's eyes, living out of the fullness of your relationship with him and enjoying the journey every step of the way. To me, these things add up to a life lived from that coveted place called peace. I'm grateful to say that after hundreds of prayers, a year of tears, and buckets of sweat, it's the place I call home these days.

TAKING BACK WHAT'S RIGHTFULLY MINE

When I got back from *The Biggest Loser* campus in August 2007, I felt that in so many ways I had neglected my child. It hadn't been on purpose, of course, but something about the string of experiences on the show helped me see what a truncated existence I had asked Noah to live. My sedentary lifestyle and my fear of socializing had taken a

terrible toll, and I wanted to do something to make it up to him. So I took
him to Disney World, just the two of
us.

> The day I took Noah to Disney World
> was the first day that I wore a
> sleeveless shirt in public in years.
> It was a day of celebration on so
> many levels.

At the end of an unbelievably fun
day of riding on roller coaster seats
I hadn't fit on for decades, Noah and I
stood in line for the monorail that would take us back to the parking
lot. He was standing behind me in line and didn't notice much of what
unfolded ahead of us, but I surely did. Twenty inches away from me
stood a young girl—probably ten or eleven years old—and two adults
who appeared to be her parents. As far as I could tell, she wasn't misbe-
having. But she must have said something that didn't sit right with her
father, because the next thing I knew, he cocked his right hand into the
air and in one swift *whoosh* slapped the young girl across the face. My
jaw dropped just as the mother—with swaddled infant in her arms—
stepped quickly between her husband and her daughter. She obviously
didn't want to cause even more of a scene, but the instantaneousness
with which she reacted made me wonder if abuse was a pattern for this
family.

> Even when you feel you aren't worth
> the fight that's involved in changing
> your life, you find that someone or
> something else is—like wanting a
> better life for Noah and wanting to
> protect that little girl.

Before I counted the cost of my own
reaction, I caught the father's eye and
said quietly, in a measured tone, "You
sorry son of a gun." Except "gun" wasn't
exactly the noun I chose.

My mother raised me *never* to talk
like that, and when the syllables fell out
of my face, I just knew Mickey or Minnie
or another official character was going to show up and toss my foul
mouth right into Disney Jail. But somehow, my anger felt justified. And
so I kept going.

"Take one step toward me," I dared the man. "I wish you would. I
wish you'd take one step toward me, because I would see to it that you
were sprawled out on the deck long before you ever reached my space."

I knew he wouldn't budge, and he didn't. Beneath their threatening
veneer, abusers are cowards. Not to mention awful excuses for fathers.
I wanted to put loving arms around that little girl and let her know that

she did not deserve to be treated that way. I wanted to assure the mother that there was a better life out there waiting for her, a life beyond cyclical abuse. But I didn't. I had done all that I could do, and I had to let that be enough.

I have no idea if my words—harsh though they might have been—changed that man. But I know that they changed me. For thirty-five years I had avoided all forms of confrontation and controversy because I was too insecure to draw attention to myself and too weak to take a stand. But *that* person wasn't at Disney that day. A new me was there, and as I spoke each syllable that afternoon, I felt long-awaited strength start to rise.

On campus, Jillian had taught my fellow contestants and me how to defend ourselves using our bodies, through kickboxing and Tae Kwon Do techniques, and for the first time in my life, I actually felt like I *could* defend myself—and even a perfect stranger—if I had to. Something in me knew that if that man had taken two steps toward me he really *would* have been laid out at my feet, pleading for mercy and repudiating his evil ways.

I'm not a violent person, honest. But for once I was equipped to fight for what was right.

For once, the Julie that God had created stood immovably, wonderfully firm. For once, I felt a sensation rise up that could only be called my soul's *strength*. Plus, if things had turned ugly in a jiffy, I could have grabbed Noah and just run for my life. Strength manifests itself in a number of ways, and one of them is knowing when to cut your losses and bail. But even if I fled on foot, I would have thanked God for stamina to sustain me. It's stamina I did not possess even thirteen months ago.

Jillian Michaels explained to me that she always trains from the outside in. When a person learns how strong she is physically, she begins to feel powerful on the inside.

My mom lives exactly twelve miles away from our house, and the thought has hit me on several occasions that if for some odd reason I needed to grab my children and run to her house (if we were accidentally locked out of our condo, if our car wouldn't start, if an armed madman was on the loose), I could actually get it done. I'd be pooped at the end of that two-and-a-half hours, sure. But eventually, we'd get there, no sweat. There is something very empowering about that realization. I call it the gift of strength.

In the movie version of John Grisham's book, *The Pelican Brief,* Julia Roberts plays the character of Tulane University law student Darby Shaw. Struck by the recent assassinations of two very diverse Supreme Court justices, she decides to nose around and find out why they were killed.

She winds up uncovering an illegal plot between the president of the United States and an evil oil magnate who's working overtime to bribe him into overturning environmental law, and she puts her findings in a brief that she shows to her law professor, who then hands the paper over to the FBI for examination. Soon afterward, the law professor is found dead.

Darby grows concerned that she'll be the next target, and so she goes on the run. (But not before she enlists the aid of a newspaper reporter named Gray Grantham, who is played by the premier specimen of humankind himself, Denzel Washington. But I digress.) The greatest scene in the movie unfolds when Darby finds herself cornered in an old deserted barn and can hear the bad guy's car drive up. She plots her escape and then flees through the fields, gunfire erupting at her heels.

What the bad guy doesn't know is that day after day after day, Darby had run her little heart out on her living room treadmill—just in case her life was ever in danger. All that training finally paid off, and mine is finally paying off too.

Strength of character. Strength of person. Strength of my physical frame. These are the strengths that I now live out, and fat will *never* steal them from me.

Surround Yourself with Positive Influences

Years ago *Saturday Night Live* came out with a character who could kill a festive gathering in four seconds flat. "Debbie Downer" would show up at her friend Ronnie's thirty-fifth birthday party, for example, and when offered a piece of yummy birthday cake by the host say, "None for me. With all the refined sugars we're eating, America's experiencing a virtual *epidemic* of juvenile diabetes." As the rest of the group's shoulders slumped in the awkward silence that always followed Debbie's remarks, you'd hear the strains of the deflating, downer-chords play: whan-*whan*.

When I started to make positive changes in my life, I unwittingly became a real-life Debbie Downer. And nobody likes Debbie Downers. I always had been the Funny Fat Friend, but now that I was slimming down, increasingly, people were uncomfortable around me. They assumed I'd judge their food choices, criticize their lack of exercise and suck the fun right out of the room. All of a sudden the people I knew and loved felt not encouraged but indicted by my improvement. It was a reaction I hadn't expected.

Before I went on *The Biggest Loser*, my closest friends and I had a girls' night about once a month. Most of us were overweight, and it was a night when we could shove our diets aside for a few hours and feast on all our favorite indulgences—which always included Oreos, nachos and other pillars of wholesome healthfulness. Interestingly, when I came back from campus, nobody wanted to have a girls' night with me. "We can't have *that* type of food . . . *Julie's* going to be there!" Whan-*whan*.

"Girls, it's still *me*!" I wanted to remind them. "Even without a six-inch stack of nachos on my plate, I'm still the Julie you know and love!" But it was no use. They weren't too sure what to make of my weight-loss progress, and I wasn't too sure what to make of them.

I learned a valuable lesson during those first weeks back: When you undergo dramatic change, there is a period of time when you exist in a lonely middle ground. For many months I no longer fit in with my fat friends, but I wasn't part of the "skinny club" yet either. I was a girl without a group, which for a social butterfly is the worst kind of girl to be. Did I want to feel accepted, or did I want true transformation more? On some days that was an *impossibly* tough question to answer.

Over time I sought out a support system of people who really did want the best for me, whatever that might mean. I needed a handful of friends who would push me toward my potential, who would pick me up when I floundered and who would cheer for me over even the smallest success. And interestingly, as I surrounded myself with those positive influences, my old friends came around too. They saw that despite my outer transformation, the inner me was still the same. They resolved to stick with me, no matter what my weight. And finally, they stopped with that annoying whan-*whan* every time I entered a room.

CHAPTER 3

Weight That We All Carry

I T'S A *THE BIGGEST LOSER* tradition that, every season, participants come up with personal mottos that represent the reason they're on the show to begin with. Sometimes the phrases are printed on flags that fly from flagpoles soaring high above the campus. Other times they're emblazoned on (really, really big) T-shirts so that contestants can *wear* why they're there, which was the case for my teammates and me, the season we were all on the show.

Early on in my *The Biggest Loser* experience, one of the show's producers approached me and asked about my motto. What was I really trying to accomplish? she wanted to know. What was my *real* motivation for leaving my husband and son behind in Jacksonville, traipsing to the other end of the country and subjecting myself to six-hour workouts and a diet frighteningly devoid of fried foods every day?

My first few responses were things like, "To fit into Jillian Michaels' jeans" and "To bring sexy back." But then I took a more thoughtful turn. "The real reason I'm here," I admitted, "is because I *never* finish what I start. I want to finish what I've started, for once." The producer nodded a knowing grin as she jotted down what I had said.

My family and friends could attest to the fact that I was never exactly known as a "completer." I'd quit relationships. I'd quit college. I'd quit the pursuit of a thousand dreams, most notably my dream of being in shape. But this time would be different. *This* time on this show, I would finish what I'd started, for once. I'd show everyone—those same doubting friends and family members, as well as every guy I'd ever dated during those brief, slimmer days who might be watching the show thinking, *Whew! Talk about a narrow escape!*—I would show them *all*, and I would show myself, that I could finish something just once.

Or that's what I told Jillian and my team, anyway, the day we were handed our shirts.

WHAT WE REALLY HUNGER FOR

My teammates and I were sitting around one day in our black-team bedroom, just hanging out and chatting about how much better our accommodations were on campus than in the desert. Even a sparsely decorated oversized dorm room felt luxurious by comparison.

Jillian came bounding into the room, a stack of black T-shirts in her arms. She was wearing one of those pairs of jeans I so desperately wanted to squeeze into someday, and a white tank top that boasted bulging muscles popping out from both armholes. The girls on our team—as well as the guys—secretly coveted Jillian's physique. Whether any of us would actually ever *attain* it was another matter entirely.

> My teammates and I loved how buff Jillian was, until those moments when she threw her ripped self on our backs while we were forced to run up a hill. She may be slim, but *you* try hauling a hundred and twenty extra pounds around during your next workout!

Shirts were tossed to each of my teammates, and then a shirt soared through the air toward me. We all unfolded them with the pride of a rookie NBA player who has just received his first jersey. "What do they *say*?" Jillian pressed us with a smile.

Some of the mottos were funny, and some were poignant. But all of them eventually would serve as helpful insights into the hearts and minds of my team. In that moment, we were acknowledging not only why we were there, but why the rest of our team was there too. It was a level of understanding that made us want to fight from that day forward, not only for ourselves, but also for each other. These people weren't just competitors; they were now family—real people with real lives and real reasons they just couldn't quit.

My teammate Jez was first up. "To kick fear's butt," he said, as he read his shirt aloud. "I'm tired of being afraid of everything." Being overweight had always been Jez's excuse for why he couldn't accomplish the goals he had set for his life, and he feared what would happen once he was thin. Would his dreams all magically come true? Or would he realize that being fat wasn't his problem after all . . . and *then* what would be left to blame?

Hollie went next. "To practice what I preach," her shirt read. She was a schoolteacher and cheerleading coach who was very demanding about her kids' dietary habits and their dedication to exercise. She desperately wanted to show her students that she was committed to living by the standards she had set for them.

"To be a *rock star*," Isabeau piped up with a wry smile. Blonde, beautiful Isabeau, who was a singer/songwriter with towering musical dreams.

"To be half the man so that I can be twice the man," Bill said with pride. He told of the time he went to ride a roller coaster with his daughter but couldn't wedge himself into the seat. His daughter, who constantly worried about her dad's weight, tried to console him, but her words only made him feel worse. "Kids shouldn't have to wonder if their dad's going to be around," he said. "I want to lose half of my weight so that I can be twice as active in my kids' lives," he said.

Bill's twin brother Jim then spoke up: "For me, for them, forever," he read with a satisfied nod that silently honored his wife and his kids, "*that's* why I am here."

And then it was my turn. "To finish what I've started, for once," I said as I propped myself up on my elbows and held up my shirt.

Jillian caught my eye. "What does that mean to you, Jules?" she asked. "Tell me about your shirt."

"I *never* finish what I start," I said. "I mean, I've started to lose weight a hundred times. I'm here to *finish* it . . . once and for all."

There was real meaning behind what I said, and as I glanced down at my hands after I'd said my piece, I halfway expected to see them coated in grains of sand. Of course they were perfectly clean. But the residue of the afternoon spent in the desert hotel the previous week, just God and me and the realization that I was *worth* the dreams I felt compelled to chase, still coated my mind and my heart. *He* knew I had it in me to finish what I'd started. And now I was starting to believe him.

For once.

～∧∼

I've spent the vast majority of my life being fat, and I've had plenty of fat friends along the way. What was surfacing for my *The Biggest Loser* teammates as we learned about each other's goals only served to validate what I've long believed: for nearly every obese person I know, physical weight is just a cover for the emotional weight he or she bears.

I saw a psychiatrist on TV one time who was counseling overweight teens and their exasperated parents. "What are you *really* hungry for?" he asked each of the kids. "I mean, aside from the food, what is it you crave?"

The kids' responses caused tears to spring to my eyes. How easily I could relate. How easily *any* obese person could relate.

"I just want time with you!" one teenager cried out to her mom, a single woman working two jobs to support her family.

"Acceptance," another said as he looked sheepishly at his overbearing father.

"Approval from the other kids at school," a young boy said. "I'm tired of them teasing me because I'm fat."

I too had been hungry for those things—for approval and acceptance and a sense that I mattered—and I, too, had tried to eat my way full. But food would never be able to satisfy the sort of deep-down hunger I felt.

WEIGHT OF ANOTHER KIND

Since my days on *The Biggest Loser*, I have done a fair amount of public speaking. I stand before women's groups and MOPS (Mothers of Preschoolers) meetings and community gatherings, and without exception when I get to this part of my story—the realization that my physical weight wasn't just about diet and exercise but was reflective of deeper turbulent waters rushing far below the surface—I see streams of tears chase their way down scores of cheeks.

Audience members frequently approach me after a talk to tell me that my before-and-after photos hang on their refrigerator as a daily reminder of their need to finish what they've started, for once. What a surreal thing, to think that such a simple statement could have such a wide-reaching effect.

"I went to the show thinking the only weight I carried was the kind that can be measured in pounds," I explain. "All those years of being overweight, I never knew there were other burdens I was carrying; I had become a master at diverting the frustration I felt toward everyone else instead. My family told me that my weight was my problem, but I thought that *they* were the problem—*their* criticism, *their* negative attitudes, *their* disappointment with who I was. I would push all the blame onto them and go on my merry way, filling the role of the happy fat girl—Jokester Julie—never once having to admit what lurked beneath.

We all carry weight that God does not intend for us to carry. Call it the human experience or call it sheer insanity, but somehow we walk through this life tethered to things that serve no purpose but to weigh us down. For some people it's anger—a boiling rage they feel in their soul. For others, it's the quicksand of a lifetime of racked-up regrets. For still others, it's the dreadful quandary of feeling insignificant in their own skin.

It could be a financial weight, the weight of fear over infertility, the weight of deception—living two or three lives or more. Like me, it could be as straightforward as a terrible lack of self-esteem.

It could be a weight we've chosen to pick up, or a weight someone else has placed on us—abuse. Neglect. A lifetime of being misunderstood.

But whatever the weight we carry, it's proof that there's always far more to the story than what shows up on the bathroom scale.

～⋎⋏～

When you think about it, it really is lunacy that we voluntarily lug around so much extra weight. Wouldn't it be easier to walk and run and sleep and *live* without all that? Speaking from personal experience, it's a heck of a lot easier to pretend to be perfect—whether weighted down or not—than it is to admit when something is wrong. Or at least that's how it seems. The truth of the matter is that eventually we crumble under the weight of the façade we try so hard to hold up. It's scary to confess, for instance, that we struggle with insecurity—that despite our confident cover, we're not who everyone thinks that we are. Or who everyone needs us to be. The reality of admitting who we really are? That can feel heavier than the physical weight we bear.

Men and women often come up to me after a talk I've given and with brushed-away tears speak of their struggles with weight. They talk about how they are *consumed* by the extra forty pounds they are carrying, and how they are at their wit's end regarding how to lose them. I look into their downcast eyes and see so clearly the real battle they fight.

I see the fear. I see the insecurity. In some cases, I see the remnants of verbal abuse. "Your physical weight is the least of your worries," I want to say. "Don't you see the bigger picture here? Truly, now, what are you hungry for?"

They don't know it, but they have on a goal-shirt I can read. It's written all over their faces, all over their hearts, all over their words. "Look down and read your *real* goal," I yearn to cry out. "Be willing to face the hard truth."

> I saw a sign at the airport the other day that simply asked, "What have you got to lose?" What a meaningful question—and in the context of carrying weight we were never intended to carry, one both you and I must frequently ask.

There are people who would find such joy on the other side of a major change, but something deep inside says, "Losing the physical weight is only going to force me to take a closer look at the real reason for my burdensome state." And man, can that message mess with a person. They buy into the lie—as I did—that they're not worth the effort, they cast aside the lightness of life and they pad their way back toward the fridge. They want genuine change. They just don't want it badly enough.

It's incredibly frustrating to see people with all the potential in the world dig in their heels and refuse to change. Your heart wishes you could lift every extraneous burden off of them, that you could just hand them the wings they will need to soar. But the truth is, we have to face our weights for ourselves. The move is ours alone to make. Which, by the way, is why my Weight Watchers experience at age eight didn't work. My well-meaning mother had a vision for me that I hadn't quite bought into myself. And despite her noble intentions, it was my move, alone, to make.

My team's goal-shirts carried so much meaning because the words were more than mere slogans; they were tangible proof that the six of us were no longer comfortable in our pain. Each of us finally knew what we were hungry for, and we were determined to persevere until we were really and truly full.

DECIDING TO SEE WHAT'S UNSEEN

Jillian Michaels has a philosophy that when you begin to change your body, the rest of you changes too. As physical strength powers up, emotional weights power down. It's a theory I agreed to pretty early on, because when you wake up one day and realize that you can work out for ninety minutes straight without vomiting, it really is true: Suddenly, you're wildly intolerant of the fear, the regret and the insecurities you carried your whole life.

The challenge, then, is hanging on until you see that new you emerge.

When my teammates and I started to push ourselves physically, our various weights—fears, insecurities, assumptions—tried to push back against our progress. It was tempting to use that as an excuse, to whine that it was utterly inhumane to make fat people do skinny-people things and that if we *were* made to run up a steep hill, for instance, there should at least be a stack of Oreos at the top.

But we knew that for the sake of our goals, we had no choice but to hang on—just a little while longer, a little more sweat, a few more reps ... hang on.

—∿∿—

To date, the largest man to compete on *The Biggest Loser* is participating in the season that's airing as I write this book. He weighed in at 454 pounds his first week on the show and was given Jillian as his trainer, poor guy. Last week the camera caught him on a treadmill, walking when he was supposed to be running. In typical Jillian-fashion, she hopped up onto the base of the treadmill, looked this young man in the eye and said, "Run!"

He kept walking.

"I said *run!*" Jillian bellowed.

"My legs hurt," he whimpered. "I can't run!"

Jillian stared at him for several seconds as the viewing audience held its collective breath. Then, with a surprising amount of tenderness, she asked, "What is *really* wrong with you?"

He choked up as he kept walking, his gaze firmly fixed on his feet. "All I can focus on is that I'm hurting," he said. "I can't focus on where I'm headed with this whole thing because I can't even imagine myself not-fat.

"I've *never* been not-fat," he continued. "I've *never* pushed through pain. I've *never* been where I'm going, and I can't for a second imagine myself there."

One of my favorite worship choruses says, "I want to know you; I want to see your face. I want to know you more." It's a song sung to God, but the lyrics took on fresh meaning for me during my days on *The Biggest Loser* campus. I did want to know God more through my experience on campus, but I also wanted to know more of the woman he had created me to be. Like the contestant on the treadmill said, though, I had never known that person. I had never met her. I had never seen her face. And it's hard to pursue a vision you just don't see.

I wanted to know what the burden-free Julie looked like, who she would be. I knew she existed, and that she had been ordained by God, but where was she hiding? And how was she going to be found?

During the finale show that caps off every season of *The Biggest Loser*, contestants get to rip their way through large sheets of paper that feature life-size images of each person's "before" body. On more than one occasion during those early days when I craved a vision of the me I would become, I'd daydream about that finale-moment. I'd be falling apart during an especially rigorous workout, and instead of talking to me about the agony I was experiencing, Jillian would come up to me and say, "So, Jules, are you going to wear red lipstick to the finale? I think red would be good." Or, "About that finale: are you thinking slacks or a dress?" Or, "Will your hair be up or down? Are you doing heels, or what? You're *short*, you know."

> I wound up wearing black pants, a black strapless top and a rhinestone-studded belt to the Season 4 finale. With four-inch heels, by the way.

Jillian already knew what I was slowly sorting out: If I could just catch a glimpse of who I'd be on the back side of all my hard work, the work wouldn't seem so hard after all.

DARING TO LAY DOWN THE WEIGHT

If part of the life experience is acknowledging the weight we were never intended to carry, then the other part is learning that it's possible to lay it down.

Hebrews 12:1 says, "Therefore, since we are surrounded by such a great cloud of witnesses, let us throw off everything that hinders and the sin that so easily entangles, and let us run with perseverance the race marked out for us." I had read that verse a dozen times before, but I'd never noticed how relevant it is to the process of losing weight.

What finally enabled me to start visualizing the "me I would be" was the practice of thinking about contestants from *The Biggest Loser* seasons previous to mine. I'd think about the players who had gone before me and who had endeared themselves to me by their hard work and their determination to honor their goals. And I'd think about the *dramatic* transformation they'd known as a result of refusing to quit. It was yet one more example of my being accidentally biblical in my approach to life. Without intending to, I'd crafted my own "cloud of witnesses" that could inspire me and push me and see me through to the end.

For once, I could see the Julie that God intended me to be, the less-burdened woman who had been hiding within. For once, I felt my body changing and those extra weights melting away. For once, I was doing it—I was actually finishing what I had started.

For once.

My newfound appreciation for that verse in Hebrews has caused me now to believe that *everyone* can throw off the extraneous things weighing her down. The writer of that verse didn't approach the idea timidly. It's not like he said, "You know, give it a little thought, and if it seems like a good idea to you, then maybe get rid of your weight."

Far from it. It's more like, "Get the weight *gone*, girl. Get it gone!" Remember the great cloud of witnesses. And throw off what hinders and entangles you. Think about who's gone before you, and choose now to lay down your weight.

I originally wanted to be on *The Biggest Loser* because I thought it was going to be fun. I wanted to be the cute, peppy, happy-go-lucky girl who made everything cheery and everyone laugh. But I got there and realized that the joke was on me. You see yourself differently when you are forced to acknowledge your weight, and ultimately to lay it all down. I felt crippled in every way while I was on campus: At various points along the journey, it seemed I'd been stripped of every form of support—emotional, physical, spiritual and more. But it would take being broken in every possible way before I'd agree to get my weight gone.

And so it is with that verse in Hebrews 12. The instructions found there only work when you stumble upon a crossroads and dare to take the riskier path. For me, that crossroads was the intersection of streets named Big Change and Big Forever. Would I embark on "big change" or would I settle for being "big forever"? Which path would I choose?

My self-talk went something like this: "Decide today that you want this change badly enough to pursue the person you deserve to be, or say to yourself *right now* that you're going to be content with being fat every day for the rest of your life."

I was thirty-five years old and facing a do-or-die situation. *Which path should I choose?*

───∿∿───

Years ago when Mike and I were potty-training our son Noah, we noticed that Noah would always go crouch in the corner when he had to poop. We'd say, "Noah, we can see you hiding over there. Do you need to go potty?" To which he'd reply, "No!" just before producing poopy pants.

He was old enough not to poop in his pants. He had been *trained* not to poop in his pants. And he *hated* the sensation of walking around in that awful poop-in-the-pants state. So why did he stick to his crouching routine? Because he wasn't ready to make the effort to stop.

Finally Mike and I decided that Noah would be banned from wearing his favorite Thomas the Train "big boy" underpants until he proved to us that he would go to the bathroom *in* the bathroom instead of hiding in the corner and lying his way through another poop. From there, things shifted.

There's a point in our lives when we are supposed to be babies. We're supposed to be fragile and dependent and needy and weak. We're *supposed* to poop in our pants. But then comes the point of awareness that it's time to put aside childish things and live in the fullness and richness and "adultness" of who God has created us to be.

At some point we must quit hiding, rise from our crouched position and decide in our hearts to grow up. *That* is the crossroads I was standing at. I had been hiding in a corner, trying to mask the stench of my obesity and its requisite weights. I knew that it stunk. Everyone *around* me knew that it stunk. But only I could make the decision to clean up the mess that I'd made. Maya Angelou says that, "When we know better, we do better."[3] And although it took me more than three decades to get there, at last I would prove I knew better.

───∿∿───

There is a third aspect to the verse in Hebrews 12 that inspires me every time I read it. "Let us run with perseverance," it says, "the race marked out for us." Now, you tell me: Is it even possible to run—let alone to run *with perseverance*—when you're fat and unhappy and an emotional wreck? I dare you to say yes.

I came across a quote one time that says, "Perseverance is the hard work you do after you get tired of doing the hard work you already did." That about sums it up.

At the end of our season on the show, the remaining contestants and I had to complete a challenge that involved dragging a giant forty-pound scale behind us as well as the equivalent of whatever weight we had lost to that point in the game. The weight was added to our scales a little at a time, and as the challenge went on it became increasingly difficult to race back and forth. It was such a clear picture to me of how tough it is to soar when you're dragging dead weight.

Back then I had no idea what race God had marked out for me. Still don't, as a matter of fact. But this much I do know: However the road winds and wherever it leads, it will be vastly easier to run in a sloughed-off-weight state. And I've got the proof to support it.

When my teammate Isabeau auditioned for *The Biggest Loser*, part of her driving motivation was that she wanted to fit in with her family—her brother, her mom and her dad—all of whom were "normal" size. Sure, she wanted other things, too, like pursuing a songwriting career, becoming a bona fide rock star and wearing off-the-rack jackets from Urban Outfitters. But underneath all of that were those "deeper waters"—the emotional weight of feeling ostracized from her own family.

Every year Isabeau's family ran a 5K race together, which she had never been able to run. It would bring her to tears to talk about how every summer she'd sit on the curb, waiting the half-hour for them to return. "It was inconceivable to them that I'd ever participate in that run," she told me one day. "We all had just accepted the fact that this was 'their thing' that I didn't do."

Between Isabeau's time on campus and our season finale, she ran that race

The first time I ran a road race, I cried the entire first mile of the nine-mile total. I couldn't believe I was actually achieving something I had yearned to do for thirty-five years.

with her family, all 3.1 miles of it. She wasn't rail-thin when she ran, but she was definitely carrying less weight—physically, emotionally, in *every* regard—and on that day Isabeau soared.

After the Season 4 finale, my husband and I had my goal-shirt encased in glass and hung it in our den. To this day it serves as a reminder of the lifelong commitment I made.

I think about her achievement now and remember every drop of sweat that got her to that race. I remember every hour in the gym. Every wind sprint we were forced to run. Every doughnut we refused to eat. Every *everything* that brought the new "us" into being. And still today I know she'd agree that it was worth every ounce of that work. To feel light on your feet on a God-ordained path—is there a better reward than that?

People ask me whether I kept that goal-shirt, and my answer's always the same: Of course I kept that shirt! It's the *motto* that I changed and now can leave behind. I already "finished what I started, for once." And now I'm determined "to *continue* what I started, *forever.*"

Move More and Eat Less

The most frequently asked question I get from people who are trying to lose weight is this one: "How did you do it?" They approach me in grocery stores, in restaurants, at my son's soccer games, everywhere I go, it seems, and want to know exactly what I did to drop my weight.

What they expect in reply is some complicated formula that I followed to the letter. I can see it in their eyes. Which is why I know that my actual response is always something of a disappointment.

"If you want to lose weight," I explain, "you have to move more. And eat less."

They stare back at me as if to say, "No, really. Tell me what you did."

But that is, in fact, what I did. It's what every fat person who lost weight did, unless they went the surgical route.

The Biggest Loser taught me many nuances of diet and exercise that I never knew existed—how to balance carb intake, how to structure a workout regimen so that you remain injury-free, how to overcome negative self-talk when you think you just can't go on—but when it was all said and done, my big takeaway was this: The only way to lose weight is to burn more calories than you consume. You have to move more, and you have to eat less. Period.

When I was overweight, I would circle the mall parking lot for forty-five minutes straight, looking for a parking spot that was inches from the door. I could have entered the mall, done all of my shopping, and returned to my car five times in the time it took me to hunt down a fat-person's spot. These days I pull in, I park and I walk.

I move. I move more.

Likewise, prior to losing weight, a typical weeknight dinner involved swinging through the drive-thru at McDonald's after Noah's soccer games and ordering a double cheeseburger, a large order of fries and a large Coke. I'd put down a full day's calories in one meal flat, and often follow that up later with a fresh batch of cookies at home. Lord, have mercy.

I'm not a purist when it comes to fast food now, but I've definitely reined in my routine. I eat, but I eat less. And I eat far less fast food.

Those same people who ask how I lost weight probably go home, look in the mirror, find a terribly obese person standing there and feel utterly overwhelmed. I mean, where do you start when you need to lose one hundred pounds? With my advice fresh on their minds, all they can think about is that it's hard to "move more" when you can barely move, and it's hard to "eat less" when food seems to be your only friend.

That's certainly how I used to feel.

But here's what I'd tell them if I had the chance: "Your excess weight didn't appear in one day, and it won't go away that fast either. I don't care where you start, but start somewhere. Move a little bit more, or eat a little bit less, but do one of those two things right now."

Walk to the mailbox. Walk to the grocery store if it's around the corner. Heck, walk even if it's a mile away. Ditch your fast-food habit, if only for one day. (If you're in the drive-thru lane while you're reading this book, put the book down, throw your car in reverse and go home! You'll thank me in the morning.) Replace soda with water for even a week, and see what kind of benefits you feel. Do five laps around your living room during commercial breaks, I don't care. Just move! Move more. And eat—you guessed it—less.

Part Two

Jell-O Bones and a Bucket of Tears:

My Surreal Existence on Reality TV

CHAPTER 4

The Terrifying, Tumultuous Trip
toward Thin

I N THE 1991 movie *What About Bob?* Bill Murray plays the hilarious character Bob Wiley, an insecure, neurotic and quirky recluse who self-admittedly has a few "problems." One day he is referred to a psychiatrist, played by Richard Dreyfuss, and in an early scene sheds light on the exact nature of his dilemma.

"Here's the simplest way to put it," Bob says. "I worry about diseases, so I have trouble touching things. In public places it's almost impossible. I have a real big problem moving."

"Talk about ... *moving*," says Dreyfuss' character, Dr. Leo Marvin.

"As long as I'm in my apartment, I'm okay," Bob explains, "but when I want to go out, I get ... weird."

"Talk about *weird*," comes the advice.

"Talk about weird. Well, I get dizzy spells," Bob says. "Nausea. Cold sweats. Hot sweats. Fever blisters. Difficulty breathing. Difficulty swallowing. Blurred vision. Involuntary trembling. Dead hands. Numb lips. Fingernail sensitivity. Pelvic discomfort ..."

If you never saw *What About Bob?* and your life seems strangely incomplete, now you know why. Put it in your Netflix queue today. Few movies are funnier than this one.

You get the feeling Bob could go on this way for hours, delineating the symptoms faced by an irrational hermit, symptoms that sound strangely like those also faced by obese people trying to work out for the very first time. Thankfully, Bob's litany is interrupted.

"Bob," says Dr. Marvin as he scans his bookshelves, "a groundbreaking book has just come out that might help you." He pulls the book from the shelf and hands the copy to Bob.

"*Baby Steps*?" Bob asks as he takes in the title.

"*Baby Steps*," confirms Dr. Marvin. "It means setting small, reasonable goals for yourself, one day at a time, one tiny step at a time. For instance, when you leave this office, don't think about everything you have to do to get out of the building. Just think of what you must do to get out of this room, and when you get to the hall, deal with that hall, and so forth. You see? *Baby* steps."

"*Baby* steps!" Bob cheers as he rises to leave and takes small shuffles toward the door. "Oh boy!"

———∿∿———

Several months after I'd been on the show and had made the transition from the madness known as "Jillian Michaels' workouts" to the madness known as Margie's, I'd see the baby-steps approach play out in living color.

A new girl named Sharon showed up to be trained one day, and immediately Margie pulled me aside. "Julie," she asked, "can you please help me look after her? She's never really worked out." It was an assessment that would be proven true during our very first hour together.

Partway through the seventy minutes of sprints, races and drills, I looked over to find my newfound, overweight friend barfing for all she was worth. She was exhausted, miserable and obviously physically sick. "Sharon," I said as I approached her, "you simply cannot quit. I know this is hard, but you have to keep going, just one step at a time." She nodded as she stood up from her keeled-over position and attempted to pull herself together.

Months ago I posted Sharon's story on my MySpace page and was in awe over the reception it received. My favorite reply came from a young woman in Mississippi, who wrote,

"I know exactly how Sharon feels. I'd let myself gain so much weight over the last nine years that I was no longer happy in my own skin. I recently started exercising, and six hours after my first cardio workout I could not move. Muscles were hurting that I didn't even know were there, but three days later, I went at it again. I'm finally sticking to a schedule now, and for the first time in my life, instead of saying, 'I'm *going* to do it,' I'm actually *doing* it!"

Amazingly, she persevered through the rest of that workout and despite being sore for the entire week following that debut actually showed up for round two of the torture two days later.

During our second seventy-minute training session together, I checked in on Sharon between drills to make sure she was still alive. As I approached her I noticed that tears were streaming down her cheeks. "What is it?" I asked as gently as possible.

"I don't know," she whispered through choked-back tears. "I really don't know why I'm crying."

I cupped her hand in my hands, looked her straight in the eyes and said, "I do. I know *exactly* why you're tearing up." She met my gaze in anticipation of what I would say. "You're crying for three reasons," I continued. "First, you're crying because you are completely embarrassed about letting yourself get to this point. You can't believe that *you* of all people are this horribly and uncomfortably fat.

"The second reason you are crying is that this is the hardest thing you have ever done, and physically, it just plain hurts.

"And third, those tears are tears of pride. You're proud that you're actually *doing* this."

Sharon nodded so rapidly that I thought her head might wobble right off her shoulders. "How do you know all of that?" she finally asked.

I told her that on so many occasions on campus, I had shed those very same tears. I too had followed the baby-step progression, from embarrassment to pain to pride, and while I wouldn't trade the end result for all the money in the world, I vastly underestimated what it would take to walk that path.

"MUST I REMIND YOU I'M FAT?"

I didn't fully know how much weight I carried all of my adult life until I tried to run it up a hill. The first time Jillian asked me to jog for five minutes straight—no stopping allowed—I thought I'd literally burst into tears. Sure, she had first prepared my fragile knees by working to build up the muscles that surround them, but when I heard her demand that multiminute run I knew I was a goner for sure. I was writing my obituary in my mind's eye as I pulled on my socks and shoes. "Julie Hadden—loving wife, mom and friend. Sadly enough, that twenty-foot jog just did her in!" What a pitiful way to go.

Halfway through the run that I was sure I would not survive, I looked at Jillian and wanted to scream, "I'm a fat person! Do I really need to remind you of that? I'm fat, and fat people like couches and French fries and drinks that have fizz, not death-wish jogs in the blazing sun!"

"Welcome to your new world, Jules!" Jillian sneered as if hearing my thoughts. She had been running backward faster than I was running forward, and as she did a one-eighty and raced off into the distance, I heard her cheer, "Keep going! It doesn't get better than this!"

Prior to my *The Biggest Loser* experience, the only form of physical activity I engaged in was the kind that involved walking from the living room to the kitchen for a refill on snacks, or from the car to the house after picking up Noah from school. I guess there were other examples, but they reflected accidental exercise at best. Clearly that had all changed drastically, now that I was on the show.

The worst part of being on campus wasn't the fact that I was denied my French fries and fizz. Nor was it the fact that Jillian made me complete a near-fatal run. It's that those things happened not just once but on a sickeningly daily basis. In the spirit of referencing Bill Murray movies, it was like I had been dropped onto the set of *Groundhog Day*, where every twenty-four-hour period mirrored the awful day you thought you'd already lived through.

As a frame of reference, for my entire life leading up to the show, dragging luggage through an airport represented the most rigorous workout I'd known. Well, that, and sweating my way into a swimsuit during those dreaded pageant days.

A typical day on campus involved getting up at seven-thirty, grabbing a bite to eat and hitting the gym before Jillian arrived so that once she was there, our homework assignment was complete. Typically that homework involved an hour of cardio—such as spending twenty minutes on the stair-climbing machine at level eight, followed by twenty minutes on the elliptical machine at 150 revolutions per minute, followed by twenty minutes on the stationary bike or the treadmill. After that, we'd engage in one-on-one workouts with Jillian. And oh, how I hated those.

Some of my teammates actually looked forward to the individual attention, but for the life of me, I don't know why. I'd refuse to make eye contact with Jillian each morning when she'd ask our team, "Okay, who's up first?" Thankfully, my teammate Hollie typically jumped at the chance to get her "Jillian time" over with; from the safety of my treadmill I'd watch every exercise Jillian put her through so that I'd be prepared when I was called on. When it finally was my turn, my ever-present thought was, "Great day, let this be over soon."

After those excruciating one-on-ones, we'd have to log another hour of independent exercise before we could take a short break for lunch. Our afternoon schedule looked strangely the same: individual training with Jillian, followed by an hour of work on our own. Talk about exhausting! My flabby little self didn't know what to think, after all I was asking it to do.

The most intense days of all were the ones that involved a challenge in addition to the normal stuff of campus life. We'd be awakened at 3:00 AM and told to get "camera ready" as quickly as possible, which usually involved a shower, team-colored workout clothes and an attempt to look at least halfway awake.

My teammates and I would plod downstairs to eat an apple and some almonds, even as I offered up a silent prayer—"Seriously, Lord, if you'd deliver me a cinnamon roll, I'd be *far* more pleasant to be around." We'd then pack a lunch for ourselves and climb into a van that would drive us to the challenge location ninety minutes away. I always thought I'd be able to sleep during those van rides, but my plans were futile at best. Between the chatter of my teammates, the potholes in the road, and the rising sun casting bright beams across my face, it was no use.

The single common denominator uniting a very diverse group of eighteen original contestants for Season 4 was that *nobody* ate breakfast prior to their time on the show. Eat breakfast, people!

Once on-site, we'd spend another hour preparing for the physical part of the challenge. Sports-training staff members would tape our feet and ankles, give us instruction on the nuances of the challenge and then set up cameras and microphones. By the time the challenge actually started, the sun was high in the sky.

Each challenge took thirty to forty-five minutes to complete. If the show's host, the lovely and talented Alison Sweeney, was asked to redo certain shots because of audio blips or lighting issues, it could take longer, but usually we'd be done in less than one hour's time. Afterward,

I was incredibly enamored with Alison Sweeney at the beginning of the show because I had seen her for so many years on *Days of Our Lives*. She still starred on that show while she was working with *The Biggest Loser*, and often she'd come to our set immediately after leaving the set of her soap. We all loved to harass her after her flashback scenes on *Days*; she'd arrive at our show with hair that still boasted a 1950s bouffant or 1970s flyaways.

each contestant had to sit for interviews about the challenge itself, answering questions like, "How did you feel when two *blue-team* members outlasted you?" and "Walk us through your initial strategy . . . why did you think you might win?"

It took more than two hours to run everyone through the interview process, so when it wasn't our turn, we'd grab a seat and eat our sack lunch. When everyone was finally done, we'd load back into the van and head home. Incredibly, even after a tiresome morning like that, we'd get back to campus and have to unload the van, empty the coolers and put everything back in the appropriate kitchen cabinet or refrigerator drawer. So much for being TV celebrities! Since when do stars do their own chores?

Then, into a fresh set of workout clothes and on to the gym we'd go.

⌐∿∽⌐

After our painstaking series of workouts, we'd then head back to the house. We would prepare and eat dinner, which seemed always to consist of a small grilled chicken breast, half a cup of veggies, a small side salad and a glass of room-temperature water—*again*. Oh joy.

The Bodybugg is an armband device that measures your caloric intake and expenditure. We would have loved them, except for the fact that our trainer could log online and tell whether or not we were burning calories while she was away. Made it a *wee* bit harder to cheat.

We'd clean up the kitchen, moan about how exhausted we were, wait in line to do our "confessional" recordings on camera, write a few letters to family members who were cheering us on from home, update our online Bodybugg, moan some more about how exhausted we were and then whimper our way to sleep.

It was a far cry from the life I'd known in Jacksonville. And things would only get worse.

THE TROUBLE WITH JILLIAN

When the black team was still operating incognito in the desert, a production assistant approached Jillian with a video camera during one of our workouts to ask her about the strategy she employed when training a team. "Tell us about your approach, Jillian," the guy said. And in response, Jillian shed light for millions of Americans on the truth of what makes her tick.

> Contestants weren't allowed contact with loved ones until well into the game—no phone calls, no letters, no e-mails, no nothing. Finally, by week eight, I was allowed to call Mike. No sweeter sound had my ears ever heard than that particular "Hello?"

"My plan is the same, season after season after season," Jillian said as she then punched one fist into the palm of the other hand: "Beatings, beatings, beatings. And then some more beatings." Whether or not we appreciated her approach, evidently it had been working well for her. At this writing, out of the six seasons that Jillian has appeared on, a member of her team has won every single time.

> Jillian Michaels also has won every season of *The Biggest Loser Australia* on which she has appeared, which makes her an *international* training threat.

Still, on those frequent occasions when I needed a way to ease the pain that she so fervently loved to inflict, I'd dream up new reasons to detest the trainer who has a strange affinity for abuse. While I could write an entire book on the trouble with Jillian Michaels, I'll try to contain myself to a top-ten list of sorts. Here they are, in no particular order.

SHE CAN'T COUNT

On a near-daily basis Jillian would lead a small group of us in cardio drills. She'd say, "Okay, everyone, twenty jump-squats, starting now." She'd begin counting as we obediently crouched down low and then sprung up high, but when we got to twenty, mysteriously, we were not done. "Five more!" she'd holler, just when we were pulling back to take a break. "Really, Jillian," Hollie would protest. "You've got to be kidding."

Obviously, she was not.

The extra five would become an extra fifteen in the end, and my teammates and I would despise her even more. The first twenty were tough enough, let alone an agonizing total of thirty-five. I stand by my case: She cannot count. But that was hardly the worst of her quirks.

SHE IS NEVER WRONG

The only thing more annoying than a person who thinks she's always right is a person who is, in fact, never wrong. Enter Jillian Michaels.

For instance, it would be mere hours before a weigh-in, and I'd say, "I think I lost six pounds this week." I mean, I know my body best, right? Jillian would shake her head immediately and say, "Nope. You only lost three." Or, "Are you kidding? You clearly lost eight." Of course, come weigh-in time, she always was dead on.

Jillian also knew our personal limits better than we did. During one especially awful workout, Isabeau was running on a treadmill when Jillian came into the gym. She made a beeline for Izzy and said, "Harder! *Faster*, Isabeau. Move!" Through labored breaths, Izzy panted out her reply: "I *can't*, Jillian! I'm already going as fast as I can go!"

Jillian, of course, took that response as a challenge. She reached around and punched buttons on the treadmill's control pad until Isabeau was nearly flying, she was running so fast. As soon as Izzy successfully completed the thirty-second interval, with Jillian counting down every single stride, she heard Jillian shrieking at the top of her lungs as she left the gym, "I AM NEEEEVVVVVER WRONG!"

Closer to home, weeks into my *The Biggest Loser* experience, Jillian decided to take me off of all of my medications, which included Ortho Tricycline to combat the effects of my polycystic ovary syndrome, and Metformin for my glucose intolerance and pre-diabetic condition. Understandably, I was nervous about it, but she assured me that in three weeks' time my body would adjust. Twenty-one days later,

> Jillian was so concerned about my polycystic ovary syndrome that she made contact with some of the world's most renowned doctors to find out how I could convince my body to lose weight. The meds I was taking were being used preventively—to regulate my hormones, mostly—and those doctors and the show's doc agreed unanimously that if I was going to begin normalizing my hormone levels through better diet and exercise patterns, then I could discontinue my habit of popping pills. Thank goodness!

you guessed it: My plateau of piddly two- and three-pound weight-loss weeks was jolted, and I finally began to see results.

Never wrong. Never, ever, ever wrong. It's annoying, but it's true.

SHE CLEARLY LACKS COMPASSION

If you're overweight, it's tough to tip yourself over and walk on your hands and feet, but "bear crawls" were one of Jillian's favorite exercises from day one. She'd divide us into duos and wrap resistance bands around the waist of one member of each team. "Get in back of them," she'd holler to the ones without the bands strangling their bellies, "and don't let them get up the hill!" Talk about misery. With us pulling against them, our beloved friends and teammates would then tip over into the bear-crawl position and try with all their might to ascend the hundred-yard hill.

I remember one situation when this was the drill *du jour*, and all was going well. That is, until Hollie cried. Keep in mind, Hollie was not much of a crier. But on that particular day she'd simply had enough.

Jillian noticed Hollie hesitating, and so she grabbed the resistance band that was wrapped around Hollie and said, "Are you going to do this, Hollie? Or are you going to *quit*?"

The rest of us kept moving and tried to avoid eye contact with Jillian. We hated to see Hollie get picked on, but it was better her than us.

Through the corner of my eye I saw Hollie tip herself onto all fours, her heavy, heavy weight coming down hard on her hands. Her neck looked constricted as her chubby cheeks covered her eyes. Sweat ran down her face and pooled on the ground below.

But still, she forced herself up the path.

In the face of an emotional breakdown, I'm sure some trainers rush to the person's side, wrap a loving arm around the person's neck, and say, "Oh, you poor thing. Here, let's have a Snickers and take a break." But not Jillian. Far from it. She'd rush to your side, all right. But only so that she could fire a closer-range shot that was sure to take your sorry self down.

SHE HAS NO CONCEPT OF TIME

Jillian would send one of my teammates or me to retrieve something from the house during a workout and become irate when we finally returned. "You should have been back in *three* minutes!" she'd accuse whoever had been sent on the errand, forgetting entirely that it was a five-minute walk from the gym to the house ... and therefore a ten-minute walk round-trip.

SHE POSSESSES ZERO PATIENCE

Jillian would tell us to eat lunch when we were between workouts and then thirty seconds later, obviously angered by the fact that food was not finding its way to our faces yet, say, "I thought I told you to *eat your lunch*!"

"Hello!" we'd fire back. "We have to cook it first!"

SHE'S A SNEAKY SABOTEUR

Once we finally *did* get our lunch prepared, Jillian would control our portions through the use of condiments. If she felt like we'd had enough to eat, she would upend the ketchup bottle or unscrew the salt shaker and destroy the remainder of our meal. And she wanted to be our *friend*?

SHE IS CONSUMED WITH ALL THINGS "IMMUNITY"

Whenever our team competed in a challenge or a temptation activity, Jillian only wanted for us to assume risk if we would be guaranteed immunity. The reward could be a priceless video made by a loved one, a much-needed full-body massage or five thousand dollars in cold hard cash, and still Jillian would not budge. Family meant nothing and money meant nothing, because there was only room for one goal, and that goal was immunity, immunity, immunity. "Who cares if you win five grand, if it costs you a week in this game?" she'd rant. And as always, Jillian was right.

SHE HAS A SPECIAL DISDAIN FOR SEATS

Jillian loved to lead our team in "spin" classes. She'd circle up the stationary bikes, tell us to take our pick and find a seat and then promptly proceed to remove them—the seats, that is. She'd rev up all the bikes as high as they would go and then come jump on my front wheel. There I'd be, pedaling as though my life depended on it—because it did—huffing and puffing out prayers to God and fending off Jillian's added resistance until the magical moment I heard the word *Stop*.

SHE INSISTS ON FOOD GOING IN...

From day one, the black team was instructed to bring snacks with us to every workout. If you forgot it, sweet heavens, the universe would utterly come to a halt. "I asked you to bring your SNACKS!" Jillian would roar upon discovering delinquency in the ranks. I'm sure that camera operators and production assistants stationed in the gym who heard that little reminder thought that Jillian was looking out for our own good. "What a kind and thoughtful trainer she is," they must have thought. After all, wouldn't any trainer worth her biceps want her trainees to eat healthy, frequent meals?

But that wasn't Jillian's motivation at *all*.

In reality, Jillian preferred to beat the snot out of us, and she knew we needed nourishment to withstand it.

Beatings, beatings, beatings—she was a woman of her word.

...AND DOES A HAPPY-DANCE WHEN FOOD COMES BACK OUT

On the heels of one workout in which Hollie did, in fact, remember to bring her snack, Jillian circled up the black team and asked us to have a seat. We were all exhausted, and as Jillian stood in the middle of the circle, giving her best attempt at a pep talk, I couldn't help but notice the teammate sitting directly across the circle from me.

Evidently Hollie had brought her food in a plastic grocery bag, and now the empty bag was hanging around her face, its handles hooked over both of her ears. I snickered a little at the sight of my friend, which caught Jillian's attention. "What's so funny?" she said, genuinely curious.

She swiveled around to see what I was looking at, and when she took in her trainee with a barf bag on her face, she just had to know more. "Hollie, honey? What's *up*?"

But of course Hollie could not reply. For days on end our bodies had been detoxing from all the "clean" eating and incessant workouts we'd endured, and Hollie had some business to tend to. With all eyes on her, she drew her knees toward her chin, and, able to hold her cookies no longer, completely and thoroughly barfed. Which sent Jillian into full-fledged dance-mode.

I'm not sure when it began, but by our season on the show, Jillian had crafted a puke-induced dance of joy. Why was she so elated about such a terrible turn of events? Because it meant that her beatings had taken effect, that her poor, suffering contestant had actually worked out *that* hard.

It's a little difficult to describe without nonverbals, but essentially she squats down, throws her hands in front of her thighs, thrusts her butt into the air and swings her hips in ever-widening circles while squawking out strains of sheer delight.

Try though we did to contain ourselves for Hollie's benefit, my teammates and I finally dissolved into a fit of laughter. By the time we composed ourselves, Jillian was on the floor in happy-baby position, kicking her feet in the air and crying hysterical tears. "That's fan*tas*tic!" she cheered over poor Hollie's condition. "She's carrying a puke-purse on her face!"

⌒〜∧〜⌒

Surely you're with me here in deeming our trainer a little unstable at best. For all the reasons I've cited—not to mention a training philosophy that includes not one or two or three but *four* occurrences of the word "beatings"—I dare say Jillian is just a *little* south of sane.

Still, for all her craziness, we loved her. She was our trainer and confidante and yes, she'd even become our friend. Her commanding presence had commanded us, and our trust for her ran deep.

INSANE IN MORE WAYS THAN ONE

The implications of working out that long and that hard, for that many days in a row, were many.

After about two weeks, every bone in my body felt like it was made of Jell-O. I knew I'd hit an all-time low when I realized that for four days straight I had been crawling on all fours to the bathroom because I was too exhausted to carry my own weight. Exhaustion can do funny things to a girl, making trips to the bathroom and showering incredibly difficult.

On the night that my teammates and I found out we had been cast for Season 4 of *The Biggest Loser*, J. D. Roth,

> Surprisingly, I grew accustomed rather quickly to having a video camera in my face twenty-four hours a day. I just hoped one wasn't rolling each time I *crawled* my way to the ladies' room. How pathetic.

the show's executive producer, told us that contestants from previous seasons eventually found themselves facing such significant physical pain that they could no longer wash their hair. They simply could not lift their worn-out arms that high.

One evening when Hollie and I happened to be in the communal showers at the same time, I saw my friend cave to the trend. Too fatigued to move her arms, she instead grabbed her bottle of Pantene, gave it a good squirt toward the wall, let her head fall forward and rotated her neck in small circles until the blob of shampoo found its way to her hair. Talk about *exhaustion*.

Hollie doesn't remember the episode today, which is testimony to God's grace. I liken it to women who forget the pain of childbirth right after it happens, which is pretty much the sole reason we don't have a world made up of families with just one child.

The next morning, as was the case nearly *every* morning, another exhausted teammate, Jim, served as our alarm clock. Who needs a buzzer when the guy sleeping thirty feet away from you wakes you up every day with deafening moans and groans? "Ow, my *knee!*" he'd cry as soon as his feet hit the floor. Or, "Oh my *back*, my *ankles*, my arm! Ow, ow, *owww!*"

> There actually is no such thing as a "last-chance workout" on *The Biggest Loser*. The term was cooked up just for TV. I *wish* we would have had them, because that would have meant that other workouts were *less* intense in nature! In actuality we worked out six to eight hours a day every day, and every hour was just as hard as the one that had just passed.

Still, despite our body's creaks and groans and wails and pleas, toward the end we wanted to win the grand prize so badly that we would do the craziest things.

> Before *The Biggest Loser*, I could barely walk for three consecutive minutes without becoming winded. Every time I go to the gym in Jacksonville these days, I find it odd that people leave after "only" working out for an hour. My, how things have changed.

We would watch the other teams come into the gym, and if we caught wind of the fact that they were going to work out for an hour, we'd stay in there an hour and two minutes just to mess with them. Who cared if we were in excruciating pain? It was worth it if it meant that a black-team member would win!

My teammates and I also started staking out our favorite equipment, such as the calorie-blasting stair-climbing machines. If Hollie got into the gym first, she'd hop on a stair-climber and throw her towel on the one right beside her. When a blue- or red-team contestant approached it, intending to climb on, she'd say, "So sorry, but Julie already called it." In fact, I *hadn't* already called it. In fact, I was still in the kitchen eating breakfast. But what are friends for, if not to keep everyone but *your* team from taking home the ultimate prize?

Once on the coveted stair-climbers, my teammates and I would stay put for as long as we could convince our legs to move. With every stride we were keeping someone else from losing weight. Ah, the splendor of a little spirited competition!

Somewhere along the way various players even participated in voluntary workouts, on top of the already ridiculous workout regime our trainers had established for us.

One morning, blue-team member Neil snuck off to the gym at 5:00 AM to get in an early workout. To his surprise, he found my teammate Bill sprawled out on the floor. Bill evidently had been working out all night long and must have caved to utter exhaustion. "Oh my gosh," Neil thought, "he's *dead!*"

Wasting no time, Neil stepped right over Bill and mounted his beloved treadmill. I told you, didn't I? *Crazy.*

Later that day, several of us hunted down Neil and demanded an explanation. "*Really*, Neil? You didn't even check to see if Bill was *alive* before you worked out?"

"Hey," Neil replied, "I figured, at least there's *one* down."

> Surely you remember Neil. You know, the guy who water-loaded one week and gained seventeen pounds, only to lose thirty-three the next week and make the rest of us so mad? I know, I know: It's a *game*. Still, we were mad.

We were becoming insane, every single one of us, which was fitting, given where we happened to be living at the time—at a bona fide former insane asylum. Read on.

⌇⌇⌇

Every contestant on Season 4 thought he or she would be competing at *The Biggest Loser* Ranch, site of Seasons 1 through 3. Far from some dusty primitive campground, *this* ranch was actually a posh mansion. So, while we knew we'd be absolutely tortured while on-site, at least our surroundings would be pretty.

You can imagine our dismay when we realized that Season 4 was going to be billed as "*The Biggest Loser* University"—complete with cold and sterile dorms.

Come to think of it, *real* dorms would have been better than where they chose to house us in the end.

In passing, we had learned from one of the production assistants that our "dorm" was actually a former clinic for the mentally ill. Sometime during that first week on campus, long after the rest of our team had fallen asleep, Isabeau and I were talking to each other from our respective beds. Suddenly we noticed that some of the windows had sawed-off bars on them. I sat up in bed and took in the long room that we stayed in, eyeing the series of beds that lined the wall. "This was the *hospital* ward!" I whispered. It felt like we were in a war scene, where all of the injured soldiers are lined up in a row—a metaphor that wasn't lost on me at all.

Oddities abounded at the asylum. Old pharmacy rooms still had those Dutch doors I remember from childhood Sunday school classes, where the top and bottom halves work independently of each other. The hallway that ran down the middle of the facility seemed to span forever. On one side were various rooms that had been used as wards, and on the other side were cages where they probably had performed lobotomies. Nearby were still-operational vegetable fields, and depending on the way the wind blew, we'd wake up to the smell of either strawberries, which was great, or onions, which was less than great.

Contestants from past seasons would drop in for visits every once in a while and rub in our faces just how atrocious our living conditions were. Until that point, we hadn't really noticed. It was like living in a third-world country and having someone show up and say, "You know, in America we have running water." And you go, "You *do*?"

We had a comfortable room, a paved walkway that led to fully outfitted gym, and teammates that were becoming more like family every day. Despite the rigors of our routine, like little Mary Lennox in her lovely Secret Garden, who found a little slice of serenity in the most unlikely of situations, the asylum was our refuge—for us, a home-sweet-home.

WHEN PAIN GIVES WAY TO PROGRESS

My team and I not only got used to our mad surroundings, but eventually we got used to Jillian's madness too. And truth be told, some of the lessons she taught us I will carry with me all the remaining days of my life.

There is a sign that hangs in *The Biggest Loser* gym that says, "Feel the fear . . . and do it anyway." It's a quote from Jillian, and a philosophy I would come to embrace. Through her constant encouragement—if you can call it that—I would learn that progress doesn't show up unless discomfort comes with it. And oh, how she knew how to bring us to that point. I go to the gym these days and see people on treadmills, going three miles an hour on a 0 percent incline. Come on, now. You've got to work harder than that!

Here's my on-campus takeaway, free of charge: If you are able to carry on a conversation while working out, then you aren't working out hard enough.

Another of Jillian's exhortations was, "Remember: It's just exercise."

One of the greatest rewards I received from my *The Biggest Loser* experience is the ability to walk into any gym in any city today and not be embarrassed by how I look. What a gift!

During those weeks when we were working out in the gym in Hermosa prior to our on-campus appearance, it wasn't uncommon for us to cause quite a stir. We'd walk into the local 24 Hour Fitness and immediately hear whispers and gasps as people noticed that Jillian Michaels was leading our pack. From that moment until the moment we left, all eyes were on us.

One day Jillian was training Jim, who physically was the strongest member of our team at that time, when some random guy rushed up to her and said, "You're *killing* him! Quit *killing* him!" Jillian took a step back, sized up the guy, and then said with a level voice, "Do you have *any* idea who I am?"

In the man's defense, he was, in fact, genuinely concerned that Jim was going to die. And understandably so, given how it must appear to normal people who see Jillian train for their very first time. But she—and Jim too, for that matter—understood what all of us had come to know: Once your body is strong, everything else is just exercise. I would need to remember that when I was back home after the show and depressed about gaining a few pounds. "It's just exercise," I'd tell myself when I felt like giving up. "You're used to this, your body craves this and if you persevere, you'll find your target weight once more."

> On the show we were trained to be on a par with professional athletes, and although it may take time and effort for me to meet a particular goal these days, I honestly believe that, physically speaking, there is *nothing* I cannot accomplish.

Can I give you one more tidbit from my favorite trainer? "It never gets easier," she'd say to us every day. "*Ever.*" And you know what? She was right.

Even now, it is not easy. It's not easy to work out one or two hours a day, five days a week. It's not easy to make wise food choices when French fries taunt me at every turn. It's not easy to dig deep for motivation to stay healthy and capable and strong. But I do it anyway.

I do it because I would rather suffer the pain of progress than the pain of being fat. I would rather celebrate the joy of well-made choices than the joy a cupcake can bring. I would rather leave a challenging legacy of healthfulness to my family and friends than the cheap one marked only by fun.

I look back and can't *believe* what my body was able to do during the show. I was irritable and in agony much of the time, but I did it. And when my long-hated weight finally found its way off, what a sight for sore eyes was the new me.

———◦∧∧◦———

During week thirteen of my *The Biggest Loser* experience, I won a twenty-four-hour trip home. More accurately, Hollie won it for me. By that point in the show there were eight contestants left in the game, and she beat the lot of us in a twenty-four-kilometer triathlon. The prize? Not only immunity and a home-visit for herself, but immunity and a home-visit for another player of her choosing. Praise Jesus and all things holy, she picked me.

I remember looking up when I heard my name called, thinking, *Me? Little ol' me? Great! Let's go!*

It was a mad dash home. Hollie and I flew through the shower, grabbed a few articles of clothing from our room and hopped in the van that was waiting to take us to the airport.

I remember walking up the sidewalk in Jacksonville in my T-shirt, flip-flops and jeans, with butterflies flapping their way through my stomach. Mike told me later that it was the first time in nearly eight years that I had worn jeans, but who was counting?

Immediately I spotted Mike and Noah and our puppy Flower, and the tears just started to flow. It had been three months since I had seen them last, and the woman's heart in me simply came undone.

Approaching them, life fell into slow motion. I stretched over my son to kiss my husband before realizing that I had been intercepted mid-stride by Noah. For the first time in his life, he was able to wrap his arms all the way around my waist. What a thrill!

After a lovely—and nutritionally safe—lunch at Subway, a camera crew took Mike, Noah and me to the beach so that I could give them a glimpse of what a "real" workout entailed. I went easy on them, but even so, they were whipped.

Thirty minutes into a measly routine of commando crawls, push-ups, mountain-climbers and leg presses, Mike's legs collapsed under his own weight. He was sweating and out of breath and his body was clearly done—*Mike*, mind you, who is six feet one and strong as strong can be, under regular circumstances. Sad, sad man. *Pitiful*, even.

> Prior to *The Biggest Loser* experience, Mike and I probably ate out five or six times a week. The richness of the food, the gigantic portion sizes, the desire to eat all that you paid for—nothing about that trend was good.

> My darling husband had lost twenty-eight pounds on his own while I was on the show those first few months. *Twenty-eight* pounds, and without a lick of torture from the likes of Jillian Michaels. Where is the fairness in *that*!

I had lost thirty-eight pounds by that point in the game, and as Mike took me in that day, I remember thinking, *This is what it looks like when your husband is proud of you.*

Of course, he had always been proud of me. Perhaps what I really meant is that for once, I agreed.

William Shakespeare once wrote that, "To climb steep hills requires slow pace at first."[4] I look back on my four months on *The Biggest Loser* campus—as well as the strenuous months that followed—and realize that while I started turtle-slow, I still made it all the way to the top. There's something to be said for baby steps.

There's something *big* to be said for small steps.

Start Now!

It's never wise to begin a diet inside a restaurant, but I found myself in that un-enviable situation on more than a few occasions during my yo-yo dieting days. My family and I would wake up on a lazy Saturday morning and decide to go to Cracker Barrel for breakfast. "No problem," I'd say. "I'll just order an all-veggie egg-white omelet and a cup of coffee, no cream."

My strategy worked, until the freebies showed up. Before I knew it I was sitting in front of a side of hash browns, a basket of biscuits, a dish of thick gravy and a large glass of juice . . . in *addition* to that all-veggie egg-white om-elet. A few dozen swift bites later I'd mourn the good intentions that had gone awry once more.

Before long, it would be time for lunch, but instead of making a healthy food-choice, I'd think, *What kind of diet starts with hash browns and biscuits and gravy?* The day was obviously already shot, so who cared what I ate for lunch? With a spirit of rebellion in full swing, I'd pull through the McDonald's line, order whatever I wanted and disappoint myself just a little bit more.

I'd follow the same line of thinking for dinner—gorging on pizza or excessive desserts—and then awaken the next morning with a self-induced sugar high and a mild state of depression over the sorry choices I'd made.

The cycle I describe would have been tolerable if it had been the exception instead of the rule. But that was not the case. Day by day, week after week I would indulge the downward spiral until I finally was so disgusted with myself that I simply had to make a change. Like any addict knows, the binge is a blast until you wake up one day and say, "How the heck did I get here?"

On those how-the-heck-did-I-get-here days, my hopes would be dashed, my self-esteem would be shot and my pants would be far too tight. "I can't believe I let myself get to this point again," I'd moan, as if moaning could make anything better.

—⌒∧∧⌒—

Several years ago I went to Las Vegas for my thirtieth birthday. I'm not much for gambling, but I had set aside a whopping forty dollars that I was willing to lose—and lose it I did, one precious nickel at a time. I camped out at the nickel-slots because the dollar-ones were far too risky; I'm a *mom*, for heaven's sake, and moms are known for carefully measuring risk and never assuming more than would be wise. Plus, we're cheap. We like two-for-one deals and anything that's free, which is why I always had so much trouble turning down the hash browns that accompanied my otherwise-healthy breakfast.

I dropped each of those nickels into the machine with incredible care because I had set a limit of forty bucks for myself, and I was determined to stay within it. But let's say that instead of forty dollars, my limit had been *fourteen-hundred* dollars. And, just for the sake of illustration, let's say that I went absolutely crazy, blew eight-hundred bucks before 10:00 AM, and then, feeling depressed and disappointed over my failure, took the remaining six-hundred dollars and tossed it into the first garbage can I saw. You would think that I had lost my ever-loving mind, right? You'd say, "Hey, just because you wasted the first part of your money doesn't mean you have to trash the rest!" You'd tell me to start now being wise with my money so that I didn't waste all that was left.

Months after that Vegas trip, I bought a cup of coffee at a gourmet shop, and printed on the back of the paper cup was the phrase, "Treat your calories like hundred-dollar bills."

In that instant, something inside my mind clicked.

What that disposable coffee cup was telling me was that even when I screw up at breakfast, I don't have to blow the balance of my daily calorie allotment. I could make a fresh start at *any* hour of the day, and spend the next hundred calories I ate as wisely as I would spend my cold, hard cash.

The line of thinking is helping me make better choices these days. When I veer off-course, I stop, find the path and move toward it as quickly as my short legs can get me there. Better still, I am learning to plan ahead so that those tangents are fewer and further between.

Every night, in addition to thinking about what's on my family's agenda the following day, I think about how many calories I plan to spend. If we're going to have to rush from school to soccer practice, for instance, then I know to toss a few Ziploc bags of almonds and raisins in my purse. If I know that friends are having us over for dinner, then I can call ahead to find out what will be served so that I can plan the rest of my day's calories accordingly and possibly even offer to bring a side dish that I know I can actually eat. If I know that Mike is craving Outback Steakhouse for dinner, then I can figure out exactly what I'll order. If I know that I am in need of a giant piece of chocolate cake, then I can drop that six-hundred and eighty calories of Betty Crocker yumminess into the plan.

If you were heading to the mall to buy a Prada purse, you'd probably research how much it was going to cost you first. I'm just suggesting that the same care be taken with food.

Admittedly, there are times when I walk into a situation unprepared. Maybe it's a restaurant I'm unfamiliar with. Maybe it's a venue that doesn't allow outside food. Maybe it's a birthday party where I have no idea what will be served, which is precisely the situation I found myself in last weekend.

A woman I know was hosting a tea party for a mutual friend, and as I eyed the spread before me I realized there was nothing *remotely* healthful there. The tea sandwiches were made with white bread and were oozing herb butter from all sides. The brownies were covered in ganache and topped with sugared raspberries. Even the iced tea was swirling with excess sugar. What was a girl to do?

I didn't want to offend the hostess by refusing to eat, but how could I stick to a calorie count when everything was so bad for me? I decided I'd set a *food* limit instead. Making my way through the line, I selected four small tea sandwiches and one dessert—and I requested plain iced tea that I could add a little stevia to and be fine.

All morning I drank as much water as I could stomach, in hopes of flushing out my system, and I avoided Starbucks en route back home. I felt so proud of myself for sticking to my plan that just after noon I went for a three-mile run. One good decision had led to another good decision, and then another on top of that. How much better that upward spiral felt than the downward one I knew so well!

This is the power of starting right now—wherever you are, in whatever situation you find yourself. Instead of making excuses and putting it off, let *this* hour be the start of making the change that will bless you the rest of your days. Spend your calories as you would precious hundred-dollar bills, and you'll rack up a string of good decisions in no time.

CHAPTER 5

Psychology 101 and
The Biggest Loser Campus

FOR MOST OF MY adult life I was a huge fan of the sweater-set—you know, a stretchy sleeveless shell topped with an even stretchier button-down cardigan. They come in every conceivable color and at $24.99 on the JCPenney sale rack, it's well within the reach of many women to own the full rainbow of options.

For most fat people, their clothes closet starts to resemble a uniform shop over time, and my uniform hinged on the beloved sweater-set. It was comfortable, coordinated and covered a multitude of flaws. Additionally, I never had to think about what to wear each day. The only downside was that I didn't exactly exhibit variety. If it was a weekday, I'd wear a sweater-set and capri pants. If it was Sunday, I'd wear a sweater-set and a skirt. If it was date-night with my husband, I'd wear a sweater set and black slacks. Easy as pie, right?

Although I no longer wear sweater-sets, I miss the practicality of that second layer. Still today I never leave home without a jacket; even in hot, humid Florida I'm *always* the one in the group who is freezing cold.

When it was time for my final audition for the show, understandably, I was nervous about what to wear. To nobody's shock, I opted for the sweater-set, but my rationale went deeper than you might think.

From the beginning I seemed to be positioned as the "stay-at-home mom with PTA hair," and as I made it further and further through the interview process, I figured my attire ought to reflect the woman the casting people believed me to be. Ever the people-pleaser—some habits die hard.

I'm not entirely sure how "sincere and sweet" became my persona among production staff from the show, but the common refrain I heard each time I interacted with any of them was, "You're such a nice person, Julie, and you're obviously a very caring mom. I'm just not sure . . . well, I don't know if you're *cut out* for this game." I'd walk away from those interviews thinking, "What does *that* mean?"

The only explanation I ever landed on was that it was more than a little intimidating to tell a group of strangers about my deepest, most heart-wrenching struggles, and something about that process left me more subdued than usual. Instead of being bubbly, effusive Julie, I became Esther standing before the king. I was waiting for the golden scepter to be outstretched instead of barreling my way through. As I look back now, it's like the other contestants had road rage, and I was the granny in an Impala, just puttering down the road. Easygoing, lovable and happy to be out for a nice Sunday afternoon ride—that's how I came across, and the implications of that impression would be severe.

"I think you're cute and adorable . . . and America will *love* you," I remember the show's psychologist telling me following my initial assessment with him. "I just don't know that you have what it takes to make it on a show like this."

There was that uncertainty again—were my chances all but shot?

Shortly after that psych assessment was the red-velvet-chair interview with J. D. Roth and friends. Toward the end of that interview, I was shocked to hear J.D. speak roughly the same words I'd heard from the psychologist. Had they compared notes? Was this a conspiracy to keep me from achieving my dream?

"You seem sweet and nice . . ." J.D. began. I stared at his mouth as he spoke but the rest of his words became a mumbled blur. I was tired of settling for less than what I truly was capable of, and something inside of me snapped. They aren't going to cast me because I'm nice? I don't think so! I may be a Pollyanna, but I'm not your *average* Pollyanna. I'm a Pollyanna who has done beauty pageants, which makes me a Pollyanna who *knows* how to fight.

Enough, I thought. *I'm putting an end to this now.*

As I sat before J.D. and the others, I felt nervous but resolved. "If I perish, I perish,"[5] Queen Esther had said just before her big speech that day, and suddenly in that moment, I could relate.

Still holding J.D.'s gaze, I said with a perfectly straight face, "Don't let this sweater-set fool you. I did *pageants*, remember? I *know* how it feels to pull a knife out of my back."

J.D. was speechless. My metaphor had connected. Pageant girls are known for being perfect and polished, but they're also known for being fierce. You don't want to mess with them, and in six seconds flat I had assured the show's casting team that my competitors wouldn't want to mess with me either.

I had the mom-bob haircut. I had the ever-stylish sweater-set. And, evidently, I had the attention of J.D. Now all I needed was the chance to prove I had the emotional chutzpah not just to get through an interview, but to *win*.

HIGH HIGHS AND EVEN LOWER LOWS

Life during *The Biggest Loser* was a roller coaster—complete with high highs, low lows, and stomach-flipping spins. And if a roller-coaster ride is jolting for a normal person, try riding one when you're morbidly obese. In the first forty-eight hours flat, I went from feeling thrilled about being on the show, to feeling abandoned because I didn't get picked by the red or blue teams, to feeling exhausted after my first workout in the desert, to feeling elated because I slept *great* my second night at the budget motel. Up, then down, then up, then down—would it be like this forever?

Over the next three days, I felt rejected upon being kicked out of the gym, imprisoned by the sheer weight of the body I was living inside, suffocated by my mounting insecurities and self-reproach, depressed by the fact that I was *still* secretly sneaking snacks and utterly alone as I figured out that food remained my only friend.

A totally unhelpful reality on campus was that the production crew had a snack table that was always stocked. If I had a dime for every diet Sunkist that Hollie and I stole, I'd be a rich, rich girl.

From there I'd do a downward spiral into feeling silly that someone as incompetent as I had made the show, overwhelmed by looking in the mirror and realizing just how far I had to go, insignificant when I saw the workhorses I was competing against, guilty because I'd left my family in order to pursue a self-focused dream, embarrassed when I stood on the scale for the first time, remorseful when I recalled all the things my weight had kept me from doing and angry as I recounted all that fat had stolen from me.

It wasn't pretty.

But then, just as surely as the spiral had descended, it would arrest itself and start moving the other way. I felt *grateful* to have been selected out of the quarter-million who had applied. I felt *powerful* when I ran my first mile. I felt *triumphant* as the pounds finally began to come off. And with every baby step I took, I felt *freed* from long-held fears.

The physical strain of the game was real, but it paled in comparison to the emotional battles I fought. It's far easier to whip a set of biceps into shape than it is to strengthen a mushy mind.

<hr>

One of Jillian Michaels' mantras is, "You don't get fat because of diet and exercise alone." She knew all along what it took me months to understand, that in addition to physical weight, there is always more weight that we carry. As I've mentioned before, Jillian's theory was that if she could somehow get us to unearth those inner demons, we'd be a heck of a lot healthier as we faced the outer ones.

The philosophy made sense to me. After all, fat people can't deny bulging saddlebags, cottage-cheese thighs and the spare tire that's hanging from their waist. But they *can* try to deny the stuff that remains unseen. And for a time, my entire team and I did a decent job of denying that aside from our physical weight there was absolutely anything wrong. The alternative seemed unthinkable.

I'd lived all of adulthood behind the mask of "allrightness." I was happy Julie, bouncy Julie, funny Julie and spontaneous Julie—Julie whom everyone knew and loved. On campus it seemed that every move I made, every word that I spoke, every emotion I finally agreed to share served only to chip away at the visage that my friends and family

After my time on campus, I heard from many people back home that they had no idea I was so miserable inside. "Neither did I," I admitted every time. "Trust me . . . neither did I."

knew as "me." I knew they'd be watching the show from home, thinking, *That's not the Julie we know.*

It was agonizing to bare my soul on national TV, but I'd come to my own personal breaking point, and all I could do was just break. And exactly as Jillian had planned, by the time that breaking point was upon me, I was too physically exhausted to keep the emotional tsunami at bay.

———∿∿———

When I watched *The Biggest Loser* from home I'd get so frustrated with contestants who always cried. *What do they have to be so upset over?* I'd wonder. That is, until I became a blubbering idiot myself. I had made a sport out of stuffing my true feelings in life, but once I allowed the wave onto shore, well . . . Katy, bar the door. You've never *seen* so many tears.

I cried when I realized that I was the weakest link. I cried when I got on the scale and thought about my mother and all of her friends and my husband and all of our friends knowing my real weight. I cried when I had to vote people off the show. I cried when I thought *I* might be voted off the show. I cried when my teammates struggled and I cried when I struggled. I cried when I received praise for my hard work, and I cried when other people got more praise than I did, especially when I'd worked equally hard.

I cried because I missed my family, and then I cried wondering whether

The reason that voting people off the show was so difficult is because all of us were on borrowed time to begin with. We were all considered "morbidly obese" at the show's start, and when you eliminated a player, most likely you were eliminating one who was still morbidly obese. Most likely you were sending them right back to where they developed hypertension, diabetes and poor eating habits in the first place. And without having had enough time to make deep, sustainable changes, in essence, you were kicking them to the curb. The worst times were when I had to eliminate players who were older or heavier than I was. Those nights I felt like the selfish, inconsiderate clod who stays seated on the bus even when an elderly, disabled woman unsteadily stands there with no place to sit down.

they really missed me. I cried when I felt alone, and I cried when I realized I'd made new friends—friends just like me, who "got" what it meant to be fat.

I cried because God had allowed me to shed all those tears, and then I cried as he wiped each of them away.

Toward the end of the show, when the pool of contestants had been whittled down to the black team's final four, Jillian had a running joke she loved to tell. She'd say, "If we were all standing on top of a tall building and I told the four of you to jump off, Isabeau would try to negotiate—'Can we do it from a floor lower?' Bill would want to go even *higher* than the roof—'I can do better than this!' Hollie would cuss me out and storm off. And Julie? She'd take a flying leap on my 'go' but sob the entire way down."

Sadly, she had it about right. I had reverted back to the adolescent version of myself—at best, a wobbly, emotional wreck.

Tears, tears and more tears I cried, until thankfully, one day things finally clicked. I had been emptied and flattened and emotionally wrung dry. But by his grace, God gave me the tools I needed to strengthen not just my body, but my *mind*.

STRENGTH OF BODY, STRENGTH OF MIND

Throughout my life, many situations should have served as a wake-up call for me regarding my health . . . or lack thereof. You would think that when I heard straight from my doctor's mouth that I could not birth another child until I dropped forty pounds, I'd be motivated to change. But nope! That wake-up call I snoozed right past.

After the twenty-fifth time of hiding behind those racks at Target to avoid friends I hadn't seen in a while . . . *surely* that was a wake-up call. But nope! Still didn't opt to change.

How about the sixty-fourth occasion of insisting on sex with the lights turned off? Nope, that wasn't a motivator either.

What about my southern-born family saying, "Good *Lawd*, child, that butt is getting so *big*!" each and every time they saw me?

You guessed it: a great big whopping *nope*.

As I say, many things should have motivated me in the past but didn't. And I know I'm not alone in this. I know overweight people who have lost friends to heart attacks and then the following week hear their own doctor say, "You'll be dead in five years if you continue this way." Think that prognosis causes them to change? Nope, not even *close*.

I know people who try to donate blood and are told by the nurse that their blood is so bad it just can't be drawn. Surely *that's* motivation to change. I wish it were, but nope.

There are friends who can't walk up a flight of stairs without gasping for fleeting breath, but even that doesn't faze them at all.

Honestly, it would be far easier to judge all those people if I weren't so much like them myself. Despite what my doctor, my family and my sex life told me, it wasn't until *I* was motivated to change that I changed.

Still, if I really wanted to achieve my deeply desired goals, I'd have to learn to hear from those who had my best interest at heart.

TRUST FOR THE TRUSTLESS

One of the most sobering realizations I made during my *The Biggest Loser* stint was that I had spent a good portion of my life not trusting a single soul. And while it's true that I was the only one who could motivate me, at some point, even that revelation would warrant trust. I was about to get schooled in the annoying nuances of trust—for my trainer, my team and myself.

When you are separated from your family, your friends and all indications of home, and you can't yet trust the competitors you're trying to outlast, you seek out whatever lifeline you can find. Whether I liked it or not, Jillian was going to have to do.

Because of her stick-to-itiveness with contestants who appeared on previous seasons of the show, Jillian had proven her worth to me vicariously. But at the beginning of our time together, I wasn't sure I trusted her with *me*. She seemed ruthless. Harsh. And lacking a certain southern charm. But over time I'd look past all of that. The day would finally dawn when I'd see Jillian as someone just like me.

PLACING TRUST IN MY TRAINER

Early on in the show, the black team gathered together under a tree after an afternoon of normal, challenging workouts. We were all still getting to know each other, and getting to know Jillian as well.

She pulled us all in for a team huddle because we had a weigh-in the very next night. "Guys, Bob's a great trainer, and I'm sure Kim will compete hard, so I'm going to lay out for you the only advantage I see for us," she began.

As she spoke, she passed out copies of two of her books, *Winning by Losing* and *Making the Cut*.[6] "Inside, there's a survey about whether you're a fast oxidizer or a slow oxidizer," she continued, "and I'm going to craft individual eating plans based on how you respond ..." My mind was chasing other thoughts as Jillian's voice continued to fill the air.

I stared at the cover of one of the books and saw Jillian's flawless figure staring back at me. She was captured in a pristine pose, and the lighting was just right. I glanced up at her in real life and then glanced back down at the book in my hands. She was the same here as she was there—how was it *possible* to be that ripped?

She jabbered on and on—something about focusing on the weigh-in and making sure our food intake was what it needed to be—but all I could think about was her body that was perfect and my body that was not. The contrast, admittedly, was tough to take in.

When Jillian finally came up for air, I took advantage of the pause. "Jillian?" I said. "Do you mind if I ask you a question?"

Undeterred by the interruption, she said, "No, honey, of course not. What's on your mind?"

I looked around at my teammates and mustered the courage to respond. "When you look at us," I said, "are you ... *disgusted* ... by what you see?"

To this day, I have never again seen the look that appeared on Jillian's face when I posed that question. It was a strange mix of pity and anger, of horror wrapped up in devastation that the subject would even come up. After nearly five full seconds, Jillian spoke. "Of *course* not!" she answered. "Why on earth would you ask me that?"

I hadn't meant it in the harsh way she was taking it. I meant the question sincerely, and in the same obvious vein as asking a teetotaler if she is sickened when she sees a drunk slouched on the sidewalk, clinging to a near-empty bottle of scotch.

"You're someone who cares a great deal about fitness and her body," I started. "I mean, it's clear that you take good care of yourself. ..." I looked up at her eyes, which were looking back at mine, and kept going. "I just figured that unfocused people like us must absolutely repulse a disciplined person like you."

Apparently it took two therapy sessions worth eight-hundred bucks to get Jillian over our little exchange. "How could Julie *think* such a thing about me?" she had asked her therapist, who wisely responded, "Julie doesn't think that you are disgusted by her and her teammates; Julie *herself* is the one who feels disgusted."

A few days later, when the entire black team was in the gym working out, Jillian garnered my trust even more. She walked toward us while we ran our hearts out on the treadmill and said with a sincere grin, "I get how you guys feel, you know."

It was an uncommonly empathetic comment, coming from her.

Sure you do, you tiny, ripped liar, I thought but certainly did not say.

"No, seriously," she replied as she took in our skeptical eyes. "I'll bring the pictures to prove it."

The next day Jillian showed up to our workout with the promised photos in hand, and as I scanned the images before me, my jaw fell slack. The shots were taken in the 1980s, so I excused the bad perm and ridiculous attire. But what was with the unibrow, the distant look in the eyes, the sixty extra pounds? Oh. My. Gosh. Jillian *did* know how we felt. She hadn't always been the stunning woman my teammates and I gawked at every day. When she yelled at us and demanded our best, it's because she had been there herself. And she knew what it would take for us to reach our potential, the same way she had stretched to reach hers.

When I go to the gym these days and see a heavy girl just *killing* herself on the elliptical machine, I can't help but cheer her on. I know what she's feeling, because I've been there myself. And although she can't yet see it, I know exactly how she'll feel when she's fit.

In the time it took for me to look at one photo, my trust in Jillian was sealed. She wasn't an evil tyrant; she was a chubby girl who'd been reformed. And now she was determined to help others find similar reformation too. Learning to trust her intentions—and her actions—would pave the path for me to trust others too. My teammates, for instance, and eventually even myself.

PLACING TRUST IN MY TEAM

Back on day ten of the special brand of torment known as *The Biggest Loser*, the black team had made its first appearance on campus. Under the cover of darkness an unmarked van dropped us off just outside the gym. Quietly and with a fair amount of urgency, we scurried into the weigh-in area, where we would wait for the other teams' arrival. After almost half an hour, we heard the chatter and the footsteps of red- and blue-team members who were making their way to the gym. My heart raced and I thought about how stunned they'd be to see us standing there, the six men and women they left stranded at the Last Chance Café back on day one of our collective experience. Would they be able to tell how hard we'd been working in the desert for ten days straight?

As the blue and red teams neared, two giant doors emblazoned with *The Biggest Loser* logo slid open so that they could enter the part of the gym that was designated for weighing-in, and the first thing they saw was the black team standing on risers at the front of the room. Jaws dropped, eyes widened and audible groans could be heard as Bob, Kim and their shocked teams saw Jillian standing before them, her hands stuffed into her back pockets and her muscular arms bursting out from both sides. She wore black motorcycle boots that stretched to her knees with her skintight jeans tucked inside and a posture that said, "Come and get us. We dare you."

After the shouts of sarcasm and laughter died down and the others got settled onto their team risers, Alison said, "Red team . . . blue team . . . meet the *black* team." They were not amused. They had established their rhythms, their routines and their strategies for success. All they saw when they looked at us was one big fat disruption.

The first few days with our newfound competition would not be pleasant ones. They wouldn't let us sit at "their" tables during mealtimes and ostracized us at every opportunity. We were clearly the nerds, and they were the cheerleaders and jocks. While they may have taken some satisfaction from making us feel estranged, what they did not consider was that social lepers stick together. The trust that was forged among the black team during those early "outcast days" likely led to our undeniable domination in the end.

My trust for others was expanding, but would I ever be able to trust myself? In due time I'd be invited to find out.

PLACING TRUST, FOR ONCE, IN MYSELF

At nine in the morning, about three months into our *The Biggest Loser* experience, after pulling on a fresh black-team T-shirt and packing a lunch, my teammates and I were driven off-campus for the day. Evidently, we were going to be put to work to see what it was like to live in the real world for a change. As the campus became a dot in the rearview mirror, I was sobered by the reminder that there existed an entire universe outside of our happy *The Biggest Loser* bubble, a universe we were all going to have to return to someday. I know I wasn't alone in wondering if I'd find a way to survive.

Suddenly we were characters in that M. Night Shyamalan movie, *The Village*, in which a group of people, led by the town's elders, had been living a simple, peaceful life in a secluded place sometime in the 1800s. Or so they thought. Through a wild series of events they came to discover that their village was nothing but a facade. In reality it was 2004, and a fast-paced, modern world was spinning all around them.

How do you survive when your airtight bubble bursts? It's the question that was on all of our minds as we stepped out of campus life for the day.

After I finally grew accustomed to the idea of being thrust into the real world for a full day, I then discovered that our real world would involve a pizza parlor. And putting me inside a pizza place is like asking an alcoholic to fill in for the bartender—some things just aren't wise to do.

We walked from the car to the pizzeria, and I could smell the pepperoni from the parking lot. "It's okay, belly," I soothed. "We're gonna do *just* fine." Once inside, the manager introduced himself to us and then showed us to our appointed stations. Not only would I have to *smell* the toppings, but, evidently, I'd have to *touch* them too. I looked down at the giant buckets full of crumbled Italian sausage and grated mozzarella cheese and thought, *Surely life is not this cruel . . .*

Pizza in any form is my kryptonite. Thick crust, stuffed crust, toppings galore—however you care to serve it is absolutely fine with me. On our once-a-week "high-calorie" days on campus, other contestants always wanted variety—Chinese food one week, hamburgers the next— but not me. I say if there is any opportunity for pizza, then pizza is what

I still eat pizza, but now I stick to veggies and thin crust, which has about 180 calories a slice instead of a thick-crust-supreme's 350 or 400. I decide ahead of time how many slices I will eat and then after removing *only* that amount, I shut the box and give away the rest. Left to my own devices I could eat well over half the pie. And who wants to work off *that* calorie count?

must be consumed. At the job site that day, it was like I was sick in the hospital and a long, lost friend had stepped into my room. "Where have you *been* all this time?" I wondered aloud as I stared down at a pile of thick pepperoni circles. "I've missed you more than you can possibly know!"

In the end, the experience was cathartic. Like someone with a terrible fear of heights surviving a skydiving debut, I had stared down my biggest fear—at least as it related to food—and won. I had trusted myself in the most untrustworthy of situations and proven that I could prevail.

TENACITY FOR THOSE WHO LOSE HEART

There were other tools God gave me for sorting out the tangled mess of emotions I held, like *tenacity*, a character trait I'd never before possessed.

Sometimes my goal was making it through the day; sometimes it was making it through that particular workout; and sometimes I had my focus narrowed down to nothing but the very next movement. "You can do it, Julie," I'd reassure myself. "You can lift up your arm one more time."

When things got tough, tenacity said keep going. I could either keep going, or I could do nothing, and doing nothing simply wasn't an option.

During one workout in particular, Jillian made me stand on the gym floor and then jump onto a plyometric box that was eight inches off the ground. I know, I know, eight inches is nothing. But it might as well have been Mount Everest for the mindgames going on in my head. I've never been a good jumper, and as I thought back on the two painful knee surgeries I'd endured my thoughts just got the better of me. "Jump!" Jillian screamed to my face, but flat-footed there I remained. In that moment I knew beyond the shadow of a doubt that I'd fail. But then tenacity whispered, "You can do this. Just try."

I would ice my knees after an especially challenging run and sit there thinking the entire time, "Maybe I should just give up. Maybe this game's not for me." My bones and my background were telling me to quit, but tenacity held me there. "You've quit every time before," I would think. "You're *here* because you've quit, in fact. But a quitter is not who you are."

One of the perks of being on a TV show is that the equipment we used was second to none. When my knees throbbed after a tough workout, trainers would take me to a recovery room and give me an automatic-icing brace to rest my knee in for a while. *Ahhh . . .*

To finish what I've started, for once—would my actions prove my mantra true, or would I cave to weariness and doubt?

In those moments I knew that if quit on that day, I'd be quitting every day 'til I died. I imagined myself five or ten years later, looking back on that give-up moment and wondering who I might have become had I allowed my newfound tenacity to have its way in my mind and my heart.

⌒∧∧⌒

Sometimes, during our "dark-day" workouts, when cameras weren't rolling and things were a little more laid back, music would be played in the gym. One morning a member of another team brought in a CD with Suzie McNeil's song titled "Believe."

The first time I heard her beautiful, ragged voice strain out the chorus to that song, it felt like my heart took flight. "If you just believe," that chorus goes, "you can move mountains with dreams. The higher you climb, the better it gets, 'cause you will see things you'll never forget . . . if you just believe."

The higher you climb, the better it gets—based on the experiences I'd known to that point, I could think of words no truer than those.

So many things tried to squash my belief, but tenacity just kept plugging along. When I'd been passed over instead of placed on a team, my belief took a pretty big hit. When I finally got to campus and realized nobody wanted me there, again, my belief took a hit. When I was losing two pounds to everyone else's fifteen, my belief suffered quite a blow. When I was achy and fearful and just plain overtrained, my belief nearly bottomed out.

Before I left to be on the show, a friend sent me a care package with a bracelet inside. Hanging from the thin cord were tiny baby blocks that spelled out the word *believe*. At the time, I thought it was nothing more than a sweet gesture, but as the show went on that bracelet became a precious symbol of the tenacious spirit God was forging in me.

"You will see things you'll never forget," I'd sing to myself, "if you'll just believe."

How badly I wanted to see those memorable things—the pride in the eyes of my husband rooting for me from home; the delight on the face of a son who craved an active mom; the satisfaction in my sigh after I'd fit into a size-six dress.

Each time I heard that song, my belief was renewed that as long as I kept going, I might just conquer the whole wide world.

Belief was necessary at every turn, it seemed—belief that we were inspiring an entire nation to greater healthfulness, wholeness and strength; belief that we were inspiring each other to reach the goals each one of us had set; belief that with even mustard-seed-size faith, *nothing* was impossible for us.[7]

TIME . . . JUST GIVE IT TIME

If there was a third part of being rescued from my emotional tailspin, it was the divine reminder that real change takes real time to accomplish.

For me, weight came off slowly—at least slowly by *The Biggest Loser* standards. They say that on average a dieting person should lose two pounds a week, but when your competitors are putting up numbers like thirty-one and thirty-three, your three pounds seem pitiable at best.

My first three weeks on the show saw me drop a whopping eight pounds, but it was better than having gained it. "A gradual ascent before you soar," Jillian assured me as I stepped down dejected from the scale one time. How I hoped she'd be proven right.

Week four showed up, and I was the last member of the black team to be weighed in. I stepped on the scale and stared at the floor as Alison Sweeney announced my previous weight of 210 pounds. "Julie," she then said, "your current weight is . . ."

The numbers rolled up and down and all around like a Las Vegas slot machine as I prayed and swayed and waited for them to stop. "Your current weight," Alison continued, "is 203. You lost seven pounds this week."

To say I freaked out would be an understatement. I tried to take in what Alison had just said but believing that surely I had heard her wrong, I swiveled around and looked at the giant display board behind me to check my current weight for myself. Sure enough, a glowing "203" was posted there, in all its marvelous, miraculous glory.

"Shut UP!" I screamed from the scale, which is another way of saying, "I am so excited by this news that I could just pee in my pants"—which I almost did, actually.

Seven pounds, gone forever from my body! *Seven* pounds. It was the biggest loss I'd ever known, and I was elated and ecstatic and full of joy. I screamed some more and then did a little dance

> The giant *The Biggest Loser* scale is bogus. In reality, we were weighed in at a doctor's office the morning before TV-time weigh-in. Sorry to burst your bubble. (If it's any consolation, we really didn't know our individual totals until they were revealed at the fake weigh-in.)

just me, myself and I, before I agreed to come down from the platform where I'd seen my hard work paid off. Maybe, just maybe, I would one day reach my goal. Maybe it would just take a little time.

THE SUN, THE MOON AND A MUCH-NEEDED MASSAGE

Partway through the show, Alison informed us that we'd be flying to Jamaica for the week. Warm sunshine, beautiful weather, stunning surroundings—what more could we ask for? Truly, aside from a reprisal of Jillian's madness-in-the-desert workouts, the getaway felt relaxing and replenishing and fun.

When it was time for all three teams to compete in our challenge, we were told to change into bathing suits and then to meet out at the beach. Fifty yards from shore were three platforms floating in the ocean and a raft tied to the front of each one. Alison explained that the first team to get all of their members from the platform to the shore would win an afternoon of pampering, including a deep-tissue massage. Oh, how I wanted that massage. I *always* want a massage. I'd take a massage

With Jamaica's humidity and without the show's stylists in tow, Jillian's hair grew larger with each minute we were there. She didn't care much about her ever-expanding 'do until the rest of my black-team friends and I began to tease her mercilessly and call her "Monica" from the TV show *Friends*. The episode we were referring to involved Monica and the gang visiting Barbados, where the humidity was so bad that she decided to get corn-rows. We would have suggested the coif-controlling idea to Jillian except that things didn't work out so well for Monica: A few days after she sported her bead-and-shell-adorned rows, she got them caught in the shower curtain and almost injured herself permanently.

now if someone offered one. "We *have* to win this," I declared to my team as we swam out to our designated platform.

It didn't always happen this way, but for some reason, during this particular challenge, the black team just killed the competition. I'm not bragging here; you can watch the footage for yourself. Sure, we had a few early spills as Bill got used to the pulley system, but soon enough he found his sea legs and garnered a healthy lead.

While Bill made his way to shore, the rest of us hung out on the platform, laughing ourselves silly over the fact that former-football-player Phil could not stay balanced on his red-team's raft. He'd pull himself up to a standing position and get four feet across the water before overturning himself into the ocean. A ten-foot-high splash would drench his teammates before he'd sputter and splash his way back to his raft.

After Bill got to shore it was my turn to go. I steadied myself on the too-small raft, crouched down as I coiled the rope around my wrist, and held on for all I was worth. Fortunately, smooth-as-silk Bill coasted me all the way in to shore, where I high-fived him and geared up for Jim.

Bill and I would pull Jim atop the water just as smoothly, and then the three of us would work to bring Jez across. Jez was our fourth and final player to get to shore, and as he stood up on the platform and readied himself for his ride, he noticed that the red and blue teams hadn't pulled even one person in. It was a slaughtering, I tell you. A *slaughtering*!

Jez stood up proudly on his raft, his big butt high in the sky, and coasted toward his three teammates, who were cheering hysterically from the beach. It wouldn't be until later that we'd hear how Jez had mooned the other two teams his entire trip to shore. Ah, victory is sweet.

L ater, during that long and lovely beachfront massage, I considered how far I'd come. For the first time in a long time I was perfectly relaxed, I was completely content and I sensed strength rising from within. "You're *doing* it, Julie!" I said to myself. "You're stronger, both body and soul."

The new me was finally emerging, the "me" God was shaping me to be. And as I caught sight of her for the first time, *those* tears were tears of joy.

Find an Inspiring Image and Focus on It Every Day

Maybe it's Jennifer Lopez's curvy derriere, or Beyoncé's lean torso or Kelly Ripa's fresh and pretty face. Perhaps it's Eva Mendez's flawless skin, or Eva Longoria's perfectly petite frame. Whatever it is you desire, when you're vying for transformation, it's critical to keep an image of victory in mind.

The on-campus gym where my teammates and I worked out was home to a well-stocked display of *The Biggest Loser* memorabilia from previous seasons, and because I was particularly inspired by Season 2's Suzy Preston, I gravitated toward her "stuff." I'd try on her trademark horn-rimmed glasses and hold up the weigh-in tank top she wore to her grand finale and picture myself in her slimmed-down state.

Eventually I would shrink to the size that meant I could have worn the top, which both astounded and delighted me.

Additionally, I kept an old pageant dress and the size 34B long-line bra that I wore at my wedding beside my bed while I was on campus. They both represented eras of my life when I was smaller than my norm, and as I looked at them longingly each night I'd envision myself fitting into them once again. Not squeezing myself into them with gritted teeth, mind you—but wearing them comfortably, and preferably with room to spare.

In the end, that pageant dress wound up being far too big for my post-*The Biggest Loser* size. You should have seen my smile.

On those days when my weight-loss goal seemed utterly unattainable, images of healthy celebrities and of me at a smaller size kept me going strong. I'd look in the mirror and see myself becoming more of the "me" God had created, a version of myself that truly I'd never known.

Whether it's an old photo of yourself, a piece of clothing you one day hope to wear or a celebrity who embodies the fit appearance to which you aspire, keep an inspiring image close by and focus on it each and every day. Remind yourself that with God's help, you possess the power to become precisely who you and he envision you to be.

CHAPTER 6

The Spiritual Side of My Weight-Loss Struggle

THE FIRST FEW WEEKS of my *The Biggest Loser* experience were tumultuous to say the least. My body was stunned. My emotions were erratic. And my spiritual condition? Well, let's just say it left much to be desired. I had all the book-knowledge a girl could want about things like mercy and grace and love, but a very limited understanding of who God was. It was the equivalent of reading forty-five cookbooks cover to cover but never once setting foot inside a kitchen. I had learned much about God along the way—and at some level I even knew him. But would I ever really lean on him and live out that knowledge?

How I hoped the answer was yes.

I got "saved," as we say in Southern Baptist circles, when I was thirteen years old. At the time, I'm not sure what I thought I was being saved from: I had heard so many dramatic stories at church about people being rescued from drug addiction or habitual shoplifting, but as a pimply adolescent with a squeaky clean record, my biggest concern was how to avoid getting caught for couple-skating at the roller rink on Friday night. Would I even have a testimony worth telling? I certainly had my doubts.

> I still love to roller-skate. I can't quite figure out the whole roller-blading thing, but a girl can't be good at *everything*.

"Everyone has fallen short of God's perfect standard," our pastor said consistently. "Everyone needs a way to bridge the gap that our

95

How superficial was it that a primary reason I wanted to get "saved" was so that I could walk down the red-carpeted aisle, stand at the front of the church and have my name announced, get a free Bible and enjoy a swim in the giant baptism tank a few weeks later!

shortcomings create, and the only Bridge that can do it is the person of Jesus Christ." Originally I professed my faith primarily because it was simply the "thing to do." But over time I'd realize the truth of the matter, that despite my tame testimony, my pastor would be proven right.

For a while after accepting Christ into my life, I tried to get by riding the coattails of my mother's strong beliefs. I knew that God existed, I knew that he was bigger than I was and I knew that when I died one day, I was definitely heaven-bound. But I was thirteen and a little perplexed about how to really live out the Christian life. To think that a deity wanted a personal relationship with me was more than my prepubescent brain could grasp.

In my mind God was something of a wise but distant dictator who existed only in the fictional realm. Sort of a cross between Santa Claus and Obi-Wan Kenobi with an attitude. Whenever I wanted something—a new outfit, an A on a test, a boyfriend—I'd send my wish list to the "ultimate" North Pole, crossing my fingers that I had been good enough to see my wish come true. The times when I was left longing, I'd up the ante on my allegiance to the dos and don'ts I'd been taught. In the Baptist

Despite how I felt about all of those Wednesday-night services, I met some of my closest friends in the context of the youth group at church. The same is proving true these days for my son Noah, who is also found at church nearly every Wednesday night.

church of my youth, at least, good things came to "good" Christians—those who did not drink, did not dance and did not miss a single church service. I felt certain that extra credit was issued for Wednesday-night attendance, because I seemed to find myself there whenever midweek rolled around.

When I left home to be on the show I had very real concerns about what God and his faithful followers back at my church would think. Once in LA, I'd be skipping church for weeks, if not months, on end. There would be no church clothes, no hymns, no Wednesday-night worship and no preplanned corporate prayer. What's more, I would be "laboring" on the Sabbath by competing or working out. Talk about a Baptist no-no of *gargantuan* proportion.

Funny how in hindsight I see how much I linked Christian habits and behaviors to my security in Christ. Of course I knew that it was in actuality impossible to lose my salvation. But it would take me years to live from the freedom of knowing I was safe in the grip of God's grace from the moment I first believed.

I knew that everything was about to be taken from me—my family, my friends, my church and my routine. What I didn't know was that God would replace them all with his powerful, personal presence.

ALL ALONE, OR SO I THOUGHT

One of the most interesting aspects of being on *The Biggest Loser* was the ubiquitous presence of cameras and production crew. It wasn't uncommon for my teammates and me to be interrupted even during the most grueling of workouts in order to be interviewed for one segment of the show or another. To be sure, it was a situation that elicited a mixed response: A break was always welcomed during one of Jillian's workouts, but who wanted to be punished by her upon returning to the gym?

> There were microphones everywhere on campus, it seemed. They were in our bathrooms, in our bedrooms and in the dining room where we ate every meal. There were precious few locations that weren't wired up with a mic, but Hollie and I found each and every one and swapped secrets the entire season long.

Fairly early in the show, one of the production assistants pulled me from a treadmill and asked me to come outside to talk on camera about my thoughts on the experience thus far. It was maybe two minutes into our little chat when I saw her swivel her head toward the cameraman and with a heavy sigh say, "Cut." Still the people-pleaser of the bunch, I asked if I'd said something wrong.

> Jillian pitched a massive fit every time anyone interrupted our workouts. I later learned from production crew that they used to draw straws to determine who had to enter the gym to remove one of her team members for an interview.

"No, it's the bells," she said, and nodded toward the distance behind me. "We'll start over when things quiet down."

I had been so focused on whatever it was I was saying that I had failed to notice the majestic church bells pealing their noontime chime. I looked toward the church that I could not see and closed my eyes as the bells finished their song. *I thought my faith was stuck in Jacksonville, God, but you're clearly here with me now.* I sat perfectly still while I awaited his reply, anxious for conversation with the one I'd kept at a stiff arm's length.

"I know you thought you were alone here," he seemed to say, "but I've been with you all along."

"*Here?*" I thought with a small, wry smile. "They let you come to *Hollywood?*"

───⌇⌇───

E very fifteen minutes from that day forward, I noticed those church bells ringing. They chimed on the quarter-hour, on the half-hour, at fifteen 'til and when the top of the hour came—how had I missed them before? Regardless of what we were doing, sound technicians would curse and all production activity would cease. But for me those bells weren't a source of frustration; they were a reminder to talk to God.

I was away from my church, my pastor and the familiar to-dos of my youth, and yet it was in the midst of that utterly stripped-back state that I came face to face with God. My rules were being replaced with relationship, and my faith felt fresh and new.

EXACTLY WHAT I NEEDED, EXACTLY WHEN I NEEDED IT

S o much of my sanity while on the show came in the form of song. I've always loved to sing, and I tend to resonate with the world around me "lyrically" more than in any other way. As I tucked myself further and further into the strong, sturdy embrace of God during those first fresh-new-faith weeks, I took greater and greater pleasure in praising him through song. Jillian's beatings became far more tolerable as I learned to sing praises to the One who wanted to be my *real* Trainer, Jesus Christ, and a chorus that became a staple for me on campus still brings me joy today. "You are my Shield," the lyric goes, "my Strength,

I wasn't the only one on the show who loved to sing. Obviously singer/songwriter Isabeau could hold a mean tune, but so could red-team-member Bryan, who had made it to the top thirty on *American Idol* the previous season. Talk about star power!

my Portion, Deliverer . . ." I would sing each of those roles of Christ and feel my spirits and my own strength rise. As I learned to declare how I was starting to view God, he met me right at my point of need.

MY SHIELD

M y teammates knew about my faith in God from pretty early in the game. They'd hear me talk about my perspectives on life and love and leaving a faith-based legacy, and they'd joke, "We'll make you a deal. You start the Church of Hadden, and we'll come!"

I'd reply with a good-natured laugh, knowing in my heart that God was shielding me from being the oversensitive people-pleaser I'd once been. For so many years I had sought approval in others' satisfaction. If everyone else was pleased with me, then I assumed God was pleased with me too. If they were disappointed, well, God must feel that way too.

But that couldn't have been further from the truth.

God wanted me to see that in him I could find protection, in him I was accepted and loved. Amazingly, the bolder I became about sharing my faith, the stronger his protection around me grew. "You *are* my shield," I'd tell God as though he'd forgotten. "My shield and also my *strength* . . ." I had sung the song so many times back home, but I was meaning the words this time.

MY STRENGTH

W hile I worked out on campus, much of the spiritual knowledge that I'd acquired as a kid came to mind. (Six-hour workouts could even drive pagans to pray.) I recalled the verse in Psalm 139 that says my body is fearfully and wonderfully made. I remembered 1 Corinthians 6:19, which says that our bodies are temples of God. I was reminded that my body had been created to worship him, and that my frame was intended to be strong.

I thought also about Bible characters who exhibited strength in the midst of tough situations. The one that rose to the surface immediately was the story of David and Goliath—a reference even Jillian would cite to motivate me toward greater success.

During a long treadmill-run, I'd think about tiny David facing the nine-foot-tall Philistine with nothing but a few smooth stones, and I'd regain faith in the fact that despite my small size, I could and would prevail. "You're going *down*, thunder-thighs! You don't stand a *chance*, big belly!"

My "insurmountable" circumstances were *nothing* for my mighty God. He had been faithful to give me a once-in-a-lifetime opportunity to reclaim the life he so badly wanted me to live, and I wanted more than anything to be found faithful in return.

With each dawning day and every small goal achieved, my faith in the goodness of God rose. I had spent most of my life seeking purpose, security, companionship in a thousand different places. I'd just never looked to him.

But that was about to change, and in highly dramatic fashion.

MY PORTION

A few weeks into *The Biggest Loser* experience, I told all of the other contestants that if a new car was ever the reward for a challenge, I would win the thing, hands down. "This isn't *American Idol*, Jules," they'd tease. "They don't give away cars on this show." But still I stood by my claim.

Soon after Noah was born I felt compelled to quit my full-time job as a customer-service rep and serve as a full-time stay-at-home mom. Mike was completely supportive of my desire, but as we crunched the numbers, we realized that in order for my dream to come true we'd need to get rid of our second car. Mike worked clear across town, which meant that I would be left stranded on a near-daily basis. *Surely* we could make the arrangement work . . . couldn't we?

On the same day that the ten remaining Season 4 contestants were placed into teams of two, we were told to convene on the field adjacent to the on-campus gym. Once outside we noticed stacks and stacks of garbage—pizza boxes in one pile, ice-cream containers in another, paper coffee cups in a third, a mound of empty chip-bags next to that. And then came the cans. Before our eyes two giant recycling trucks dumped out more than two and a half tons of aluminum cans, which represented the soda that the ten of us had consumed in our lifetimes thus far. The sight of them made me feel simultaneously sickened . . . and thirsty.

The challenge, we were told, would involve hauling the soda cans across a field, up a ramp and into a huge metal bin, and the team with the highest number of pounds logged at the end of half an hour would win. "This is a challenge every team is going to want to win," Alison said before we got started, "because it has a prize that *everyone* wants."

On cue, two Ford Hybrid SUVs rounded the bend, causing tears to spring instantly to my eyes. The thought of that particular prize being offered during *this* particular season of the show was almost too much to take. I buried my face in my hands as I considered the implications of winning the challenge . . . and a desperately needed new car.

After orienting us to the nuances of the competition, Alison yelled, "Go!" and we were off. My duo-partner Bill and I raced a full football-field length to the small mountain of cans, stretched our shirts out to create makeshift buckets, gathered up loads of aluminum cans and raced all the way back to the ramp. Back and forth and back and forth we went, never wavering, never stopping, never dropping our loads too soon.

> The pile of cans came to us straight from the dump. During the challenge I enjoyed the lovely stench of dead birds and stale beer, which ran down my arms the entire time.

Fifteen minutes into the competition Bill and I were in first place with forty-one pounds of cans collected so far. It's probably a good thing we didn't know our ranking; believing we were behind made us fight that much harder to win.

After what seemed an eternity, the horn sounded, signaling the end of thirty minutes' time. All ten contestants collapsed on the grass.

As I caught my breath and waited for the team tallies to be revealed, I

> Bill later told me that his speedy progress during that competition was due to the fact that he picks up leaves on Long Island every fall in much the same way—diving a big sheet underneath the pile and then scooping up as many as he can hold. Thank goodness Bill does his own lawn!

thought about the sacrifice that Mike and I had made six years prior. I thought about the freedom I longed to enjoy once more.

Finally, Alison spoke. She announced the bottom three duos and the amount of weight each had hauled, which meant that now it was down to two teams—Amy and Kae, and Bill and me. I couldn't even look at Alison, I was so nervous. I blew all of the air out of my cheeks as I reached down to hold Bill's hand. "Please, oh please, oh please, oh please"—I think those were the profound words I prayed.

"One duo hauled seventy-five-point-eight pounds," Alison said rather cryptically. "The winning duo hauled ninety-eight-point-four pounds," she then said to everyone's oohs and ahhs. Alison paused dramatically before continuing, and I couldn't help but peek at her with anxious anticipation. "The duo who won gets these," she said as she jingled two sets of car keys. At the sight of those keys I reached for my knees. My stomach was a jumble of knots.

Still peering at the ground beneath my feet, I heard the words that made my spirits soar. "And that duo is . . . Bill and Julie."

With that, of course, I cried.

———〰———

To this day, when I reflect on the can-challenge from that amazing afternoon, I think about how God lovingly returned to me what he had willingly allowed to be removed. Mike and I had been determined to create a situation in which I could be an at-home mom, but admittedly it was never fun to be stuck inside all day with a toddler and no place to go. There were so many times when I wanted to take Noah to the park or run a few errands with friends, but God had other, more significant goals in mind. Like helping me learn to stay the course, for instance, even when things got hard.

After being handed the keys to my beautiful new Ford, I climbed into the driver's seat and marveled at every square inch. Leather seats, a CD player, a sunroof—it was far nicer than anything I ever would have bought for myself, but isn't that just like God? I thought about the verse in Ephesians that says God will give us exceedingly abundantly above all that we can ask for or think.[8] And I thanked him for being true to his word.

"*I'm* your portion, Julie," he seemed to say in response to my thoughts. "And I'll provide for you to the end."

MY DELIVERER

My shield. My strength. My portion. And, my *deliverer.*

As I began to look to God to supply every single thing I needed, I witnessed him releasing me—"saving" me, as it turns out—from the things that had held me captive for years: legalism, an overemphasis on trying to please people, fear, heaviness both in my body and in my heart. At every turn, he was fulfilling his promise to help me bear up under what life had thrown my way.

"God is faithful," 1 Corinthians 10:13 says. "He will not let you be tempted beyond what you can bear. But when you are tempted, he will also provide a way out so that you can stand up under it." There were plenty of temptations for me on campus, but *you* try sneaking a Snickers with the God of the universe standing right by your side. "I'm with you in this struggle," he'd remind me, "and with my help, you're capable of making choices that are wise."

"WAIT, SO IT'S *NOT* ALL ABOUT ME?"

What is interesting to me as I reflect on the spiritual awakening I experienced while on campus is that somehow I thought that God had orchestrated it just for me. Julie had a need, and Jesus decided to meet it. Julie shed a tear, and Jesus bent over to catch it. Julie suffered a little pain, and Jesus rushed over to soothe it.

I would come to discover that I had gotten the whole thing entirely wrong. God had not revealed himself to me in a personal, powerful way so that I would be comforted only; he had gifted me with his presence so that I could extend that comfort to others—both on the show and beyond.

One day I was grabbing a bite to eat in the kitchen when Jillian motioned me over. "I need to talk to you," she said quietly.

I felt sure that I was in trouble.

Looking into Jillian's eyes, I saw seriousness lingering there. What could I possibly have done to make her this mad?

As I would soon find out, her intensity had nothing to do with me.

"Hollie's stepdad just called," she said in an even tone, "and the news is *really* not good."

Hollie's mother had been diagnosed with cancer years prior and although the terrible disease had lain in remission for a long time, evidently it was relapsing now. When Hollie accepted a slot on the show, her mom was faring pretty well. How could Hollie have known that during the same season she would pursue her lifelong weight-loss dream, her own mother would suffer such a terrible fate?

The production crew had told Jillian that Hollie's mom didn't have long to live. Now Jillian was supposed to break the ridiculously tough news to the girl who was finally finding her niche on the team. "Hollie is just now taking ownership of her own body," Jillian whispered to me. "This is the opportunity of a *lifetime*, and she's finally giving it her all."

Jillian, of course, was right. But equally true was that Hollie needed to do what was best for her and her family. She would decide to go home that day, to be close by when the woman who gave her life finally bid this life good-bye.

> I missed Hollie so much when she left to be by her mom's side. Isabeau and I would lie in our beds at night and talk about how the game was totally different without our good friend. We knew then that we'd *never* vote off Hollie.

As the other black-team members and I helped carry Hollie's luggage to the car that would take her to the airport, the game seemed to screech to a halt. All of my concerns about inspiring a nation dissipated into thin air as I realized the person needing inspiration the most was standing right beside me. Until that point I had begged God to be with *me*, to help *me*, to give strength to *me*, and to comfort *me*. But with this sudden turn of events my eyes were finally fixed on someone other than myself. Now my prayers were for Hollie—that *she* would sense God's presence, his help, his comfort, his peace.

"Your ways really *aren't* like my ways," I told God. "This was never about me at all."

WORDS I NEEDED TO HEAR

When Jillian first learned of my faith in Christ, she had some fun at my expense. "Oh man, I got me one of those crazy Born Agains on my team!" she'd joke.

"Jillian," I'd clarify, "born-again is an adjective, not a noun. I'm not 'a born-again.' I *am* 'born-again!'"

> Jillian actually made this comment to another born-again Christian, Pete Thomas from Season 2, who happened to be visiting the set of the show that day along with his wife. Pete chuckled at Jillian's comment and said, "That's what you used to call *me*!"

She'd just laugh as she sauntered away, but the irony of her remark stayed behind. Jillian may have pretended to misapprehend what it meant to be a follower of Christ, but hadn't I done it for real? All of my legalism and distance and fear-based behavior—did I know what it meant to relate to God at all?

In retrospect, I know that I could have accomplished my weight-loss goal without the help of *The Biggest Loser* show. What I don't know is whether my faith could have been remade by any other approach. As I learn more about the God I love, I find it more and more plausible that he flew my flabby butt all the way to LA for four solid months just so I'd be still enough to hear him speak. I thought I needed the big, dramatic experience in order to become the woman I wanted to be. But as it turned out all I needed was him.

I learned so much while I was on *The Biggest Loser*, about arm curls and calorie counts and how to make plain ground turkey taste absolutely delicious. But perhaps the most profound lesson I took away was how to walk with God. As I continue to sort out what that truly means, I find myself clinging to three divine refrains that God gave me while on the show. They represent the words I *still* need to hear, each and every day—words I pray will bless you as well.

"ACCEPT MY LOVE"

M oments after my son Noah was born, a nurse cleaned him off, swaddled him tightly in a blanket and laid him on my chest. I peered at that tiny bundle through tear-clouded eyes and thought, "I love you more than words can express." Which was sort of an interesting response, given the fact that he really wasn't very cute. Noah weighed four pounds dripping wet, his bug-eyes were too big for his face and his limbs fell at odd angles like a baby bird that had been dropped from a tree. But the moment I saw him, I loved him—not because he was magnificent, but simply because he was mine.

It's the way I have come to understand God's marvelous love for us.

"I love you unconditionally," he says, "not because you're magnificent, but just because you are mine. You don't have to be faster, thinner, prettier, smarter or more organized to warrant the love that I feel.

"I see you, I accept you, I know you, I desire you . . . I am your Father, and I am near. Accept the love you find in me, and I will walk with you every step of the way."

It was the first counsel I sensed God giving me regarding how to walk closely with him—"Accept my love, Julie. It's my heartfelt gift to you."

"OFFER YOUR LIFE"

The second piece of divine advice I got was to offer my life up in service of God. It was imperative that I learn my whole purpose for living is to love and serve God so that I can then go love and serve the people I come across.

Here's the deal: I hate public speaking. And yet, since my time on the show, nearly all of the high-impact opportunities I have been given involve some form of public speaking.

Funny, God. *Very* funny.

So, I accept the engagements. I show up. I speak from my heart, sweaty pits and all. Each time, I coerce the stomach butterflies to fly in formation at least until I can vacate the stage and then look heavenward with this thought: "You endured the cross. Clearly I had to endure that."

Speaking still scares me to death, but I know that God has given me this opportunity for such a time as this. And *not* seizing it scares me far more than seizing it ever will.

It always amazes me when people show up at the places where I've agreed to come to speak. Talk about a relief! Their presence would make for a fantastic ego boost, except for the fact that I know they're not there because of me. I am not rail-thin, I am not particularly eloquent and I tend to lose track of time. Obviously, they are not there to hear me. They are there to hear of my *struggle*—a struggle that they see themselves in.

In my view, it is far more inspiring to hear of a person's struggle than to be told of her great success. What endeared me to Hollie was not the person she presented herself to be. It was her struggle over her mom that would draw me toward her in the end. Likewise, it was not Jillian's picture-perfect abs that invited me to care deeply about her life. It was when I understood the struggle that she had one day won that her heart would be knitted to mine.

Struggles are powerful because they tend to reveal a glimpse of where God is working in the world. He loves us in the midst of our struggles and longs for us to look to him for strength. Certainly I never would have signed up for the pain and the pressure I faced while working to drop half of my body weight, but now that I'm on this side of the equation, I see God using the agony for good.

One of my favorite Casting Crowns songs says, "Are we happy, plastic people under shiny plastic steeples, with walls around our weakness, and smiles to hide our pain? If the invitation's open to every heart that has been broken, maybe then we close the curtain on our stained-glass masquerade."[9] Everyone has a facade up that makes us appear to be perfect, but you and I both know there's another "us" behind that mask. If only we'd be freer in revealing our areas of struggle . . . just think of the bridges we'd build between our hearts and the hearts of others we meet.

I have a feeling that even on my dying day I'll still be wishing I were better at offering up my whole life to God. Maybe that's the point, that this is a never-ending process and therefore a way to stay close to him. This much I do know: real living only surfaces when you're seeking *total* surrender to God.

These days I am nothing more than a broken vessel who yearns to be used by God. Whatever he asks me to do, I'll do it. Wherever he asks me to go, I'm in. For the first time in my life I find myself flat on my face, fully trusting, fully yielding, fully expecting great things as I rely on God for each breath. My cup now runs right over, and my soul is soaring high.

If only I could celebrate with a *little* slice of chocolate cake . . .

"LEAVE A LEGACY THAT POINTS TO ME"

C an I share the third piece of encouragement I received? "Leave a legacy that will undeniably point to me," God seemed to tell me while I was on the show. "Whatever accomplishments you amass, whatever successes you enjoy, always make sure that your victories point to me."

There's a passage in the Bible I came to appreciate even more while I was on campus for those four months. In Luke 19, Jesus is about to enter Jerusalem, the city he loves. His disciples are walking ahead of him, whooping and hollering and cheering their shouts of praise for all of the miracles they'd seen Jesus do, when a group of legalistic Pharisees who were standing nearby told Jesus to shut them up. Evidently they were a bit too joyous for the Pharisees' bland taste.

Jesus turns toward the Pharisees and says nine words that make my day every time: "If they keep quiet, the stones will cry out."[10] With subtle but powerful language Jesus was teaching a bunch of legalists how to praise him. And somehow I could relate because I was learning to praise him for the first time too. I acknowledged that I was living and breathing and moving and competing not just inside a TV-show set but inside the magnificent creation of God. For once I was sensing his presence—and it was personal, relevant and *real*.

I want my legacy to be that I praised God at every turn. Until I breathe my last breath, I want to praise him for the mountaintops and praise him for the valleys. I want to praise him for my history and for a future that seems so bright. I want to praise him for my husband and for my children and for my friends. I want to praise him for my body—which, though imperfect, carries me through each and every day. I can walk. I can run. I can build muscle mass and confidence and strength. And for those things, I'll always be grateful—gratefully full of praise.

The contemporary Christian band Watermark released a song years ago that echoes the heart of this theme. In "Gloria," they sing, "I wish I could crash like the waves and turn like the autumn breeze, in an effort to praise you. I wish I could smell like the forest, the fragrance lifting a mighty chorus in an effort to praise you."[11]

They go on this way, wishing they could cry out praise as effectively as rolling thunder or falling summer rain but then acknowledging that we humans have limitations when it comes to such things. When the chorus rises, the lead singer expresses her praise the only way she knows how—by singing "Gloria."

> *Gloria!*
> *Glory in the highest*
> *Forever I will hide myself in Thee*
> *Oh, Gloria!*
> *Glory in excelsis Deo*
> *Gloria!*
> *Gloria!*
> *Gloria!*[12]

I get what the singer is saying. How I wish my praise for God were as powerful as thunder! While I was on *The Biggest Loser* campus, I used to wish my praise could have rung out like those church bells or smelled like the sweet strawberries whose scent often woke us up. Knowing those things were impossible, I'd praise God the only way I knew how.

With every minute on the treadmill, my soul was saying, "Gloria!" With every healthful handful of almonds eaten, my lips were speaking, "Gloria!" With every quiet prayer mouthed when I was too tired to actually speak, my heart was crying, "Gloria! Glory in the highest! *Forever* I will hide myself in Thee."

Although you and I are limited creatures, we can praise God still. We can do what God calls us to do. We can strengthen ourselves—body, mind and soul. We can accept his great love. We can offer up our lives in service to him. We can leave behind a legacy of faithfulness to all who knew us well.

———～ハ～———

T he first weekend I was home after being on the show, I couldn't wait to go to church. Sunday morning showed up with crystal blue skies and bright, warm sunbeams, and a sense of distinct, divine hope that I'd missed.

As I stepped into the auditorium I realized that while everything was the same, it was altogether different too. The people were nicer, the music was sweeter and my attitude had been remade. How true it is that you don't really appreciate something until it has been taken away from you for a while. I had been in church for all those years without enjoying all that it means to be "in Christ." Funny how I'd overlooked him until I encountered him in a gym.

I sang a solo that weekend, Babbie Mason's "He'll Find a Way," and as I looked out from the platform at the loving eyes looking back, I couldn't help but think about how these were the people who had been praying for me for four months straight, the people who had been caring for me from afar every second I was on the show. "You did find a way, didn't you, God?" I thought as I belted out the chorus. "You found a way to break through, to be near, to beckon me toward authentic faith."

It wasn't the church of my youth that had been the problem. It wasn't legalism's rules that had led me astray. The chasm between God and me all that time was one of my own making. And how grateful I was when it was finally bridged. "When you're feeling at your weakest," that Babbie Mason song goes, "Jesus will be strong. He'll provide an answer when you find all hope is gone. He'll find a way."

I couldn't agree with her more. God always finds a way.

Set Small, Achievable Goals, and When You Reach Them, Celebrate!

It may seem like a small accomplishment to you, but the first time I was able to walk into church, sit down and cross my legs, I thought I might have to stand right back up and do a happy dance. Prior to my *The Biggest Loser* experience, I was barely able to cross my *ankles* while seated, let alone try to cross my legs.

Similarly, the first time that my son Noah was able to sit on my lap without being pushed off by the enormous roll of fat surrounding my midsection, grateful tears sprang instantly to my eyes.

Then there was the time I walked into a clothing store and was approached by a saleslady who was anxious to help me find a new outfit. She eyed my frame so that she'd know which clothes to pull and before spinning around to retrieve them said, "Hmm . . . looks like you're a size six." I could have kissed her, I was so elated. "Say that again," I said with a smile. But sadly, she'd already walked off.

When you're working toward a monumental goal, progress can seem hard to come by. No matter how hard you try and how faithful you are to your exercise and diet routine, you can't seem to get to the crossed-legs, child-on-lap, surreal-size-six stage. I get that. I *lived* that for many, many months. And what I noticed on those *will-I-ever-be-thinner-than-this?* days was that the only way I could keep my sanity was to set small, achievable goals for myself—and then to celebrate like *crazy* once I reached them.

Those smaller goals were all over the map in terms of importance, but as I look back now I see that each one played a role in my overall success.

When I had already met my calorie limit for the day and turned down a piece of chocolate cake, *that* was a real goal achieved.

When I finally didn't have to wear plus-size clothes, *that* was a real goal achieved.

When I saw an old friend and didn't duck out of sight, *that* was a real goal achieved.

When I weighed in lighter than my wedding-night weight, *that* was a real goal achieved.

When I could actually do a cartwheel, that was a real goal achieved.

And with each goal I achieved, I had fresh reason to celebrate.

Part of my celebration strategy from the start was to make sure my rewards did not revolve around food. Although the previous Julie would scoff at these words, there is much more to life than food. It's even possible to socialize with friends without the event being consumed by food. Who would have thought?

My advice if you're stuck in a progress-less state is to try rewarding your small achievements with other senses than taste. Call a friend and share your success. Do your next workout in freshly cut grass—it's the scent of celebration you won't soon forget. Write your spouse or another family member a note of thanks for supporting you along the way. Look at yourself in the mirror and simply experience self-appreciation for once. Now *that's* a way to celebrate!

Right now my "small, achievable goal" is to complete "The River Run" next month, a race that winds through the heart of Jacksonville, Florida—complete with challenging hills and long, flat stretches alike. It's the largest 15K in the United States, and trust me, seeing my feet cross that finish line will be all the reward that I need. For thirty-five years I have watched tens of thousands of people finish that race, never once thinking I could ever keep up with them. Live bands perform at ten different locations along the race course, and I have a feeling I'll be singing my heart out every long-awaited step of the way.

Break up your goal into small goals, and reward yourself as you greet each success. Before you know it you'll be smooching your sales staff and lacing up your running shoes too.

Part Three

At Home in My Own Skin:
Returning to the Old Life
I'd Somehow Never Lived

CHAPTER 7

Eight Pounds I'm Glad I Gained

I'VE ALWAYS BEEN a fan of crime fiction, and in my view there's none better than Patricia Cornwell's book *From Potter's Field*. It's part of the series that stars Detective Kay Scarpetta, a former medical examiner who retired and then became a private forensic consultant who was still utterly consumed by her work . . . and Italian cooking, which is why I *always* get hungry when I read about her life. Anyway, what's so amazing about Cornwell's writing is that just when she has you totally enthralled in one part of the plot, the chapter ends, a new one begins and that new one is about a completely different subject. "Wait," you think as you flip the page, "weren't we just in Central Park, staring at the poor girl who was killed by a mysterious murderer and left in the freezing cold wearing nothing but a trench coat and an Atlanta Braves baseball cap? And now it's Christmas Day and we're sitting in a hotel lobby? What did I miss?"

The story lines always wind up being related in the end, but all along the way you're desperate to understand how. Interestingly, I would discover after my *The Biggest Loser* experience that I only loved being kept in the dark and guessing at every turn when those things were happening to a fictional protagonist instead of happening to *me*.

I can't remember exactly when I picked up my first Patricia Cornwell book, but it was probably when I worked late-night shifts at CSX Transportation years ago. I handled paperwork for train orders coming out of various big cities. I loved that job! I loved the people, the setting and the fact that I got to read good crime-fiction when things were slow.

Throughout my entire reality TV stint, God was orchestrating such a magnificent series of captivating twists and turns that now as I look back on those days my breath is all but taken away. What's more, the masterly story lines he was writing would build to a climax that was far more exciting than Scarpetta solving a crime. They would lead to a little boy named Jaxon, Mike's and my adorable, adopted son.

INFERTILE MONTHS, UGLY MONTHS

Part of why I auditioned for *The Biggest Loser* in the first place is because I was at my wit's end. I knew that I had a medical condition—polycystic ovary syndrome—and I knew that obesity only exacerbated the problem. If I could get on a show like *The Biggest Loser*, then I might be able to lose weight once and for all. And if I could lose weight, then maybe I would be able to overcome my medical condition, get pregnant again, deliver a brand-new baby and live happily ever after. That was my plan—bing, bang, boom. Little did I know that God had a very different plan in mind.

Mike and I had loved Noah's infancy and early childhood so much that we decided we'd wait until he was three years old before trying with any intention to conceive again. We wanted to be just as present and enthralled with our second child as we'd had the luxury of being with Noah. What we didn't know at the time, of course, was that pregnancy the second time around just wasn't meant to be.

Those infertile months were ugly months. Around the time that my period was supposed to start, I would wait on pins and needles, wondering if *this* was the month we'd conceived. I would drop fifty bucks on pregnancy-detection sticks, and another fifty on ovulation kits once I realized that our efforts, yet again, had been in vain. The good stuff of intimacy quickly was replaced with clinical calculations of temperatures and fluids and calendar counts, and before long my husband and I both were sad and spent and heartsick to our cores.

In the same way that you never ask a woman her age or her weight, never, ever ask her when she's going to have another child, or a first child, for that matter. Who knows what raw nerves you might hit.

Just a little friendly advice, free of charge from me to you.

As each menstrual cycle showed up, so did Mike's overly emotional and spiritually exhausted wife. The everyday bits and pieces of life just did me in. We'd make a quick trip to the mall, for instance, and as soon as I'd catch sight of an apathetic teenager with a disheveled toddler hanging off her hip, I'd dissolve into tears. "*Seriously,* God? I've actually been trying to get pregnant, and yet *she's* the one with a child? Why would you choose *her* over *me*?" I had love to offer, care to extend and a heart that truly desired another child. Would the Giver of that desire really refuse to fulfill it?

It's interesting to me now that I would be ridiculously grateful for one of those "unplanned pregnancies" in just a few short months' time.

⌒〜ᐱ〜⌒

After a string of babyless months, Mike and I agreed to begin fertility treatments. If you ever need a totally demoralizing experience, just pay a visit to your local infertility clinic. The staff is nice enough, but as you stare at the hopelessly blank faces of the people sitting in the waiting room, you get the distinct sense that both you and they must have done something *terribly* wrong. Women and men are supposed to be able to conceive babies, and they both feel a little less human when they cannot.

In her memoir, *Inconceivable*, author Julia Indichova describes what it was like to be told by her doctor that although she had delivered a perfectly healthy daughter years prior, she could no longer become pregnant. (Could I ever relate.) It would have been fine for Indichova, except for the fact that she and her husband Ed so deeply wanted to be pregnant again. She was in and out of fertility clinics for months on end, desperate to crack the code on conceiving another child, and the end result of all those visits was, in her words, a certain "narrowing" of herself.

"I feel a narrowness in my chest," Indichova writes, "a constriction that keeps me from taking a deep breath. I think of the impersonal narrow corridors, leading to examining rooms. I think of narrow lovemaking zeroed in on the one thing that's unattainable. I realize how afraid I am to open up to the sadness, afraid to let Ed see . . . I must keep moving. I can't just sit around agonizing over my options while my childbearing days gallop away from me. I must fight against all the grave faces that say it's useless—all these appointments, all this flapping of my wings."[13]

I could have written those very same words because for me, the fight was equally tough. But for all the agony infertility elicits from women, it levels an equal blow to men. Men, for example, were not made to point semen into a plastic cup with a whole waiting-room's worth of people hovering outside. Their egos aren't meant to bear the walk of shame from that waiting room out the office door, down the hall and to the parking lot, where the car is waiting that will encase what is always a painfully silent drive home.

Time and again Mike and I would cradle nothing more than a God-given desire, fearing only a worst-case scenario would be born. There were no answers to our questions about whether the treatments would work. There were no answers to Noah's questions about why the sibling he so diligently prayed for just wasn't showing up. There was nothing but more and more questions. And a lot of waiting around.

WHEN BABIES AND FAITH GET FORMED

U nbeknownst to me, in the same month that I discovered I'd been cast on Season 4 of the show, a single mom in Jacksonville discovered that she was pregnant. It would be many months later that she and I would cross paths and string together the timeline of our mutual journey. But now with those pieces intact, I see God's perfect hand of provision at work.

In those early days after being cast, I remember crying out to God. "Please heal my body!" I'd plead. "Please help me finish what I've started so that Mike and I can conceive." Who could have known that at the very same time another woman who was roughly my age was crying out to God too.

"You hear about these circumstances happening to other women," she would later write, "but as a thirty-two-year-old single woman, this was new territory for me."[14] Like so many women who find themselves single, pregnant and deathly afraid, she immediately sought out easy answers. "I knew I needed to make a decision," she says; "I just didn't know what decision to make."[15]

As God worked in her mind and body, he was working in my mind and body too. Hour by hour, day by day, I noticed that as I made drastic changes to my diet and forced my arms, my legs and my abdomen to endure endless hours of exercise, the symptoms of my condition disappeared. No longer was I losing my hair. No longer was my body *refusing* to lose weight. I was becoming stronger, both physically and mentally, and with strength came the rising of my hope—hope that with healing would come pregnancy and with pregnancy would come the contentment so desperately sought.

Admittedly, my body was still covered in fat, but sources other than my mirror were telling me that progress was being made.

Every week on the show, contestants had to visit *The Biggest Loser* doctor so that he could run a new body-composition scan to determine body-fat percentage, bone strength and muscle mass. It's called the iDEXA and is something like a CT-scan for your entire body. All I know is that the chart it produces is really pretty. There are bright, vibrant colors like yellow and blue, but the ratio of my colors initially gave the doctor reason for concern.

Here's how it breaks down: When you see yellow on the scan, that means there's fat. When you see blue, there's muscle. And when you see white, you know that's a bone. At the beginning of my time on campus, my iDEXA image was a big blob of yellow with a teeny-tiny piece of white in the middle—all fat with a little bone thrown in for good measure.

The doctor looked at me and said, "Julie, you have no blue. You're nothing but bone and fat." As you'd guess, it wasn't a very enjoyable conversation from that point forward.

Halfway through the show I was lying on the examination table during one of my weekly appointments and happened to glance over when my iDEXA image popped onto the screen. For the first time I actually saw *blue*. "Look!" I cheered. "I have *muscles*!"

As my body began to find strength and healing, I gained confidence that anything really *was* possible with God. During those days when my faith was being formed that he really could change something as seemingly fixed as my decades-old body composition, he was forming another miracle too.

For many months, Jaxon's biological mother had all but denied the fact that she was carrying a baby, simply because she didn't know what to do. "I hid my pregnancy and contemplated the issue for months," she admits, "not knowing how my family would react to the situation. . . . Finally, after many sleepless nights, I made my decision to place my child for adoption."[16]

As she tells it, there was an ad in a local circular for a Christian adoption service called "Angelic Adoptions" that a friend of hers found and forwarded on to her. Despite her internal confusion, she couldn't help but be drawn to the name. Several hours of deliberation later, on a cool, crisp December day, she decided to make a call.

THE REAL REWARD FOR MY HARD WORK

On Thursday, December 13, 2007, I flew from Florida to California, eagerly anticipating *The Biggest Loser* Season 4 finale. As I boarded that jet, I remember feeling stronger and more slender than I'd ever felt before. Of course, that feeling had come at a fairly steep price. I don't know about you, but when a quarter-million dollars is on the line, a girl can sink to some pretty special lows. I had spent the previous week juicing and running my way to a size four, determined to take home the prize, having no clue that the real prize would not be coming to me in currency.

Things got so insane on the exercise front that just before my finale I was running a grueling fourteen miles a day. I broke it up into AM and PM chunks, but trust me, it was still a *lot*!

Once I arrived in LA, I was ushered to a secluded room in a hotel, where I was allowed to put down my things and freshen up before heading off to be fitted for my finale outfit, spray-tanned and weighed-in. I wasn't allowed to see my trainer, my castmates or the other members of the final four, which was especially devastating to someone like me, who wilts without hourly human interaction.

I went to my stage-rehearsal, which I had to endure all by myself, with no host, no audience and no other contestants around. I practiced breaking through the paper, I practiced walking in my impossibly high heels, and I practiced smiling the victor's smile. Had I really made it this far? It was hard to contain the sense of satisfaction that was welling up inside.

The day of the finale dawned, and by the time I was escorted from my hotel room to my dressing room in the studio, I was ready to burst with excitement and pride. All of my sweat. All of my hard work. It was *all* about to be paid off, in the form of some cold, hard cash and the "first female Biggest Loser" title. How cool would that be!

Production assistants knocked on my door to usher me backstage, where the final four were positioned for their grand entrance. They held up sheets and formed giant cotton dividers around us so that we couldn't see each other as we shuffle-stepped our way in the dark. My three teammates—Hollie, Isabeau and Bill—and I giggled and chatted from inside our sheets like mischievous school children. Surely they shared my sentiment: I couldn't *wait* to see what they looked like.

As we made our way from the back hall to the rear of the stage, I could hear the crowd cheering and Top 40 music blaring through the speakers. Through the cracks of the stage set I could see the audience dancing and singing during what was obviously a commercial break before our big debut.

I caught sight of Bob and Jillian coming back stage from the other side and watched them like a hawk until Bob finally sensed my stare and looked over. It was the first time he had seen me since I had been on campus, and as he took in the version of me that was forty pounds lighter than he remembered, his jaw dropped to his chest. I laughed out loud from across the stage and motioned for him to get Jillian's attention. Without breaking his gaze he elbowed his fellow trainer. I could read his lips as he said, "Jill! *Look* at Julie!" Jillian's head swiveled my way, and as her eyes fell on my figure, I posed and laughed some more. "You like?" I joked.

> I consider it a gift that I was able to see the actual moment when Jillian Michaels saw the fruit of all her hard work and smiled. If there was one person whose approval I sought in the end, it was hers.

Her hands flew to her face, and her eyes lighted up with pride. "Oh. My. *Gosh!*" she mouthed. I blew kisses her way and then readied myself to finally take the stage.

THE ONE WHO WAS MEANT TO BE OURS

Once Mike and I were allowed by the show's producers to have phone conversations and write letters back and forth, I noticed a theme in his correspondence. Evidently God impressed upon Mike that he and

I should consider adoption as a way to expand our family. I'm not really used to hearing audible voices from the heavens, but Mike says on this issue, "God really did speak." I was more than a little skeptical.

As soon as I returned home from LA, amid the whirlwind of activity that accompanied returning to normal life after being gone for four months, Mike and I talked further about his adoption idea. That weekend we had a conversation about our possible interest in adoption with our friend Haley, who is part of our church family and who, along with her husband, had recently adopted a child through the Angelic Adoptions agency. Was this really the path we also should take? My heart was definitely growing tender toward the thought.

The very next day Haley went to the agency to complete her last batch of paperwork and overheard a pregnant woman talking to a counselor about her preferences for the type of family that would adopt her baby. She wanted her son to be part of a Christian family. She wanted him to have an older sibling who was already in the home. She wanted to know that his new grandparents lived close by and that cousins and extended family would be present to help him to grow and mature. She wanted him to have a stay-at-home mom. On and on went her list.

Haley was still there when the woman left, and she overheard the counselor say to another staff member, "I don't think we have any families that fit that profile . . ."

"I think I know just the one," Haley said.

One week after I was home from *The Biggest Loser*, in addition to implementing my new diet, my new exercise program and my entirely new lease on life, I found myself in the middle of another area of newness for me: I was filling out a profile to become an adoptive parent. Mike and I took that profile, along with a fifteen-hundred-dollar application fee and a boatload of faith, and met with the social worker who had been assigned to our case. An attorney had advised us that if "things didn't work out" with this particular baby, there were plenty of others in the system, but Mike and I shared a different perspective. We wanted to be screened to be *this* baby's parents, not *any* baby's parents.

Something—or Someone—told us that it was this little boy who was meant to be ours.

On a sunny Tuesday afternoon in January my husband and I stepped into an attorney's office and shook hands with Emily, the birth mother of our new son. Despite my swirling thoughts and anxious tummy, as soon as I caught sight of Emily, everything in me relaxed. I'm sure it had something to do with the fact that she was wearing a sweater-set—that, and a genuine, soulful smile.

When we were asked to submit a profile to the adoption agency, Mike took the lead. I read through it and offered a few suggestions and changes that only a mother's heart could muster, and then later found out that some of my additions were the very reasons that our baby's birth mother chose us. Mike was equal parts elated and annoyed. Well, maybe a *bit* more elated than annoyed.

I don't know what I expected we'd find in our baby's birth mother. A wayward teen? A drug addict? Someone with distant eyes, a sordid past and a hopeless situation on her hands? I don't know where I picked up my assumptions about the sort of woman who places her baby for adoption, but upon meeting Emily, I was ashamed of my preconceptions. She was so pretty and so . . . normal. She looked like someone who I'd find sitting next to me at church. Immediately I felt honored to be in her presence, and humbled to have been selected from all of the other profiles she'd reviewed.

With our attorney looking on, the three of us talked most of the afternoon, asking questions of each other, working hard to give earnest answers in reply. We left the office feeling clueless about the decision she would make, and simultaneously at peace that we had done everything we could do.

Later that day Mike's cell phone rang. "She selected you," our attorney said. "Without reservation, she chose you." Mike ended the call, turned toward me, and with tears in his eyes said, "She said that we're 'the ones,' honey. We have a baby boy!"

As Mike and I rushed out the door to get to a dinner party we'd agreed to attend, we had no idea that Emily would have an eventful evening as well. A few hours after she left the attorney's office, she went into labor with our son. Mike would receive a call the next morning at work to tell him that Jaxon had been born at 7:35 AM.

WHEN LONG-HELD DREAMS COME TRUE

When I first called my mom to tell her that Mike and I were think-ing about adopting a son, I remember sounding doubtful as the words came off my lips. In my heart of hearts I just wasn't sure it really would pan out. Maybe Mike *hadn't* heard from God. Maybe we were just chasing a wild, unfounded dream. But we were moving forward with the adoption—and fast—and I thought it best that I tell my mom before showing up at the next family dinner with a new baby boy in tow. Despite all of my doubts, my mom was ecstatic over our news. Instead of questioning Mike's prompting, she asked, "Are you sure God doesn't want you to adopt *twins*?"

I wanted to say, "*Easy*, woman. One child at a time." But I knew it would do no good. For years my mom had been on my case to have another child. Or six. Truth be told she would love it if Mike and I had a truckload of little ones, and if I homeschooled each and every kid. But some things just aren't going to happen, no matter how much harass-ment occurs.

For the following few days it was my mom who believed in the adop-tion dream even when I did not. And when I received word that the adoption was, in fact, going to go through, I knew exactly who I wanted standing by my side when that long-held dream came true.

It wasn't just for my sake that my mom accompanied me to pick up Jaxon. I knew how important it was to Emily that this baby would grow up in the presence of extended family, and I wanted her to see firsthand the kind of grandmother he would have. For two days straight Mike and I had been visiting Emily and Jaxon, but Mom had never come along. On one of those visits Emily's mother was also in the room. I had never met her before, and as I approached her I noticed that her eyes were so puffy from crying that they were nearly swollen shut. Her words to me were kind, but her heart was understandably breaking. She was being asked to welcome a grandbaby into the world and at the same time bid him farewell. I asked if I could give her a hug, and after we embraced I explained to her that I would love that little boy as though I had birthed him myself, every single day of his life.

She would be there, Emily's dear mother, on the day when Jaxon was placed in my care. It only furthered my desire to have my own mom there too.

We arrived at Emily's room and as I took her in, I noticed that this time hers were the eyes that were nearly swollen shut. It would be more than an hour before she would admit to me that she had changed her mind that very morning about giving up her son, but that after praying for wisdom she determined it was still the right thing to do. "I truly believe that he is your child," she would say through held-back tears. "I know this baby is yours."

En route to the hospital my mom and I stopped at Wal-Mart to purchase a car seat. Why think ahead, I figured, when you can just pack all of life into one little day? It had been seven years since we had had babyish things around the house, and I suddenly felt wobbly and insecure. Would I remember how to do the infant drill?

As a mother myself, my heart was breaking for her. But I had already fallen in love with this little boy. To think of losing him now was a shuddering thought. Still, I knew what needed to be done. "Would you like some time with him alone?" I asked, knowing full well that I might be inviting a disastrous turn of events.

My mom and I stepped into the hall and then made our way to the waiting room, where other mothers held freshly born babies as they sat ready to be released. My stomach flipped over inside of me. Would I be taking home a baby soon too?

After what seemed hours, a nurse walked toward me, swaddled child in her arms, and said, "Mrs. Hadden? Here is your son." For the first time since he'd been born I kissed every square inch of my baby, feeling at last like he was mine.

A PERFECT PLOT IN THE END

If you'd asked me even three years ago if I would ever adopt a child, my answer would have been no. Not in my *wildest* dreams. Mike and I had watched our closest friends adopt a child from Vietnam, and it was a long, drawn-out, gut-wrenching experience that cost them a small fortune in fees and wound up devastating them in the end. The baby they were to adopt would never make it into their care.

Mike and I had supported them every step of the way as they endured that agonizing process, and after countless 4:00 AM phone calls and buckets of tears, there was a bitter taste in my mouth regarding all things adoption.

In addition to fearing the process itself, I was concerned about issues of the heart. Would I be able to love an adopted child the same as one I had birthed? I remember driving down the road one day during those weeks when God impressed on Mike's heart the desire to adopt. I was talking to God about how these "impressions" were infringing on my plan. "I want to have another *biological* baby," I explained, sure that he was grateful for this helpful clarification.

I kept driving, waiting for his response.

Silence. More silence. Still more silence.

And then this: *Have you forgotten that you are adopted?*

In a divine flash of insight I recalled all of the Bible verses I had learned as a kid, testifying to the truth of those words. I had been adopted into the family of God. I had become a joint-heir with Christ, which meant that I had all of the privileges and power that he enjoyed, just as if I were his kin.

I love you so much, Julie, I sensed God saying. *I love you so much that I gave my one and only Son for you, I adopted you, and I call you my own.*

It was truth I needed to hear. And truth I reflected on as I brought Jaxon home. It was as if God were saying, "Go love your new son the same way that I love you." And that's exactly what I did. It's exactly what *we* did, Mike and Noah and me.

As my mom and I stepped through my front door, a brand-new baby in my arms, I waded through oohing and aahing friends and family members who had been eagerly awaiting our arrival and made a bee-line for my husband. And with as much pride as a man can manifest, he reached down to receive his three-day-old son. "I can't believe he's finally ours." Mike beamed.

Noah was equally elated. "That baby needs us, and we need him," Noah said when he first was told that Mike and I would be adopting a child who would become his little brother. The night of Jaxon's home-coming, after our living room had cleared out and our shoes had come off, Noah ran into his bedroom with a grin on his face. He has always been an avid collector of the brightly colored long-armed monkeys they sell in toy stores and airport kiosks, and as soon as he reappeared with an especially tiny one in hand and laid it beside his brother who was sleeping in our borrowed bassinette, I knew that all things really do come together for good for those who love God. Finally, even if in the most unexpected way, we four were family.

In that moment I felt filled up—filled up and fully present. It occurred to me that had I won the Season 4 *The Biggest Loser* title, I never would have met this baby boy. My schedule would have been a tangle of contractual media-tour commitments—appearances on morning talk shows, interviews with magazine editors, conversations with radio-program hosts, shoots for fitness DVDs and more.

When I burst through the paper photo of the old me and took the stage at the Season 4 finale, the only thing on my mind was winning it all. No sane person on the planet would endure months and months of torture and be content with second place. But now as I stared down at Jaxon's sweet, sleepy face, I saw how the plot that God had been writing made absolute, perfect sense.

The Season 4 weigh-in had come down to my teammate Bill and me. As I stepped onto the scale for one final time my heart almost went into overdrive. The numbers rolled around, taunting me while I waited for my total to appear. Seconds later, it did: *ninety-seven pounds.* Which meant that 44.5 percent of my body was officially gone. *Whew.* Even as I surveyed the buff and muscular Bill, I felt confident in the fact that I had actually done enough to win.

My palms were sweaty as I watched Bill take the scale. "Man," I said to myself, "how did he get so *strong*?" The numbers started rolling around, along with my stomach, and when they stopped, so did my heart. He needed to lose more than one hundred and forty-eight pounds to take the victory, and based on the bright yellow number that flashed on the screen, it was obvious he had done just that. *One hundred and sixty-four pounds,* that man lost. He lost a whole *me* . . . and then some!

It wouldn't be until months later that I would do the math on that finale night. In terms of percentages I had lost the first-place position by a measly eight pounds, which is exactly what Jaxon weighed the day we brought him home. The eight pounds I had begrudged, I now rejoiced in. They're eight pounds I'm *so* glad I gained.

Throughout Scripture God proves that he is a God of numbers. Really. He even has a book in there with that very name—Numbers. God says that he knows his children *so well* that he counts the number of hairs on their heads. He counts every tear that they cry. He counts the number of days they will live. He counts *everything*, it seems, and I happen to believe that he counted exactly how many pounds I would drop between my first day on campus and the finale, and that the number I'd wind up losing by would be exactly eight perfect pounds.

BEAUTIFUL AND PERFECT AND STRONG

J axon turned one on January 23, 2009, and in honor of his young life our entire family drove to the Christian counseling center that had made our little addition possible. His birth mother would be there, along with her family and the staff of the center, where Emily now worked. As we walked inside, we noticed banners with first-birthday best wishes, streamers, balloons and a delicious-looking cake complete with an icing-version picture of Jaxon that Mike had snapped the month before.

> In case you're wondering, I *did* indulge in a piece of chocolate cake at Jaxon's first birthday party. But it was a very, very small piece. And I worked out later that day. So there.

It was a precious time of celebration for us and for our boy—who was surrounded by so many people who adored him with the purest form of love.

The last time I had seen Emily was when Jaxon was three days old. I was a bundle of nerves on that day, wondering if she would really let him go. Would she keep her commitment? Would she let me see him, touch him, love him as my own?

> How amazing it is to me that today Emily—Jaxon's birth mother—helps women make the same laudable decision that she herself found the courage to make just one year ago.

But now the tables were turned. As I entered the room with Jaxon in my arms, I noticed tears welling up in her eyes. The expression on her face told me exactly what she had been wondering. Would I really show up? Would I keep my commitment? Would I let her see Jaxon and touch him and love him as though he were hers?

In the hospital room all those months ago she had been the one to say, "Isn't he beautiful and perfect and strong? Hold him—you'll see what I mean." But now it was my turn to extend the same tenderness that I had been shown. "Isn't he beautiful?" I said to her amid the banners and balloons. "Isn't he perfect and strong? Here, you hold him—you'll see exactly what I mean."

For a moment in time I was able to return the gift that had so graciously been given to me. And something about that experience felt very, very right.

~\/\/~

J axon has changed the Hadden home in a thousand ways since his arrival. The other night Mike asked me, "What are all of the good things that have come from adopting Jaxon?" I thought about it for a second and said with a smile, "Hmm ... do they have to be *good*? I mean, let's be honest ... babies are *tough!*"

And it's true—babies *are* tough. In the past year I have enjoyed no more than two decent nights' sleep. I have vacuumed up more Cheerios than should be allowable by law. I have scrounged pennies from underneath couch cushions to fund his hundred-dollar-a-week formula habit. I have felt a perpetual pulling on my leg. I have organized kitchen cabinets at least six times a day. I have wiped tiny fingerprints from every conceivable surface in our home. I have had to secure the dog-food dish so that one especially curious human doesn't dine on Puppy Chow each night. I have forsaken my beloved Kelly Clarkson CD in favor of one more round of "Wheels on the Bus." I have increased my laundry duty by five loads a week. I have never finished a conversation. I have changed sixteen thousand dirty diapers. And I have not sat down even *once*.

But even in spite of that list—which is *far* from complete, as you know if you have kids—I wouldn't trade Jaxon for the world. Because of him I awaken every morning to a bright and cheery smile. Because of him Noah has a brother to share life with. Because of him I hear the two best syllables in the English language no fewer than two hundred times a day—*"Ma-maaa!"* Because of him I know that God still answers prayers.

As a parent I thought a lot about what I hoped to teach Jaxon during his first year of life. In that timeframe he would learn to talk and to walk and to sing and to dance. He would learn the names of his family members and the location of his toes. He would learn of God's love, even if he doesn't yet fully know all that it means.

What I *didn't* think much about was what Jaxon would teach me. On a rainy afternoon shortly after his first birthday I wrote a blog post for my publisher titled, "All I Needed to Know about Life I Learned from My One-Year-Old." Here's essentially what I said:

"I'm realizing as my son Jaxon turns one that all I really need to know I am learning from him. Things like:

- It's okay to cry when you don't feel good.
- You need to eat—and eat *often*—in order to be healthy.
- Getting a good night's sleep can make the difference between a good day and a bad day.
- There's something wonderful about being held by somebody you love when you are feeling cranky.
- Before you can ever learn to walk, you have to fall down a few times. (Okay, *many* times.)
- When you take the time to notice them, even tiny, seemingly insignificant things can be amazing.
- A belly laugh really *is* contagious.
- Even the worst day can be turned around with a sweet smile.
- Everything that *looks* good doesn't necessarily *taste* good. Like red crayons.
- The squeaky wheel usually does get the oil.
- And, perhaps the most significant one of all: *Nothing* compares to unconditional love."[17]

The post generated rave reviews for one and only one reason, I'm sure: Being reminded of the simple things in life often elicits the most generous helpings of gratitude.

OUR GRACIOUS GOD

Mike and I had always said that if we had another son we'd name him Elijah. We loved that name, and we loved the character in Scripture. But when things on the adoption-front heated up, my darling husband received another prompting from God, who probably has come to realize that if he delivers the messages to me, I'll forget to write them down.

Mike said, "This child is not 'Elijah.' He is someone entirely different, a baby we never *dreamed* we'd have."

And with that, we were back to square one.

All soon-to-be parents probably go through the same dilemma when choosing a name for their child. Countless *dozens* of perfectly fine names get ruled out, all because the kid who picked his nose in your third-grade class was named Jeremiah. Or Ethan. Or Doug.

We had chosen Noah's name because its origin points to the word *peace*, and so we knew that whatever name we selected for this new little one would have to have significant meaning. At one point, Mike came across the name Jackson, but its meaning was no more profound than, "Jack's son." Um, no.

Then he found the alternate spelling, and the entire baby-naming universe shifted before our eyes. "Jaxon with an *x* . . ." Mike read from the book of names one morning. "When spelled that way, it means 'God has been gracious.'"

Bingo. Jaxon it would be.

In the Bible when God changed the spelling of a person's name, it was to establish for that person a new identity. More than anything else Jaxon would bring to our lives, we wanted him to know that he brought the Haddens a bold reminder that God has been gracious, that he is gracious, and that he will be gracious for all the rest of our days.

It's hard to imagine what God thinks and feels when he looks at the four of us today, but I like to think that as he gazes down from heaven he is proud. I think he's proud that Mike and I waited for each other and stepped into marriage pure and blameless and more than a little excited to become one. I think he's proud that from that day forward we devoted ourselves to him and chose to do whatever he called us to do, even when we didn't exactly understand why. I think he's proud that we strive to prove through our lives that God's ways are *always* better than our own.

As a young girl, I dreamed about growing up, getting married and having two-point-five kids who were very close in age—a boy, a girl and whatever God wanted for the half. I never would have signed up for two boys, and certainly not two who are seven years apart and as different as night and day. But as I think about God's thoughts toward me now, I like to picture him saying, "Yes. This is how I intended it to be all along. *This* is the story I wanted to tell."

Make Smart, Simple Choices

A book series came out a couple of years ago called *Eat This, Not That*, which presents thousands of food comparisons and tells you which one you should pick. So, for example, if you're on a road trip with your family and the tiny town where you stop to get gas has only a McDonald's and a Burger King to choose from, and they're fresh out of healthier options like salads and grilled chicken, and you're fairly certain Jillian Michaels won't suddenly pop out from behind the restaurant and give you the third degree about why on *earth* you didn't pack some healthy snacks, then you can pull out this handy guide to discover that selecting a Big Mac, which contains 540 calories and twenty-nine grams of fat, is a far better choice than opting for a Whopper with cheese, which weighs in at 760 calories and forty-seven grams of fat.

Or let's say your friends want to meet at Chili's to chat, and you've been craving dessert all day. If you had read *Eat This, Not That*, you'd know that whatever you order, it had better not be the Chocolate Chip Paradise Pie with vanilla ice cream. Why? Because at 1,600 calories and seventy-eight grams of fat, you'd essentially be eating three Big Macs for dessert. And while they're a little bit better than Whoppers with cheese, still, that's just gross.

Actually, if you've been craving dessert all day, my advice is to skip Chili's altogether and make Devin Alexander's Chocolate Chocolate Brownie Cups from *The Most Decadent Diet Ever!* (Broadway, 2008) instead. She is the author of many of *The Biggest Loser* cookbooks and host of *Healthy Decadence* on FitTV. I first tasted these brownies at the Season 6 finale in LA. She said, "You *have* to try my brownies." And despite my protests, she wound up convincing me that at fifty-four calories and less than half a gram of fat a pop, I could afford to indulge her request. A yummier brownie has never touched my lips.

Chocolate Chocolate Brownie Cups

Ingredients

Butter-flavored cooking spray
½ cup unsweetened applesauce
1 teaspoon vanilla extract
8 large egg-whites

2 cups raw sugar, such as Sugar in the Raw
½ cup unbleached all-purpose flour
1 cup unsweetened cocoa powder
2 teaspoons instant espresso powder
1 teaspoon baking powder
1 teaspoon salt
½ cup mini semisweet chocolate chips

Directions

Preheat oven to 350 degrees. Thoroughly mist two twelve-cup nonstick minimuffin tins with spray. In a large mixing bowl, using sturdy whisk or spatula, mix the applesauce, vanilla, egg-whites, and sugar until well combined. Add the flour, cocoa powder, espresso powder, baking powder and salt. Stir mixture until just combined and no lumps remain. Working in batches, fill each cup of the pans until each muffin cup is nearly full. Sprinkle half of the chocolate chips evenly over brownies. Bake ten to twelve minutes or until toothpick inserted into center comes out dry. (A few crumbs are okay.) Transfer the pan to a cooling rack and allow to sit for five minutes. Repeat process with the remaining batter, making forty-eight brownies total.

By the way, once cooked, these decadent delights freeze extremely well. After-school snacks and midnight cravings are solved!

What strikes me about *Eat This, Not That* is not the actual content as much as the premise: It's much easier to make smart choices when you know what those smart choices are. The other thing that strikes me is how many extraordinarily dumb choices I made prior to being on *The Biggest Loser*. If a book had been written that instead was called "Live Like This, Not Like That," my life before the show would have provided the perfect profile for the "not like that" part of the equation. Let me give you a quick rundown of what I mean.

Before my *The Biggest Loser* experience . . .

- I ate what was convenient, which by definition is never the same thing as what is healthy.
- I ate what was cheap (again, cheap rarely also means healthy).
- I hung around with like-minded enablers (read: fat people who love to eat!).
- I looked at the big picture that was me and figured I'd never change—so why try?

- I watched far too much TV (hint: if there is a deep trench in the upholstery that runs through "your spot" on the couch, you're watching too much TV too).
- I went to bed late and never got enough sleep.
- I slept late every single chance I got.
- I quit at nearly everything I tried.
- I tried every shortcut in existence to avoid being uncomfortable or having to work too hard.
- I blamed others for everything that was wrong with me.
- I decided that I abhorred exercise, despite the fact that I'd never really tried it.
- I allowed others to dictate my self-worth. (Ironic, given it's called "self" worth!)
- I associated all-things social with food. (Who knew it was possible to go to a movie and not order popcorn?)
- I never ate breakfast. Ever.
- I bought my coffee in fancy stores that had baristas who always put fun (read: fattening) things in it, instead of making my coffee plain and at home.
- I wore shoes that made it nearly impossible for me to walk farther than a few feet.
- I was never prepared for the day or for the fact that I'd probably get hungry every few hours.
- I went to parties, dinner engagements and every other social setting totally and completely famished.

Hardly the picture of wisdom and simplicity, I think you'd agree.

———◦∧∧◦———

Some of the greatest lessons I learned on the show came in the form of smart, simple "live like this" steps that even I could take. Here are a few of my favorites:

- Pack along a snack-size baggie of almonds when you walk out of the house in the morning. When you feel that three-o'clock crash coming on, chew on three almonds, take a deep breath and remind yourself that you're worth the new lifestyle you're living!
- Eat a light snack—an apple, a few nuts, a piece of lean deli turkey—before heading out for a party or dinner engagement so that when

you arrive, you can concentrate on making a beeline to your best friend rather than to the dessert table.

- Eat at home as often as possible.
- Make only one meal for your family, kids included. Everyone should be eating healthfully!
- When you do eat out, avoid appetizers. Save your appetite for the real meal.
- Also, whenever you eat in a restaurant, immediately cut your portion in half and ask your server for a takeout container. Put half of your meal in the container, set it aside, and know that not only will you not be tempted to overeat, but also you'll have a delicious meal for tomorrow. So smart!
- Save dessert for special occasions instead of considering it an every-day necessity.
- Drink water and nothing else. Well, okay, you can stick a little bag in it and call it hot tea if you'd like; just be sure that in a given day you're not drinking your calories. Calories should come from food. End of discussion.
- Drink water before eating. Your mind will register that "full" feeling sooner than if you eat on an empty tummy.
- Never eat while watching TV.
- Never eat while standing up, such as when you're hovering over the kitchen counter preparing your kids' breakfast.
- Don't go to the grocery store hungry.
- Once you get to the grocery store, park as far away from the entrance as possible, and thank God every step of the way for your ability to walk.
- Shop only on the perimeter of the grocery store, which is where they keep the good stuff—produce, fresh seafood and so forth.
- Always take the stairs when you have the option.
- Never buy clothing that is one size too big. You will play right into that self-fulfilling prophecy and despise yourself later.
- *Enjoy* your food instead of shoveling it in. Savor every bite for the way it is nourishing your body.
- Walk or ride a bike if what you need is close by.
- Make exercise fun by including your kids. See page 206 for a great playground exercise.

There you have it: twenty smart, simple choices that you can make today. Pick a few and give them a whirl. You'll be incredibly glad that you did.

CHAPTER 8

This Is Me Now

I AWAKENED AT the crack of dawn this morning to catch a flight to Louisiana for an engagement I agreed to months ago. My publisher ran a contest for their magazine subscribers called "New Year, New You," and in addition to all sorts of support for a full twelve months, the winner would receive a weekend visit from a personal trainer, a motivational coach, a nutritionist and me—a once-obese woman who knew well the road she was about to walk. The trouble is, I was supposed to kick off the entire weekend by paying her a surprise visit and ringing her doorbell at three o'clock this afternoon. And based on what I've just been told by airline personnel here in Jacksonville, it appears I now will be arriving in Louisiana sometime around, oh, four-thirty.

My alarm shattered the blissful silence surrounding me well before five o'clock this morning, which launched me into the crazy-person's routine of packing my suitcase, throwing together Noah's lunch for school, grabbing Jaxon's favorite blanket so that he could finish sleeping on the ride to his grandmother's house and so forth. I know, I know. I should have done it all last night. Welcome to my world.

As it turned out, I arrived at the airport on time, if not a bit disheveled. I speedily hugged and kissed Mike good-bye and rushed inside toward the ticket-counter area, where I realized that I wasn't the only person in this town who got up at an ungodly hour. There had to be ninety-five people already waiting in line, and this was the line for the *self* check-in—you know, the one that is supposed to make the entire process smooth and seamless and fun.

Not so much, today.

I finally reached the front of the line, spotted an open kiosk, swiped my credit card for proof that I am, in fact, Julie Hadden, scanned my e-ticket confirmation and then cringed as three disheartening words appeared on the screen: "Itinerary Not Recognized."

I stared at the ticketing agent standing a few kiosks over until she acknowledged my presence, and as she stepped over to my end of the counter, I said, "It's not letting me check in for my flight."

"Hmm," she said. "Let's see what's going on." She then proceeded to program the proverbial space shuttle, pausing and groaning every now and then for effect. I glanced at my watch and grimaced. Six fifty-four—thirty-one minutes until my plane was due to depart. I had blown more than half an hour standing in line, and still I might miss my flight? I silently reviewed my self-talk themes, which I carry with me for situations just like this. "You're a nice person. You're a *good* person. You're a person who loves God and country. Not to mention, there's probably at least one *The Biggest Loser* fan in the general vicinity. Keep your cool, Julie. Keep your . . ."

Ms. Agent suddenly stopped typing. "I'm so sorry, but..."

There was no way the rest of that sentence could contain good news.

". . . you can't go," she continued.

"Wha-what did you say?" I asked. Clearly I was being punked. I swiveled around, sure I'd find a candid camera staring me down.

"Yeah," she said, reclaiming my attention. "You can't go."

"I can't go? To *Louisiana*, you mean? On the flight I paid for?" *Keep your cool, Julie. Keep . . .*

"Mm-hmm. Your flight was overbooked. And we resold your ticket. But we don't have time to get your luggage on the plane anyway, so..."

"But my flight doesn't leave for thirty minutes!" I said, with a little more passion than I intended.

"Actually, twenty-nine. And there's a thirty-minute cut-off on all checked luggage."

"Wait, wait, wait. So I got here on time and with proof of a paid-in-full ticket for this flight, and now you're telling me that I can't get on my plane?"

"That is correct," she said in an annoyingly helpful tone. "But because of your trouble, I won't charge you to rebook your flight."

Keep your cool, Julie. Keep your cool. "Uh-huh. And so—"

"So we can put you on the next flight, which leaves here at nine o'clock . . ."

While she tapped out another six-thousand characters on her keyboard, I started doing the math on whether I could still make my Atlanta connection and get to Louisiana in time for the shoot. "That would work," I offered, determined to keep my cool.

". . . Oh, but that one's oversold as well. Hmm . . ."

Doughnuts were created for moments like these. Doughnuts and Ben Stiller movies. In my mind's eye I replayed the scene from *Meet the Parents*, where Stiller's character Greg Focker walks up to the gate agent, hands over his ticket, and then hears her say in a perfectly perky tone, "I'm sorry, Sir, but we're only boarding rows nine and above right now."

He looks at her stiff up-do, her rosy cheeks and her painted-on smile and says, "But I'm in row eight. It's only one row off."

"Yes, we'll be calling your row shortly, Sir. Now please, step aside."

Frustrated, Focker turns around and scans the utterly vacant gate area, finding only a custodian with a vacuum cleaner a hundred feet away who's mowing long rows into the muted gray carpet. He turns back around and gawks at the airline representative with a look that says, "Surely you're kidding."

"Please step aside, Sir," she says again, pasted-on smile still firmly in place.

And so Greg Focker reaches for his suitcase, takes four steps backward and waits while the empty room stays empty and not a single soul boards the plane.

Five seconds later, the gate agent picks up the intercom phone, tilts her perky head back and forth in cadence with her words and says to her audience of one, "Ladies and gentlemen, thank you for waiting. We are now boarding all rows. All rows, you may board now."

A totally dispirited Focker picks up his bag, takes four steps forward and hands over his ticket once again.

Back in Jacksonville, I was having a surreal airport experience of my own. "Then when do you think I can actually get out of here?" I asked with as much grace as I could muster.

"Well," said Ms. Agent, while still staring at her screen, "there's one at ten-fourteen. Oh, but whoops, it would be illegal to book you on that one because you wouldn't have enough time to make your connection in Atlanta..."

"Listen, lady, have you seen my biceps? If you don't start coming up with some viable options for getting me *out* of here, on a plane and *to* the state of Louisiana THIS afternoon, believe me, things are going to get ugly."

Actually, I didn't say that. I'm pretty sure I just stared at her, dumbfounded and deflated and ready to call it quits.

THREE MYTHS I BOUGHT

Somewhere along the way I picked up the assumption that after my stint on *The Biggest Loser*, I'd exist in a permanent state of euphoria, kind of like Maria twirling down the flower-dotted Austrian mountainside in *The Sound of Music*—thin, carefree and with a lovely song on my lips. I'd waltz my way through daily life, inspiring others to lose weight just as I had and I'd sleep restfully each night, content with the course of my life.

Travel hassles didn't *exactly* fit the picture of what I thought life would look like.

But it's been this way ever since I returned home from the show. Daily life still proves to be a struggle. Inspiring others to lose weight sometimes requires eating three meals in a row in stuffy airports and sleeping on starchy budget-hotel sheets. And restfulness doesn't really come by way of starch.

This is the problem with buying into myths—they never prove themselves true. As I look at my life today, I see three clear myths I swallowed —hook, line and sinker. The first was that, despite the fact that physical, mental and spiritual transformation had been *ridiculously* difficult from day one, after I was done with the show, surely things would get easier.

Yeah, right.

MYTH #1: IT WILL GET EASIER

Making my reentry into home-life was uncomfortable and complex and weird. Clearly, this was still my home: I recognized the furniture, the appliances and the pictures on the wall. But I had changed so much that I felt like a stranger in my own skin, not to mention in

When I came home, my house smelled like someone else's house. Every house has its own smell, right? Somehow our "smell" had changed. Moreover, because I hadn't unpacked yet, the bathroom counter boasted *none* of my things; drawings of Noah's that I'd never before seen were stuck to the refrigerator door; and life as I'd known it had obviously moved on.

my house. Sure, there were some perks. I had gotten used to sleeping in a twin bed in an un-air-conditioned dorm room, but now I found myself in a cushy king-size bed . . . and with a man by my side. What's more, I didn't have to wait in line to take a shower. I could use the telephone whenever my little heart desired. And there weren't cameras rolling, waiting to record my every move.

But the downs seemed to outweigh the ups.

On *The Biggest Loser* campus the only thing I had to focus on was working out—frequently, passionately and with as few tears shed as possible. Now I was back home, where my list of responsibilities was long. Given the new skills and perspectives I had learned the past many months, I had no idea how to prioritize all those to-dos.

In addition to reacclimating to the daily routines of life, there was a relational chasm that had to be bridged.

Noah and Mike had become so close while I was gone that interacting with them upon my return felt odd. The women in my life—my mother, my mother-in-law, my sister, my grandmother—served as Noah's surrogate moms while I was away, but Mike was the one who bore the most significant burden. And God blessed his efforts in unique ways. Mike would tell you that my being gone for months on end was the best thing that could have happened to Noah's and his relationship, and in my view, he would be right.

Before I left for the show, Noah was a momma's boy through and through, mostly due to the fact that I *lived* for the child. As an obese person it was far easier to shift the focus to my son than to risk drawing attention to myself: Noah was the air that I breathed, and he knew it. How grateful I am that *The Biggest Loser* interrupted a pattern that was destined for destruction. A boy needs his dad, and I unwittingly was robbing Noah of that relationship by trying to be all things to him, all the time.

When I returned, he and Mike were both still crazy about me, and I about them, but it didn't alter the fact that I was like a junior-high kid who switched schools and then came back two years later to discover that her best friend found a new best friend while she was gone. It was the same husband, the same son and the same setting, but somehow everything now was different. There were shared experiences that I hadn't known, inside jokes that I didn't get and a continuation of the life I'd left that I no longer wanted to live.

That last realization hit me most profoundly when I opened the door to our pantry the first afternoon I was home. I absolutely flipped out. I mean, there was Crisco in there! To my knowledge, Crisco is only used for two things: baking unhealthy cakes, and coating a cast-iron skillet. And nothing healthy has *ever* been cooked in a cast-iron skillet. Ask me how I know.

I stood there staring at boxes and boxes of fake-fruit snacks, bags of white flour, a giant jar of candy that I used to sneak on a near-daily basis, can after can of overly preserved vegetables. "I forgot they even *made* canned vegetables," I said to myself. How I missed the fresh, organic LA life I'd known.

I've seen interviews on TV with recovering alcoholics who talk about how devastating it is for them when they go back to the street corner where they used to sleep and are reminded of the poor choices they once made. They see in that slab of asphalt the laziness, ignorance, complacency and indulgence that formerly characterized their lives, and the reminders are almost too much to bear. Those pantry shelves were my own personal slab of asphalt, and as I took them in, a wave of fear washed over me like none I'd ever known. "Dear God, don't let me again become the me who lived this way."

It would prove a challenging goal to pursue, the goal of moving not backward but ahead.

———✦———

One of the things that Noah and I used to do prior to my being on the show was to bake cookies together. Before you get any wild ideas about how much of a Suzy Homemaker I was or am, I should add that they were, and still are, of the slice-and-bake variety.

We'd make them for breakfast (I know, I know) or for a snack while we watched movies on Friday night. Or Tuesday night. Or *any* night, if I'm being honest.

Once I was back home, and during the same week that I had my pantry meltdown, Noah looked at me pleadingly and said, "Mommy, can we make cookies?"

I felt badly for having been gone for so long that I would have obliged almost any request from that child. "Well, of *course*, sweetheart," I said. "Whatever you want."

We dashed to the store, pulled a sugary log of bliss from the refrigerated case, rushed back home and began to slice away. I decided that I'd make only four cookies, so that I wouldn't be tempted to eat any myself. Noah could eat however many he wanted—which would probably be two or three—and then Mike would eat the rest. Perfect plan, right? Except for the fact that the rest of that little pleasure-log was still taunting me from inside the fridge.

> You can learn so much from watching how kids treat food. For example, Noah only eats when he's hungry. Imagine that! I'll say, "Noah, why aren't you hungry? It's dinner time." He'll say, "Oh, we had a surprise snack at school late this afternoon, Mom." What a logical response, not to eat when you're already full.

Within two days' time I had eaten in its entirety what remained of the unbaked cookie dough. Had I not learned anything on the show? Jillian would have *died*.

Undoubtedly, things were not getting any easier for me, now that I was home.

MYTH #2: ONE BAD CHOICE WON'T MATTER

The second myth I bought was that one little, itty-bitty bad choice wouldn't make a difference in the grand scheme of things.

For the most part—cookie-binge excluded—I tried to eat well. And I continued my exercise trend, although I certainly wasn't working out three or five or seven hours a day. Still, despite my fairly healthy habits, almost immediately after my return home I began to gain weight again.

One day when I was strong enough to actually handle introspection, I thought honestly about what could be the culprit. Instantly, I knew the answer. I had quit drinking water, replacing it with diet soda instead.

It seemed like a small decision to me. I mean, my eating patterns were mostly "clean." My exercise was frequent. I was *undoubtedly* behaving better than I had been before *The Biggest Loser.* But without intending to, I had let one bad choice sabotage all of my progress to date.

I confided my misstep to Hollie one day, and from that point forward the harassment was nonstop. My cell phone would ring, and on the other end of the line I'd hear, "Jules, how much water have you had today?"

"Uh, none," I'd admit.

"Go get a glass and fill it up. Right now. While I'm on the phone. [Insert pregnant pause.] *Now,* Julie. I'm waiting!"

Ugh. "Fine. I'm going."

It's a fair statement to say that Hollie singlehandedly drove me to drink.

I made the same mistake with food, believing that cheating a little here or there wouldn't add up to anything significant. I'd indulge from time to time in a piece of *Cheesecake Factory* chocolate cake or a large basket of hot wings, which equals a mere *150 percent* of my daily caloric-intake goal all by itself. One itty-bitty bad choice, right? Ten pounds in less than a month, I would learn the hard way that choices *do* matter, each and every one.

MYTH #3: HARD WORK EQUALS RADICAL RESULTS

A third theme that I discovered was patently false is that hard work always equals radical results.

Between my season's finale and the next season's finale, which I had planned to attend as a guest, I vowed to myself that I'd get rid of the ten pounds I had so quickly put back on. Really, now, how hard could that be? In *The Biggest Loser* land, ten pounds was just a normal week's weight loss. I upped the ante on my workouts with Margie and committed to running on "off" days, and still it took me nearly three months to get those ten pounds to budge. *Three* months!

The truth is, it was a heck of a lot more appealing to sit on the couch and devour Reese's peanut-butter cups while watching *American Idol* than it was to tug on my Spandex and hit the gym. But even on days when I didn't feel like it, I had promised myself that I would continue what I started forever—whether I saw dramatic results or not. Every choice I made was a choice that would lead me further down the path of success or cause me to regress. That much I knew. And if it was the last thing that I did, I was bound and determined to succeed.

FINDING MY WAY BACK HOME

I'll never know where I picked up my errant assumptions about what life would be like once I was thin. But whenever expectations and reality collide, the fallout can be rough. It would take me several weeks, a boatload of self-talk and a slew of challenging conversations with family and friends to establish my footing once more, but when that initial semblance of stability entered the scene at last, I knew that all those efforts were paying off.

One of the earliest "challenging conversations" was with Noah, back on that Crisco-discovery day.

Kids love anything that resembles a game, so I decided that instead of just tossing out every food item that didn't pass muster with my new eating plan, I'd instead make the culinary-cleansing fun. I turned over a box of plasticky fruit snacks or some other, equally disgusting excuse for food, and said, "See this word, Noah? That spells *fructose*, and it means sugar." I told him to find every single box, bag or can that had "high fructose corn syrup" listed in the first three ingredients and immediately to throw it away.

Within seconds, I heard him strike pantry-gold. "Look, Mom!" he'd cheer. "This one has it, second word in the list!" He would toss the box into the already bulging garbage bag and head back to the pantry to hunt for more.

We would eventually add "enriched" to the search, after I explained what it meant in terms he could understand. "Honey, think about how sad it is when we take something good that God made, and we make it bad. That's exactly what has happened to an 'enriched' food item." I told him that when people strip back all of the wonderful, natural, vitamin-filled fibers in order to make something white and fluffy, the nutritional value of that food goes all the way down to zero. "And the way I tell if the stripping has occurred is to see if the food sticks to the roof of my mouth. If it sticks, it's been stripped," I said. "Which means we should make a better food choice next time, deal?"

I was careful to walk Noah through the fact that all of these new habits weren't necessarily about him. He's so skinny that he could eat an

Proof-positive that I was pudgy even as a kid. Here I am at Disney World with my cousin, and later, clowning around at church camp.

My pageant-circuit stint didn't land me a crown, but it did afford me a great prize: my husband, Mike, featured in our engagement picture. (RIGHT)

Whoever says being fat is fun obviously never met me during my "couch days."

I weighed 216 pounds when I headed to *The Biggest Loser* casting call. Where's the sweater-set, you ask? That would come later in the process.

Talk about a lot of humanity in one photo! I loved my Season 4 castmates and love even more the fact that we no longer look like this!

Season 4's final four: Bill Germanakos, Hollie Self, me, Isabeau Miller. The last day on campus before heading home to prepare for the finale.

Julie Hadden in jeans? Who would have thought!

(RIGHT) Small enough for Noah's small arms to wrap around me—what a wonderful thing.

Oh, baby! Look at that hot mama! I was really proud of my accomplishments when this s was snapped at the finale. Official weight: 121 itty-bitty pounds.

My fearsome and much-loved trainer, Jillian Michaels, and me at a taping for the TV show *Extra* in spring 2009.

Outside Oprah's studios: Could my smile be any wider?

(RIGHT) In gym parlance, these are what we call "big guns"!

It's a good workout whenever I can kick my trainer.

Margie Marshall and me, posthalf-marathon. Thirteen-minute miles were nothing to brag about, but completing the race with a smile on my face was.

Here we are sans all the sweat.

Backstage at the *Oprah* show, we former contestants were asked to sign *The Biggest Loser* books for audience members. It's never lost on me that every speech I give and every book I sign might just be the one small thing that encourages someone to begin walking in a new and healthy direction.

I thought I'd be the first female biggest loser, but for so many good reasons this woman would wear the title instead: the powerful and beautiful Season 5 victor, Ali Vincent.

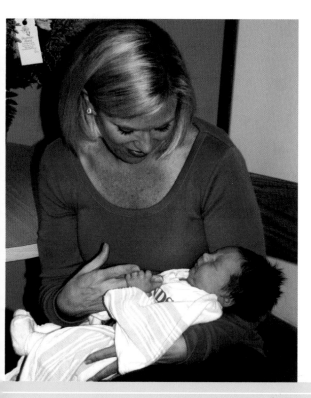

Our precious Jaxon on the day we brought him home.

Noah and his favorite villain on her bike outside a restaurant in LA.

All four Haddens—Noah, Jaxon, me and Mike—in Jacksonville, Florida, summertime 2009.

(LEFT) Park days are the best days of all. Swinging with my boy Noah.

entire chocolate cake every day for a year and not gain a single pound. But because we're a family, and because one member of our family (that would be me) tends to struggle with overindulging in things that are white and fluffy and endlessly yummy, we *all* have to agree to certain parameters so that *all* of us can succeed. In a beautiful display of self-lessness, my then-six-year-old son trotted off to his room and returned with a metal canister of candy that he kept in his closet, loot that had been collected from several birthday parties, church carnivals and trick-or-treat outings over the years. "This probably should go away too," he said with a grin, "because you know where I keep it!"

I had never been so delighted to be accused of being a thief.

When I returned home I realized that in my absence Noah had become a self-made *The Biggest Loser* version of Dustin Hoffman's character in *Rain Man*. He learned every stat from my season of the show, memorizing every contestant's starting weight, finale weight and the reason why he or she got kicked off. "Phil was too big of a threat," Noah would say with authority. Or, "I bet they got rid of Jez because they thought he could lose weight on his own at home."

Noah loved the show so much that he asked for *The Biggest Loser* action figures for Christmas. Somebody ought to start making those. Well, as long as the one representing me is the *thin* version of Julie Hadden.

Noah was so obsessed with the nuances of the show that my first few months home were spent with him grilling me about every last detail he couldn't quite figure out on his own. We dished like teenage girls, guessing people's motivations and gossiping about the actions they took. But it was that string of ongoing conversations between Noah and me that led to more serious discussions about how to live a strong and healthy life. And now, almost two years later, I think he's actually getting it. Just last week I overheard him talking to his buddy Luke during lunch, which they were enjoying outside. "Hey Luke," Noah said with a huge bite of sandwich stuffed inside his cheek, "you know your juice should always have a '100' on it, right?"

Luke was perplexed. "Huh? What are you talking about?"

"*Well*," Noah continued in his most scholarly, eight-year-old voice, "a one hundred is the very best grade. If it has, like, a 10, then that means there's only, like, ten . . . *fruit* . . . in it, and the rest of it is just *sugar*. And that's a really *bad* deal. So, whenever you buy juice, you tell your mom to make *sure* it has a 100 on the label, 'kay?"

You go, Noah. Pure fruit juice rocks.

In the same breath that I affirm Noah when he gets it right on the fruit-juice front, I encourage him to appreciate the balance I'm learning to strike. Granted, if I were a single woman, my pantry would like look a miniature Whole Foods store. I'd be able to afford all-organic produce, and I'd love feeling like I was standing in *The Biggest Loser*'s kitchen every day of the week. But I'm not single. I have a husband and two sons who need a normal wife and mom who can deal with the normal stuff of life. They need to have boys' nights when they can watch *The Munsters* and eat Taco Bell followed by a giant bowl of buttery popcorn without wondering whether or not I'll freak out. Noah needs me to show up at his school's Christmas party with cupcakes to pass out to his buddies instead of toothbrushes. Mike needs me to make a juicy hamburger for him every once in a while. It's called *life*. And I for one intend to live it. With that said, I still had some work to do if I wanted to fully embrace the post-show version of me.

———— ᴧᴧ ————

Some people who have been on *The Biggest Loser* wind up changing their entire lives as a result of their experience on the show. They get done with their time on campus, they go back home and they ditch everything that used to define who they were—their spouses, their homes, their professions and more. Really. It's remarkable, and sad, to see.

Thankfully, that just wasn't my experience.

Before the show I was extremely unhappy with me, but on other fronts my happiness-meter soared. I loved my marriage, my son, my home and my friends. I loved *all* of my life, it seemed. I just thought that a thinner version of me should be living it. Much like tolerating the absolute wrong actor being cast in your favorite sitcom, I relished the story line God had given me to experience, even when the character was altogether off the mark.

When I returned from campus, I remember thinking, "So *this* is what it feels like to have the right person in the right role with exactly the right plot." I had become the person who should have been living my life all along.

In the same way that *The Biggest Loser* experience had summoned a more fully alive version of me, the experience called out a brand-new Mike as well. While I was preparing to live a new life, he was graciously planning to help manage it.

Take today, for example. During my airport fiasco I called Mike, which surprised neither him nor me. And Mike did what he always does: He listened to me, and then he *agreed* with me. (Husbands, take note. That one step will get you anything your little heart desires.) But it didn't stop there. After intently listening to my detailed description of the annoying ticketing agent and the three flights I would *not* be on, and graciously agreeing with my assessment that life was unfair and that airports are awful and that regardless of what happened I clearly would be missing the video shoot in Louisiana at three o-freaking-clock, my husband then slid into solution mode faster than you can say "irrational woman."

Knowing that my real concern was disappointing my publisher and the team of people who had set up this whole deal, Mike's first words were, "Babe, do you need their numbers?"

God bless his soul.

"Yes," I said with an exhale. "That would be great."

It came as no surprise that Mike had those numbers on hand. He always has the numbers on hand, as well as any other microscopic detail I could possibly need to know. Mike has tremendous administrative gifts, that, candidly, I have zero use for. I like things like spontaneity and risk—you know, things that stick their tongue out at the stuff of "administration." To give you a sense of how afflicted my darling man is, he actually feels *honored* when people mistakenly assume that he's my full-time administrative assistant. There are probably support groups for people like him, don't you think?

Officially, my husband is a public-relations director who works for the government. But in addition to possessing skills that make him incredibly successful in his "real" field, he also is a stellar graphic artist and a ridiculously organized and efficient man. Let me give you just one example of how I know this to be true.

Whenever I am due to leave on a trip, Mike presents me with a folder prepared for my review. Inside the folder are pages containing every possible nuance of my travel, ground transportation, hotel and speaking arrangements. I kid you not. What's more, the pages are formatted with beautiful fonts and bright colors and laid out in the *most* intuitive way, complete with page numbers in the corners and everything. Truly, it's a work of art.

However, I should point out here that this morning as I was rushing to get myself and our two boys out the door and into the car so that I could eventually get to the airport, I shouted over my shoulder at Mike, "Do you have a bottle for Jaxon?" Of course the answer was no. For all of my husband's gifts, mothering simply is not on the list. I can't tell you how many times we've been headed to my mom's or my grandmother's house for them to watch the baby, and there has been but one pitiful wipe in Jaxon's bag. "Don't you think he'll require more than one wipe?" I ask every time. "And perhaps a diaper or two?" I'll make my way to Jaxon's room to grab wipes and diapers while scrounging through his bag to see what else might be missing. "A single jar of applesauce? *Really*?" I'm then forced to rant. "He eats *real food*, Mike. He's a *person*, not a critter. He has to be *fed*. He has to go to the *bathroom*. He has to be cleaned up *after* he goes to the bathroom. My *word*, husband. Have you been living under a rock?"

But back to this morning. "He needs a bottle, honey," I said in a slightly reprimanding tone as I made my way back inside the house. "And his blanket."

I returned with Jaxon's essentials, climbed into the front seat of the car, exhausted from the flurry of activity, and then heard Mike say, "Honey, do you have the itinerary I printed for you?"

Um, that would be no. Back inside the house I went. Seriously, if my head weren't screwed onto my neck, I'd probably misplace that too. But given the fact that I am married to Mike, I could just say, "Sweetie, where'd I leave my head?" To which he'd reply, "Ah yes, your head. I spit-shined it and left it there on the kitchen counter for you."

Friends who know me best can attest to the fact that the only reason I *ever* make it to a speaking engagement, TV interview or conference call with my publisher is that Mike whispers my to-dos as he's heading off to work. "Hey, Jules," he said just yesterday in his kindest, most help-ful tone. "Don't forget your call at three."

"Huh?" I replied.

"Yep. It's on the calendar. Don't forget."

Of course he was correct.

Mike has undeniably natural talent in this area of planning and organizing, but he wouldn't want to do it for just anyone. At least that's what he tells me. Several months ago when I could see that his helpful-ness was destined to be a trend, I said, "I just want to thank you for all that you're doing to keep my world straight. You have been so helpful, and I can't really figure out why you do all that you do, and with such a happy heart."

His response stopped me short. "Julie, this is my dream job! I love you. I'm *proud* of you. I want to make life easier for you in any way that I can. And think about it, what could possibly be better for a public-rela-tions guy than to be able to do PR for the woman I'm going to spend the rest of my life with?"

Really, now. How sweet can you get?

Still, assuming I ever make it to Louisiana for this weekend's festivi-ties, I guarantee I'll return home, walk through the door and find two very smelly sons. "Noah," I'll whisper to the one son who can speak in complete sentences, "did you *bathe* this weekend?"

The answer won't surprise me one bit. "No," he'll whisper back. "Daddy didn't make me."

And that will be the truth. Daddy *won't* have made Noah bathe, but Daddy will have laid out my agenda for Monday morning. Truth be told, I wouldn't have it any other way. Largely because of my husband's investment, I have found my way back home. Now if only I could kick to the curb the stuff that's mine alone to overcome.

FLESHING OUT THE CHANGES I'VE MADE

People tend to think that when you lose weight you also lose all the insecurities that come with being fat, but that couldn't be further from the truth. It was startling and sobering to me that while so much about me had changed during my months in LA, more about me had stayed exactly the same.

It's true: I had gained strength of mind, body and soul. But even today the frightened girl can be found deep within, the one who is terrified of letting myself down, of letting down those I know and love. That fearful one battles daily with the fighter who lives inside too—the girl who shouts, "I'll show them!" even as she understands that this is new territory, this path marked out by change. She has no idea what she's doing, but she takes it one step at a time, trusting that the training she received for four months straight will prevail somehow, some way.

As all of my personas wage war, I navigate as best I can. And on most days, I do quite well, thank you very much. It's just that a fat person spends so much of her life knowing that she's not quite enough that even when the weight is gone, the enoughness-thing still remains. When I had all that time to kill this morning, for example, I dropped by a jewelry store in the airport. The saleslady obviously recognized me from having been on the show and said, "Did you lose even *more* weight? Compared to last time I saw you, I'd say so!"

She meant those words as a compliment, of course. Why else would she deliver them with such joy?

The thing is, I heard only the insult side of the equation. If I looked thinner now, then *obviously* the last time she saw me I had weight left to lose. And if I had weight left to lose, then *obviously* on that occasion the thought ran through her mind that sure, maybe I'd done something significant on the show, but I could still stand to drop a few pounds.

Sick, huh?

The demon of enoughness comes to me in random jewelry-store interactions and in connections with good friends alike. I'll sit down to eat dinner with a girlfriend and be greeted by, "Oh, you'll never *guess* who I ran into today!" The rest of the story is always a variation on this theme: "So-and-so asked if you still looked good, and I told her that yes, you still looked *great*, and she's so happy for you!"

Again, the story is told to affirm me. But that's not at all how I take it. To me, the mutual friend's question reflects a deeper assumption that I *don't* look as great as I did right after the show, that of course by now I've failed. Each time, I want to look into my friend's eyes and say, "Next time someone asks how I look, tell her to catch a clue. She's not the only one waiting for me to fail. I'm waiting for me to fail too."

Interestingly, losing nearly half of my body's weight was just the beginning of this transformative journey. I don't particularly enjoy being eyed up and down everywhere I go. I don't particularly like it when people ask the waiter what I ordered or when they stalk me at the grocery store and judge the stuff that's in my cart. But evidently these things are what we refer to as "part of the deal." If only I could take hold of the positive and release everything else that is not. But such is the life of the recovering obese. In some ways it feels like I will have to prove my transformation every moment for the rest of my days; that is, unless I can somehow learn to stop caring more about what other people think than about what I know to be true.

———〰〰〰———

Thankfully, in the past weeks and months I have been gifted with a few coping mechanisms, courtesy of God himself. Like, for example, the ability to thank him for my Shar-Pei Puppy Thighs.

Each and every day, I make a conscientious decision to be thankful for my body. Granted, if you're Heidi Klum, the decision isn't so remarkable. But when you're me, and despite *lots* of progress on the physical front, you still retain a massive swath of deflated skin, the decision is impressive to be sure.

These days I view my excess skin as my battle scar. You read of people who come home from fighting in places like Afghanistan or Iraq and who take solace in the proof of their faithfulness—to God, to country, to themselves. In some small way, I get that now. I get what it means to fight the good fight and come home with the proof of the battle you've won. My skin used to carry everything that I hated and was the culprit for my being called names like "Thunder Thighs." I still don't have great legs, but I'll take Shar-Pei Puppy Thighs over Thunder Thighs any day of the week. My spirit is full today primarily because my skin is not.

Another way that God helps me to stay on transformation's path is to remind me that there are little victories waiting to be celebrated each and every day. I am motivated to get up early and eat a nutritious breakfast. I'm actually *interested* in working out. I can get through that workout without feeling overwhelmed or distraught. That workout can fuel my training for a 5K or even a 15K—whichever one I want. Noah and Jaxon have a mom who wants not only to watch them play but to include herself in their playtime. I can fit into clothes I previously only dreamed of wearing. And on and on it goes.

As often as the sun rises I sense God spurring me on, all along this path toward becoming the me he desires me to be. I sense it in Noah's hugs. I sense it as I carry Jaxon here and there without becoming winded. I sense it when I try on a pair of slacks that Mike has surprised me with . . . and they actually *fit*. I sense it each time someone asks for my diet-and-exercise advice. I sense it when new friends say, "I never would have guessed that you were ever overweight."

I sense it each time I lay my head on my pillow and fall asleep without feeling a single twinge of pain.

Because of the opportunity God granted me, I made my husband, my trainer and an entire nation proud. The part of the nation that actually liked me, that is. But more importantly, I made myself proud. I didn't whine, I didn't complain, and although it nearly was the end of me, I didn't despise the pain. I took it. I took every ounce of the pain that was dished out, because I knew that in the end it was pain that would lead to progress. It was pain that would pave the path to my discovering the life he'd planned for me all along.

Still, I'm a real woman who lives a real life, complete with real victories and valleys alike. I remain my worst critic, and I recognize that although I was tan, muscular and a tiny 121 pounds on the day of my *The Biggest Loser* finale, sometimes I just won't look like that.

~~~

T he moment my publisher called to schedule a cover photo shoot for this book was a low point in my day. She offered up a whole host of reasons why it needed to occur this month, and with every syllable she spoke, my spirits fell. "I'm not ready!" I wanted to say. I immediately thought that I hadn't been paying enough attention to my food or my workouts as I normally would when a photo shoot was on the books. I had been good, but I hadn't been perfect.

I know what it takes to get a decent picture of me. I require good lighting. A proper angle. Several hours in a salon, getting blonder, tanner and ready to roll. The truth is, photographers could have shot me hanging upside-down on monkey bars at the Season 4 finale, and I would have been elated over the results. But now? Now that real life has had its way? I needed more time than I was being given, and an understanding publisher too.

As it turned out, neither would be made available. The shoot was a go for sure.

I stood in seriously high heels for four hours straight on the evening of my photo session, determined to play nice and hopeful they'd get a decent shot.

The location for my photo shoot was a very cool salon in Jacksonville called The Beauty Lounge. In the middle of my session some of the staff decided to order "the best pizza in the world" from next door. "While I'm trying to be cute and skinny?!" I wanted to say. I could have died. You *know* how I feel about pizza.

Amazingly, when I saw the result of that night's hard work, I felt *proud*. I wanted to send the images to everyone I know, not because I looked great, but because I looked great for me. The woman looking back at me represented confidence, contentedness, real progress made. I spent so much of my life hating every photo that was ever snapped of me that to actually feel drawn toward one was more satisfying than I can possibly convey with words.

⌒〰⌒

It's not looking good regarding my making it to Louisiana today. In the last ten minutes I have been told via the blaring airport loudspeaker that my flight now has been moved to twelve-fifty, which means I'll certainly miss my Atlanta leg and will likely be spending the night in Georgia. For the *love*!

But logistical nightmares aside, I'm still excited about this trip. I'm ready to meet the woman who won the contest, the woman whose profile I've read and whose story I know all too well—mostly because it's so much like mine. Like I had, she's reached her midthirties without ever truly knowing good health. But also like me, she's reached a point where she is really ready to change. I can't wait to have one-on-one time with her so that I can hold her hands in mine and say, "You're not one of these tiny high-school cheerleaders who then ballooned as an adult. I get that. I *lived* that. You've *always* been chubby, and you're wondering if you'll be overweight every day from this point forward. Which brings me to why I'm here.

"This is you now," I'll continue, "but this won't be you forever. I'm here to help you dream up an image of who you'll become so that one day, you'll be the one flying all over creation and ringing strangers' doorbells with the message of hope that they need. *You'll* be the one who will have a compelling tale to tell, the story of how you once were fat but now you're thin, how that was you then, but this . . . *this* is who you are now. *This* is the real you."

A great band called Something Distant recorded a song called "The Real Me," and each time I hear it, it's like hearing my story being sung. "It's been so long," the lyrics go, "I've been held down / It's taken until now / That I could finally breathe." The song continues this way:

> *I'm not placing any blame,*
> *I'm tired of playing the same old games,*
> *In this moment, I've got to move on,*
> *And all along, I've had the strength to carry on*
> *So hard to believe,*
> *That I'm actually free,*
> *All I want to be,*
> *Is the real me.*

The last four lines of the song get me every time. "As I breathe, I can finally see. Through all the things I've been, this is the real me, the real me."[18]

What a gift this woman in Louisiana will soon receive, the gift of an entire team of people who are committed to finding the real her. It's that same gift I'll never forget.

Believe That You Are Worth It

Years ago, author Max Lucado published a story about the Wemmicks, a population of small wooden people who had been hand carved by a woodworker named Eli. The Wemmicks were as diverse as you'd expect any community to be—some had big noses and small eyes, others were short with big hands—but they had all been made by the same carver.

Day in and day out Wemmicks went around town handing out stickers to one another. People who had pretty skin or who could run fast or jump high or carry a decent tune were given stars, and people who said silly things or had chipped paint—well, they were only given dots. Punchinello was one of the "dot" people, and as a result he believed he was something of a substandard Wemmick—a Wemmick not worth his wood.

But then Punchinello met Lucia, and Lucia had neither stars nor dots on her. "That's the way I want to be!"[19] said Punchinello. "How do you do it?"

Lucia said that all Punchinello needed to do was to go visit Eli, and he would explain.

Punchinello made his way to the woodcarver's shop and was greeted with a strong, deep voice. "Punchinello!" said Eli. "How good to see you."[20] Eli picked up his creation and after taking in all those dots said, "I don't care what the other Wemmicks think . . . and you shouldn't either. All that matters is what I think. And I think you are pretty special."[21]

Punchinello wasn't sure he was buying it. He couldn't run fast. Just like me, he couldn't jump well. His paint was obviously peeling. But as if reading his mind, Eli interrupted Punchinello's thoughts. He explained that the reason stickers didn't stick to Lucia is because she had decided that what *Eli* thought about her was far more important than what all of the other Wemmicks thought. Eli told Punchinello that stickers only stick if you let them, and that as long as Punchinello came to visit him every single day, he would be reminded of Eli's care, and all of those dots would fall away. "You are special because I made you," Eli said, "and I don't make mistakes."

Punchinello turned to leave the woodcarver's shop and had the thought, *I think he really means that.* And as he did, the first dot fell to the ground.

Overweight people are all too accustomed to the "dots" of others' judgment, rejection and painful prejudice. I know, because I used to wear them. And it was incredibly difficult to avoid buying the lie that somehow I was "less than" all the thinner, star-covered people around me.

Upon losing nearly a hundred pounds I mistakenly thought that I would also lose the propensity to let other people's opinions shape my view of myself. On too many occasions since the show, I've fallen back into the old paradigm of thinking that I just wasn't all I should be. Specifically, it happens every time I open a magazine or watch TV. I see flawless skin and stunning faces and bodies that are perfect in every way, and it's all I can do to remember that I, too, am worthy, exactly as I am.

I would have to learn the hard way that you can lose all the weight you want, but unless you simultaneously lose the psychological assumption that you are inferior to other people, your weight will probably come back because you've failed to address the deeper issue that's lurking in your soul.

There will *always* be someone prettier or smarter or funnier than I am, and so with some degree of regularity, I think back on how I felt at my finale, when I broke through that paper and for once presented an image of myself to the world that I was deeply and completely proud of.

I remember that I am still a work in progress—physically, mentally and spiritually—and that God promises new mercies for *every* day.

I remember that although I am not perfect, I was created in the image of God and that he clearly makes no mistakes.

And with each and every remembrance, thankfully, I drop another dot.

You and I are *worth* the good decisions we make. We are *worth* all the abundance we can bear. God says it. I believe it. And, as Beth Moore—one of my favorite inspirational speakers—says, "that settles that."

CHAPTER 9

Dwelling Place

LAST SUMMER I received a call from the producers of *The Oprah Winfrey Show*, asking if I'd be interested in appearing with several other former *The Biggest Loser* contestants, as well as with Jillian and Bob, to show America that it really is possible not only to lose weight but also to keep it off.

I didn't need much time to formulate a reply. "Heck, yeah, I'll be on *Oprah*! When's the taping?"

After arriving in Chicago and being escorted to Harpo Studios, my friends and I were led through a rehearsal of the show. At some point during that run-through I remember taking note of the stage, the lights, the cameras and the intimate studio and thinking, "Holy guacamole. I'm going to be on the *Oprah* show. You gotta be kidding me!"

> I didn't get to meet Oprah before the show started. Evidently that's a practice of hers, so that her on-stage reaction to people will be genuine and fresh.

For years I have tuned in at four o'clock in the afternoon to watch Oprah interview world leaders and superstars, athletes and stay-at-home moms with incredible tales to tell. And now I was going to sit on that same stage? It was almost incomprehensible to me, given the fact that a mere twelve months prior I was embarrassed to be seen in public, let alone by millions on national TV.

Halfway through the show, after I heard her interview several other former contestants from my seat backstage, including Season 5's winner

Ali Vincent and my *The Biggest Loser* all-time favorite Suzy Preston from Season 2, I heard Oprah in her classic announcer's voice say, "Come on out, *Juuulie Haddddden!*" I waited for the screen to part that I had been standing behind and then walked to my center-stage mark as audience members cheered and hollered and clapped. Talk about surreal!

> The other *The Biggest Loser* contestants and I had to be ushered out quite quickly after our show so that Celine Dion could set up for her appearance on the second show that was to be taped that day. Imagine my surprise when they didn't ask me to stick around and sing back-up for her!

I approached Oprah to hug her neck and then hugged Jillian and Bob before I took my seat by their side. As the applause died down, Oprah began asking questions about what it was like to be on *The Biggest Loser*, especially given that it had meant being away from Mike and Noah for four months straight. "Who took care of your son that whole time?" Oprah asked.

"My amazing husband," I replied. "But what was funny was that everybody in town thought that I'd left him. While I was gone, nobody was allowed to know where I was or what I was doing. People in the community would come up to Mike—who by all appearances had become a single dad—and say in a pitying tone, 'We're praying for you, hon.'"

I told Oprah that when I came back from being on the show, those same people were like, "Mm-hmm, cute little blonde thang went and got all skinny to try to get back with her man! *We* see how it is."

"Oh yeah," Oprah said with a laugh, "everyone has to be in everyone else's business, right?"

"Exactly!" I replied. "I wanted to say to those people, 'Hey, cut me some slack! My absence was legit! *Really!*' But you know, people think what they want to think."

Just then producers had us cut away for a commercial break, and by the time the show resumed I had taken my seat on the front row of the audience, along with other *The Biggest Loser* contestants. Oprah was interviewing Jillian about her training philosophy,

> While I was on stage people from the audience kept waving at me. I thought they were being so sweet, and so I waved right back. It wasn't until later that I realized they were trying to get my attention to tell me that I'd left the price stickers on the soles of my shoes.

basically asking what it takes for a fat person to endure such grueling workouts.

I scanned the audience and for the first time that morning realized that I was sitting in a room full of me. Row by row I saw hundreds of thirty-something moms who were doing the best that they could. They looked pretty and polished and wore coordinated clothes, but underneath the facade I knew what life was really like.

As Jillian continued to talk about how contestants have to decide for themselves whether or not they're going to submit to the process of transformation, my mind chased other thoughts. "These women surrounding me are leading busy lives," I said to myself. "They spend all day, every day, giving themselves to everyone else and are convinced as they listen to all of us share diet and exercise tips that they will *never* be able to change. They don't have the luxury of leaving their lives for months on end. And even if they *could* do so, they probably *wouldn't* do so. They just don't see their own worth."

They were just like the old me, filled to the brim with "why me's" instead of "why *not* me's." It had probably taken a series of logistical gymnastics for them to get to the TV show that day; how would they ever be able to orchestrate their schedules to accommodate a *four-month* TV appearance?

I thought about how well I could relate to their plight, about how mere months prior I had been in their shoes. And suddenly something inside of me snapped. I had to say something. I had to say something now. I had to say something *right* now, and when I couldn't contain it any longer, I did the unthinkable: I interrupted Oprah.

"First, you have to believe that you are worthy," I said from my seat in a voice that was wobbly and weak.

The woman who has hosted kings and queens and dignitaries and even Brad Pitt threw her gaze my way and with more than a hint of shock in her eyes said, "Please stand up."

Oh lawdy, what have I done?

I stood to my feet.

"You were saying?" said the most powerful woman on the planet.

"Oh ... sorry," I whimpered in my southern little-ol'-me tone. I exhaled nervously and then kept going; what else *could* I do, given what I'd already done?

"All of these moms give of themselves day after day after day," I said, feeling stronger on my own two legs by now, "and at the end of it all, there is nothing left for them." I glanced at the women in the room and then continued, this time through heartfelt tears. "And I believe that if *you* believe that you are worth it . . . you know, I thought that my child needed more things to play with. He needed a *mom* to play with. I thought that my husband needed a wife to take care of him. He needed a wife who would take care of *herself,* so I can be there with him forever. So that's why I want to say to women—especially women—you won't start to change until you start believing that you are worth it."

> After the show, Oprah stopped me in the hallway and said, "I just want to tell you that I really love what you said out there. It is all about worthiness." And then she walked away as I floated back to my dressing room, thinking, "I just had a one-on-one conversation with *Oprah Winfrey!*"

I took my seat once more as the heart inside of me swelled. I wanted so badly for the women all around me to catch the truth of what I was saying. I wanted them to know that they had to appear on their *own* priority list before a single thing would change. Diet and exercise are the easy part; it's *belief* that is hardest to nail.

"The bottom line," Oprah said as my thoughts swirled, "is that it's about *worthiness.*"

"Exactly," I murmured to myself. "I couldn't agree with you more."

THE HANDPICKED DWELLING PLACE OF GOD

People always ask me what is the most significant takeaway or the greatest "aha" from my time spent on *The Biggest Loser* campus. And I think my answer surprises them every time. My response has nothing to do with the nuances of protein, push-ups or how to play the game. "The most important thing I learned," I instead explain, "is that you and I are worthy of living the life of our dreams."

I knew it the day I was on Oprah's show, and I know it still today.

In my view, you determine something's worth by looking to the person or thing that finds it worthy. My grandmother—Great MaMa, my family calls her—is in her eighties and on more than one occasion has asked me what I want of hers "if something ever happens" to her. I hate that question, because who in her right mind wants to think about losing a precious member of the family? But still, she persists. And my answer's the same every time.

I don't want the china that's in her cabinet or the jewelry that's in her dresser drawer. The only thing I want is something the world would place far less value on than expensive dishes and diamonds—all I want is her Bible.

Great MaMa has read that Bible nearly every day of her adult life and has underlined and made notes beside her favorite passages. That Bible to me represents the heart of who she is, and I know that once she's gone, it's the one material possession that would make her still seem near. It would only bring in a few bucks at a garage sale, but its value to me is worth more than gold. You determine something's worth by looking to the person who finds it worthy.

As God's children, then, our worth must be off the charts, because the value he placed on our lives warranted the *ultimate* sacrifice. God says in his Word that he loves us so much that at a specific point in history he sent his only Son to die for us and set us free from our sin and wrongdoing. Sure, we have value because of the contributions we make in our lives, but our intrinsic worth exists only because of God. He designed us, he formed us before we entered our mother's womb and he purposed us for great things before the world even began.

You and I are so much more than piles of lucky mud. We are intentional and intricate creations of the God of the universe, the God who gave everything so that we could live this thing called life.

I'm sure I learned as a kid in Sunday school that because Jesus Christ came to earth to serve as a divine Bridge, I could have a personal and intimate relationship with God. But it wasn't until my body began to be transformed that I embraced the idea that I'm really and truly the "dwelling place" of God. It bends my brain to think about it, but it doesn't make it any less true. The one who paints every sunset, who determined the position of every star, who raised up every mountain and who has the power to calm every storm—*that* One, *he* makes his home inside *me*. With every breath I breathe and every day I live, I can know his presence, his strength, his love and his grace.

I don't have to talk to God in cryptic thee-and-thou prayers. I can chat with him like I'm sitting across from a friend—in reality, he's even closer than that! I don't have to wait until I'm sitting inside a church building on a Sunday morning to tell him what I need. I can call out to him any hour of any day, whether I'm in a church, a café or a mall. *Anywhere* I find myself can become a sacred spot, which was news to me—a girl who treated her body more like a fairground than holy ground most every day of her life.

If you've ever been to a state fair, then you know exactly what I mean. Fair-going conjures up images of people who throw on a stained tank top, cutoffs, and flip-flops and charitably call that an outfit. They shuffle around like sunburned zombies, eating as many on-a-stick food items as they can find and then wash it all down with guzzler-sized sodas and beer. It's not exactly the picture of intentionality and reverence that comes to mind when you think about all things holy. "You're not a fairground," God would reveal to me. "You're *holy* ground because I dwell here. Now all that's left is for you to actually live like you believe that too!"

> I remember seeing deep-fried Twinkies for sale at the Jacksonville Agricultural Fair one time. Surely the apocalypse is near.

One of the things that knitted my heart to the heart of Margie Marshall—the superfit diva of a trainer who has worked with me ever since I got home from the show—is that she gets this dwelling-place idea better than most people I know. Margie's history is interesting to me because, while we find ourselves in a similar situation healthwise today, we started at opposite ends of the spectrum. I was the slothful, excuse-filled woman who couldn't seem to stop downing chocolate cake, and she was the overtrained, obsessive workout freak who almost lost everything in the name of being fit.

"God had given me a passion for nutrition and exercise," Margie told me one time, "but I took what had been given to me as a gracious gift and let it completely consume me." Margie used to prize her workouts so much that she would gladly let other responsibilities slide if it meant she could spend one more hour at the gym. Her husband and her children paid a steep price for the lesson she had to learn the hard way, but she'll tell you today that she would walk that path all over again if it meant gaining the intimacy with Christ she now knows.

When I returned from *The Biggest Loser* and asked Margie to be my personal trainer, I had no idea what my request would mean to her.

"While you were on the show, I prayed one prayer on one occasion to God," she later told me. "I felt foolish for asking him this, but in that prayer I pleaded with him to let me be your trainer once you were home. Through tears I told him that I desperately wanted another chance, that I promised I wouldn't abuse his gracious gift this time around, if only he'd let me work with you."

Obviously, God answered her prayers. In her words, "It's like God said, 'Margie, I'm going to give you back these seeds that I gave you before, but this time, I want you to plant your garden *my* way.'"

Nearly everyone I know can relate to Margie's sentiment, because at one time or another we've all mis-used the stuff that God has given us to steward. Whether it's a talent for sing-ing, a gift for organizing and planning, the capacity to write great books, star in great plays, lead great businesses— whatever "it" is, if we're not careful we're

> Looking back, it's interesting to see that God knew Margie needed me in order to live out her second chance, and I needed her in order to live out mine.

all prone to make the "it" about us. Which would be fine, except that God then gets elbowed right out of our lives. And *you* try living in a house where nobody ever acknowledges your presence. The greatest Resident our souls could ever know deserves far better than that.

THE WONDERFUL WEIGHT OF WORTHINESS

Earlier this year I had the opportunity to write an article for *Guideposts* magazine for a cover story they were doing on the secrets of making personal change stick. When I received the edited version of my story back from their publishing team, one of the writers had included a powerful title to accompany it. "Worth the Weight," it read. Instantly I thought, *Dang! Why didn't I think of that?*

The title perfectly summed up my thoughts on making big changes stick, because when you understand your inherent worth, you treat yourself and those around you in an altogether different way. You tend to say yes to the things that will honor your body and no to the things that won't. You tend to endure a little pain, knowing that the gain will be that much better. You tend to soak up every last, lovely drop of life because you understand that each one is a gift from your God. And you help others to do the same.

Those three simple words—*worth the weight*—eloquently capture the theme of my life thus far. "God doesn't think I'm a failure," I wrote in that cover story—a revelation I'd had back on *The Biggest Loser* campus. "He wants the best for me, and so I'll keep working toward it."[22] As I read those sentences now, I realize that even as I nearly caved under the pressure of Jillian's unforgiving workouts, my soul was surely getting stronger. I was finally beginning to grasp that the God who lived inside of me wasn't interested in being a silent travel companion as I trudged my way through life. He wanted to inhabit my thoughts, embody my actions and serve as the sole Lifter of my head. I had heard once that King David in the Bible referred to God as the "lifter of his head," but I'd never really known what that meant. At least not in a firsthand sort of way.

I remember hearing Oprah talk one time about how she visits young girls in Africa and constantly tells them to keep their heads up. "I never want to see your head fall sheepishly to your chest," she says to them, emphasizing her point by physically lifting little chins until young eyes meet her gaze. Similarly, God had placed his mighty index finger under my chin, causing me finally to crane my neck too. "Look up," I imagined him saying, "and see what I see when I look at you."

When I looked down, I saw only big thighs, but as I looked up the only "big" thing I found was my potential, reflected in God's eyes. "I find you *significant*," I sensed him saying, "and lovely and smart and strong. You have every reason to keep your head held high, and if you stay close, I'll help you do just that."

I think this is what the weight of worthiness feels like, a weight that surrounds you, that grounds you, that proves to you who you really are.

———◡◠◡———

Margie and I gave a speech to a local MOPS group a few months ago, and near the end of our time on stage, she shared the story of John Stephen Akhwari, a marathon runner the media calls "the greatest last-place finisher of all time."

In 1968, Akhwari had been sent to

> It was surreal for me to be back at MOPS—a group that serves mothers of preschoolers. I had to keep reminding myself that, thanks to Jaxon, I'm actually one of those again!

the Mexico City summer Olympics to run the marathon, which followed a beautiful course through town but then ended inside the Olympic Stadium. The winner of that race finished in two hours and twenty minutes; Akhwari finished in three and a half. Out of the fifty-seven men who completed the race, he finished fifty-seventh. Some feat, right?

Still, as Akhwari rounded the final bend, pain hobbling his steps and blood tracing its way down his bandaged leg, the small crowd that was still assembled went nuts. When the exhausted runner finally crossed the finish line, reporters descended on him, all with the same question on their lips: "Why did you keep running, when there was no way whatsoever that you could win?"

Akhwari seemed perplexed by the question. "My country did not send me to Mexico City to start the race," Akhwari explained. "They sent me to finish."[23]

On *The Biggest Loser* campus, God showed me who I was capable of becoming, and it was *that* girl I wanted to know. *That* girl would finish what she started, for once. And *that* girl would continue what she started forever. No longer would I need to keep tabs on all my imperfections; instead I could focus on the person my potential pointed to, the worthy woman whom God had knitted together before the foundation of the world. He wasn't judging me but loving me, and so I could start loving me too—whether I finished first or I finished last. Holding in my arms the full weight of my worthiness helped me understand what it means to live a life that's not just holy, but also whole. And nothing satisfies a searching soul more than that. If only everyone on the planet would choose to live this way! Just imagine all the good we could do.

THE TOUGHEST TRUTH TO ADMIT

Patty Gonzalez was a blue-team member during my season on the show. Like me, she was in her thirties; also like me, she carried a *lot* of baggage. As the mom of young kids, she knew what it was like to put everyone else's needs ahead of her own. She loved her children. She loved *life*. She just didn't love how unlovely she felt to herself.

One afternoon Bob Harper took his team off-campus to a 24 Hour Fitness to do a spin class. Upon arriving, the entire remaining blue team—Neil and Nicole, Ryan and Kae and Patty—mounted stationary bikes that were positioned in a circle and started pedaling for what

Bob still teaches a spin class called "The Ride" every Saturday morning at Crunch gym in LA. It remains a personal goal of mine to spin there someday!

would wind up being a grueling hour-long ride.

With flushed cheeks and sweat dripping from her brow, Patty in particular was determined to finish strong. During the last two minutes, Bob climbed down from his bike, crouched underneath the handlebars of Patty's bike and said, "Let's *go*, Patty. You are the mother of three! You are going to be a role model to many, many women out there. You know how busy it is, how hard it is to have three kids. You're taking advantage of this time.

"How hard is it to be a mom? It got you to two hundred and eighty pounds, didn't it? That's how hard it was, right? You don't want to do that anymore, do you? You don't want any more excuses. *None*, right? You're going to take advantage of every single second that we have together, *aren't* you. You're worth it, *aren't* you!"

"Yes," she huffed out through weary, panted breaths.

"Yes," Bob said. "You are. *Tell* me that you're worth it."

She got to the word "I" and then fell apart in sobs.

"Tell me," Bob said, as Patty continued to pedal furiously.

Still she couldn't compose herself enough to speak.

"Tell me you're *worth* it," Bob repeated.

Again, Patty's legs kept moving even as her mouth stayed put.

"Tell me you're worth it," Bob said once more with a gentle nod.

"I'm worth it," Patty said, as though she'd never said those words before.

"You are, *aren't* you?" Bob said. "Now tell me again."

"I'm *worth* it," Patty echoed, this time stronger.

"That's *right*!" Bob cheered. "You *are* worth it! You're going to go a long way, baby! You're worth it."

"I'm worth it." Just a whisper this time fell from her lips.

"You're worth it," Bob whispered back.

⁓⌁⁓

P atty would say later of the exchange that, "It was hard for me to say those things because it was hard for me to believe that I deserve to be good to my body. I'm just now learning to value who I am."

How well I could relate to those words. In fact, as I watched that particular episode with my family, I had tears streaming down my face. Had I been the one on that bike, I would have struggled to utter those words too. To see someone like Patty, who is beautiful and amazing and strong, choke on the words of her

> Patty wound up being voted off the very week that she spoke the words of worthiness. I hated to see her go, but I loved that before she left, she had come to believe the truth of who she is.

worthiness was a powerful sight. Why would someone like her struggle to admit the truest truth in life? Why do *any* of us struggle to admit it?

> I'm sure Bob had no idea that his words would affect not just Patty but also millions of people who were watching Patty soar. I know, because I was one of those people.

The more people I meet these days, the more I am coming to understand that the toughest truth to admit is not that we have failed; it's that we might just succeed if we try. "Our deepest fear is not that we are inadequate," author Marianne Williamson says. "Our deepest fear is that we are powerful beyond measure. It is our light, not our darkness, that most frightens us. We ask ourselves, 'Who am I to be brilliant, gorgeous, talented, fabulous?'

"Actually, who are you *not* to be? You are a child of God. Your playing small does not serve the world. There is nothing enlightened about shrinking so that other people won't feel insecure around you. We are all meant to shine, as children do. We were born to make manifest the glory of God that is within us. It's not just in some of us; it's in everyone. And as we let our own light shine, we unconsciously give other people permission to do the same. As we are liberated from our own fear, our presence automatically liberates others."[24]

I am worthy of living the life of my dreams—the moment someone finally says those words out loud and therefore agrees in her spirit that she is in fact worthy, things change. *Everything* changes! It was true for Patty. It was true for me. It will be true for you too.

⌒〜⌒

So, back to that trip to Louisiana I was trying to make so that I could be part of the "New Year, New You" contest celebration. As it turns out, despite all of my airport fiascos, I did eventually get to Monroe, and

I did eventually get to meet Tammie, the winner of the big reward. And am I ever grateful for that! It was surreal to talk to someone who is in the exact same position that I was in two years ago and who is actually looking to *me* for advice. As I conveyed heartfelt words to her about what the weight-loss journey is like, I thought, *I can't believe I'm saying these things! I feel more like you than I do me!*

On day two of my stay, several of us—Tammie, as well as her new nutritionist, her new trainer, her new motivational coach and yours truly—gathered in the front yard to do a photo shoot for the magazine. After a few group shots, the photographer asked to capture Tammie by herself. I happened to walk by as they were setting up her shot, and I overheard Tammie say to the photographer, "You're probably going to need a wide-angle lens to get *this* belly in the frame!"

I was stopped dead in my tracks.

Suddenly, everything that Jillian had ever told me about the power of negative self-talk came rushing to my mind. Back on campus I used to joke about the folding chairs that outfitted every room, it seemed. "This is an *obesity* show," I'd say. "Do they really think my gargantuan butt is gonna fit on *that*?"

Unfortunately, one day Jillian overheard me. "You will not speak of yourself that way!" she fumed.

"It was just a joke!" I'd beg. But it was no use. Punishment was coming my way for sure.

It took precious few rounds of endless jumping jacks and push-ups-until-you-puke before my teammates and I learned to speak very kindly about ourselves.

When I heard Tammie's comment, it was as though she'd scraped her nails slowly down a chalkboard. And in that moment I understood why Jillian had made self-esteem such a big deal. Later, during a private conversation, I looked at Tammie and said, "I heard the comment you made about your stomach out there." Her eyes got big and round, like those of a child caught with her hand in the cookie jar.

"I know you said it as a joke," I continued, "but I also know that you said it because in your mind you actually *believe* that it's true."

Overweight people are really good at beating everyone else to the punch so that they never have to hear words that could wound them.

I had been good at it, and Tammie was good at it too. But if she truly wanted to change, then that pattern was going to have to be broken.

"For this process to work," I explained, "you simply cannot talk about yourself in a disparaging way. If you hear those things long enough, you will begin to believe they are true."

I had turned into Jillian, right before my eyes—the one who had first uttered the words that I was now speaking.

After a long and meaningful conversation with Tammie, I looked her straight in the eyes and in essence said, "I want to hear you say out loud that you're worthy." She faces a year-long journey in full view of a massive online audience who will be eagerly cheering her on as she works toward her own weight-loss transformation, a journey that will be filled with ups and downs, victories and missteps, laughter and a bucketful of tears. I thought about the responsibilities that would be vying for her attention all along the way, including caring for her family, her circle of friends and her job as a sixth-grade teacher, and I knew that if she were to reach her goals she'd have to prioritize herself in there somewhere too.

"Tell me you're *worthy* of the effort," I said, to which she stumbled and stammered and cried.

"Believe me," I said quietly, "I know what those tears are about. But I'm not letting you off the hook. Tell me you're worth all this effort."

We went through several cycles of this—my insisting to hear those words, her getting choked up and finding herself utterly incapable of saying them—before a breakthrough finally came.

"I'm worth it," she looked at me and said. "I'm *worth* it."

"Yes, you are," I said. "Now, let's get started."

⌒‿ᴠᴧ‿⌒

I believe in the coming days that more and more people will be talking about this issue of worthiness, and, in my view, that's a *very* good thing. If you and I refuse to believe that we are worth the time and effort it takes to implement necessary change in our lives, then we'll never get our lazy butts off the couch—(oops . . . would that be considered negative self-talk?)—throw away the empty bag of chips we've just devoured and make a *good* choice for a change. We just won't. We'll never accomplish more than we think we're capable of accomplishing, and we'll never realize that capacity until we first realize that we're *worthy* of those accomplishments. I believe that principle like I believe in gravity. You can try to deny it, but as soon as you find yourself falling from the top of a building, you'll see that it's still remarkably true.

There are kids who crave our care, spouses who crave our companionship, colleagues who crave our contribution and communities that crave our service. But more importantly, there is a God who craves our *hearts*. He created you and me for a specific purpose, and nothing brings him more delight than when we desire to know him and love him and find out what that purpose is. "It's in *Christ*," Ephesians 1:11–12 says, "that we find out who we are and what we are living for. Long before we first heard of Christ and got our hopes up, he had his eye on us, had designs on us for glorious living, part of the overall purpose he is working out in everything and everyone."[25]

You are precious to God. You are purposed for good. And you are worthy of the life of your dreams.

Don't Look at the Big Picture

Recently I ran a 5K with my friend Stacey. Like me, Stacey had never been an athlete, and I knew that her first road race would bring with it a fair amount of fear and uncertainty. Actually, she'd be a nervous wreck, but I chose not to tell her that.

She kept babbling something about how there was "no way" she could run 3.1 miles without stopping, and despite the fact that I blew off her doubt, I knew exactly how she felt. I'd pitched my tent in the no-way camp once too.

I saw Stacey a few days before our race and tried to prepare her for what was to come. "Listen," I said, "here's exactly how it will all go down. When we start the race, there will be a big band playing loud music that will rev you up and make your heart pump fast. Your adrenaline will be soaring so high that when the starting-gun sounds, you won't even notice the first mile. You'll be totally consumed with weaving your way through the crowd, noticing the too-short shorts on the girl in front of you and trying to figure out how the woman pushing a stroller with triplets who also has her six-year-old by her side could *possibly* have just passed you.

"The second mile—now, that's the toughest. It will seem like it takes forever to run because your adrenaline level will have settled down, the streets will be wide open and your mind will close in on the fact that this is the farthest you have ever run. During that mile, focus on your breathing and *absolutely* nothing else. Keep putting one foot in front of the other, and remind yourself frequently that in twelve short minutes or less you'll be done. Whatever you do, remember that you will not *die* during mile two! I'll be right by your side, and I promise you, we'll pull through.

"The third mile is by far the most exciting mile of all. Mile three represents every dream you've dreamed that you believed would never come true. Your mind will race as you consider the fact that you are about to accomplish a very impressive goal, and that you are officially a runner! You'll feel like you're flying as you near the finish line, not only because you'll have caught your stride by then, but also because you'll notice that the super-fast six-year-old is now standing on the curb with his shoelaces untied whining about how he can't take another step while his do-it-all-and-do-it-well mom tries desperately to figure out how to fit him on the back of the stroller so that they, too, can complete the race. You'll hear the crowd cheering as you stretch out those final strides, and as you catch sight of your husband, who is hopping up and down like a crazy person, you'll feel that same sense of elation over what you've just done.

"That, my friend, is a 5K. It's going to be the best day of your life."

~~~

When I was on campus I followed this same approach to life. Rather than focusing on the big, scary picture, I focused on each individual frame. When I stepped onto the treadmill, I'd remind myself, "It's only an hour, Julie. Do the best that you can." When I did my dishes after a meal, I'd think, "Just scrub your little heart out. Don't worry about what everyone else is eating that smells so *incredibly* good right now." When it was time for bed, I'd say to myself, "Don't worry about how difficult or challenging tomorrow will be. Your job for these next seven hours is to rest, and rest well."

Even now I work to break down my day into chunks. "For this hour," I said just this morning, "my only goal is to get Noah to school on time." After I did that successfully, I focused on calling back the doctor. Then I focused only on bathing our dog Flower. Then I turned all of my attention to completing chapter ten of this book. One simple step at a time, I got through all of my plans and had a satisfying day in the end.

Like all worthwhile pursuits in life, weight loss happens one simple step at a time. Looking too far ahead discourages even the sturdiest warrior I know, so I find it helpful to focus on what's right before me, each and every day.

CHAPTER 10

When I Pray, I Pray for You

I NEVER WANTED to be the poster girl for weight loss. First of all, you can't be the poster girl for weight loss unless at one time you have been obese—or morbidly obese, as they preferred to call us in *The Biggest Loser* land. In normal, everyday life, people who are obese are referred to as heavyset or big-boned or, you know, the lady with the short bob and tortoiseshell glasses. But this was not the case on the show. Lest there be any lingering doubt among players and viewers alike, producers wanted to make sure we all knew that the "stars" of this *particular* show were *fat.*

Obese.

Morbidly obese, even—perhaps a mere hair's breadth away from death.

These are words that rarely connote happy, positive things. When you think of obese, you don't think of adjectives like *disciplined* and *productive* and *fit* as much as you think of ones like *overindulgent* and *lazy* and *gross.* And those descriptors weren't ones I wanted to be known for. I wanted to be known for something strong, not something weak. Yes, if I'd had the opportunity to dictate the course of my life, I would have picked a far different path for sure. Like the one walked by Miss America.

As I mentioned earlier in this book, I did pageants in my twenties and thought that if I could just overcome my "little weight issue," I would join the ranks of those who got to saunter down runways wearing a gown and a crown and pretending they were Barbie in real life. But that was before I actually met one.

My husband Mike used to judge beauty pageants, and when he migrated from that field into his current pursuits of PR and graphic arts, people got wind of his new role. In no time he had a Web site design business, which in the early days consisted largely of pageant winners. I've had the opportunity over the years to meet many of them, and I remember like it was last night the first time I actually got to enjoy dinner with a current Miss America. As expected, she was stunningly beautiful and perfectly poised and had motivation to spare. But surprisingly, when we entered the restaurant, there was no trumpet fanfare sounding, no men in tuxes awaiting our arrival with bundled roses in hand, no gown, no crown and no pizzazz at all. It was just . . . her. In jeans and a boring shirt. That was the night when I realized that for Miss America, the glamour ends the night she is crowned. Still, I was enthralled. Jeans and a boring shirt beat morbidly obese any day of the week.

Another of the Miss America winners I met along the way happened to be married to a congressman. And once I made it on to *The Biggest Loser*, he called and asked if I would address our national representatives after my season ended. He was a fan of the show and explained that many officials had been working on legislation to solve the insurance crisis that had been created by the soaring rate of obesity in this country over the past several years. "I can't believe what you all are able to do in such a short amount of time, and without any surgery or drugs!" he said during that call. "How is it possible that nobody from the show has come to Washington to help Congress understand the power of diet and exercise so that thinking can be incorporated into the bills that are put forth?"

The last time I had been to Washington, DC, was on a choir trip during my senior year of high school. Thankfully, I wouldn't be standing on risers in front of the White House wearing a pink wrinkle-free polyester dress and gigantic bangs this time around.

I was asked to come share my story and to explain exactly what it takes to see massive life-change as a thirty-something stay-at-home mom. Julie Hadden on Capitol Hill—it was a frightening thought for all who know me well.

WHAT MOTIVATES ME MOST

J axon was born exactly three days before Mike and I were to head to Washington, DC, and the thought of leaving my brand-new son was more than I could bear. There was a time when missing an opportunity like that would have crushed my spirit, but as I looked into my sweet baby's eyes, all I could think about was how *this* opportunity trumped everything else.

Unexpectedly, several months later Mike and I would be able to visit our nation's capital, and the experience was every bit as amazing as I imagine it would have been immediately on the heels of finale week.

Because of my presence on the show, we were afforded an insider's "red jacket" tour. I never saw a single red jacket, but I saw lots of other fun things. Like the inside of Dick Cheney's office. I was asked to wait in there while my DC contact momentarily ran to her office. Although she assured me that the vice president was out of town, the entire time I sat there, all I could think about was what on earth I would say to the man if he suddenly returned.

Mike and I joined a small group of VIPs who were also being given the special tour, and as each of them went around our circle and explained who they were and what they did for a living, I felt a wave of panicky heat surge through my bones. *What am I supposed to say about myself?* I thought. These people were all CEOs of this or ambassadors of that, and then there was me, Ellie Mae Clampett and her down-home husband Jethro. I looked over my shoulder at Mike and whispered with a fair amount of intensity, "Whatever you do, keep your mouth *shut!*"

Thankfully, he complied.

We walked majestic halls and retraced steps that dozens of presidents had taken. From the windows of the West Wing offices we saw the vice president's helicopter land on the south lawn. I met several of President Bush's staff and would even stay in touch with one woman whom I'd felt a connection with that day.

Truly, the opportunities and introductions I've known because of my experience on *The Biggest Loser* have been humbling and invigorating and utterly surreal. I got to meet Oprah, of course, and Larry King and Mario Lopez at dinner one night. I met actresses Vanessa Marcil and Kristen Alphonso, and consider Bob Harper and Alison Sweeney and Jillian Michaels my friends. But while it has been amazing to speak with the "rich and famous" of the world—some of whom I'd looked up to for years and years—the people who have inspired me most since the show are the ones living everyday lives. They are fighting for their families, fighting to keep jobs in a tough economy and fighting to live by selfless, God-honoring values in a world that tells them it's all about them. They are fighting for weight loss without the help of nutritionists, trainers and four focused months away from home, which is utterly remarkable to me.

They do what I could never seem to do—they get up early, they stay up late, they sacrifice their comfort and they lay it on the line—all for the sake of pursuing that one audacious goal.

WHEN I PRAY, I PRAY FOR YOU

As a wife and a mom of two boys, I rarely have any time alone. So when it comes to setting aside time for practices that feed my "inner me," the task can feel pretty tough. Take prayer, for example. While it would be nice to sit down at the kitchen table with a journal and a pen in one hand and a cup of steaming-hot coffee in the other so that I could log my prayers for the day, in forty seconds flat that journal would be covered in Crayola wax, my coffee cup would be upended and my pen would be chewed up. Welcome to the world of having a one-year-old.

Somewhere along the way I established a pattern for prayer that actually works for my life, a pattern that seems to involve two parts.

On many nights I'm so wired that when I go to bed, I just can't fall asleep. It used to frustrate me terribly, but I have come to realize that there's an upside to bouts of insomnia, and for me it involves time for prayer. Now I simply say, "What is it you want me to know, God? What is it that I need to hear?" I lie there, perfectly still, just waiting for some semblance of insight from the One who is obviously keeping me up. And while I wait, I pray.

I pray prayers of thanksgiving—for Mike, for Noah, for Jaxon, for my other family members and for my friends. I thank God for the fact that I have a soft bed to (not) sleep in, especially in this world where so many people are found lying on cold streets or in humid huts or atop mattresses made of soil.

Prayers of thanksgiving gently rock me to sleep, and by the time the sun rises, I'm refreshed and renewed once more.

I've noticed that, in addition to my evening prayer ritual, there's a morning-time habit I pursue. I may awaken refreshed and renewed, but as soon as I remember all of the to-dos I need to tackle and all the monsters I need to slay, my spirit wilts. My morning prayers go something like this: "Oh, God, give me strength." (Or patience. Or wisdom. Or a supernatural infusion of about six extra hours in this day.)

"Help me be the person I need to be today," I ask him. "Bring to mind the thoughts you want me to think. Show me the steps you want me to take. Remind me of the people who can inspire me to be the best 'me' all day long."

Depending on the day, God brings to mind different people in my life. But there are a handful of people whose lives seem to inspire me more than any others these days. I want to introduce them to you, not only so that you will be inspired by their stories, too, but also so that you will consider—perhaps for the first time in your life—that *your* story can serve as the perfect dose of inspiration others might need in order to catalyze big changes in their lives.

"GIVE ME MELISSA'S UNWAVERING FAITH"

Melissa and I have been friends since junior high, and in the years since then, we've been through it all. Together, we got caught for drinking wine coolers when we were fifteen, we walked across the stage at our high school graduation, we saw each other get married and start families, and today we watch our kids make "together" memories of their own.

Melissa was the girl in school who was always on the most attractive list and always got good grades. Her life seemed so easy, so effortless, so free. But there came a day when the peace that she had known would be shattered and her faith would be pressured to prevail.

Four years ago Melissa was getting her two kids ready for bed, when she sensed something of a *pop* and then felt a stream of water running down her legs. She was pregnant with her husband's and her third child, but surely her water wasn't breaking this early; she was only twenty-three weeks along.

She looked down to see what was happening and realized that it wasn't water at all; it was blood. She rushed to the bathroom and climbed into the tub while Chuck hurriedly ushered the children to another room. Melissa sat in a puddle of her own blood, believing that certainly her baby was dead.

When Melissa arrived at the hospital, the nurse confirmed the worst fear of all: No heartbeat could be found. Melissa lay in a hospital bed, grieving for what seemed like hours as she waited for the on-call obstetrician's arrival.

The doctor finally arrived and explained that he needed to do an ultrasound to confirm the death of the baby. As he slowly moved the wand across Melissa's belly, he said—to her surprise and his—"This baby has a heartbeat. Your child is still alive!"

Melissa came undone. Chuck says that in that split second all he could think about was the verse from the Bible story about the prodigal son: "This son of mine was dead and is alive again!" [26]

In a strange mix of relief and terror, Melissa weighed the words she'd just heard. Was the doctor's comment good or bad news? Her son still had a heartbeat, but would he ever know a normal life, given the trauma he'd just been through?

The doctor wheeled Melissa into surgery and delivered the baby, who had spent less than six months in her womb. She was so drugged up that I wasn't able to see her until the next morning, when she was finally coherent. I sat down beside her hospital bed and took her hand in mine as she wailed the most guttural sobs I've ever heard. Tears streamed down my cheeks as I looked upon the friend I'd walked home from school with and spent countless nights with and curled my hair with and worn neon clothes with. We had shared so much of life together, and yet we'd never shared anything like this. "Oh, God, please care for my friend," I prayed. "Please hold her and remind her you're here. . . ."

When Ethan was born, he was so tiny that when Chuck slid his wedding band over the baby's fragile hand, it fit all the way up to his shoulder. Ethan was so unformed and translucent that he resembled a see-through squirrel. Through his onionskin flesh, I could see veins and organs and bone. And yet he was alive. This son of Melissa's was dead and was alive again! Or that's how we saw the situation anyway. Doctors had a different take on things. Rather than offering up hope, they offered dire predictions and a recommendation to end Ethan's life support.

My friend was appalled. "I don't want to unplug his life support! Can't we give him a chance to live?" she pleaded. "Please keep working on him . . . keep doing whatever you can do."

And indeed they did, keeping their monumental doubts at bay.

Melissa eventually was released from the hospital, but Ethan had to stay behind. I don't know how many months passed during their separation—four, maybe?—but each and every day Melissa and Chuck sorted out child care for their two other children and made their way to Ethan's side. Sometimes they went to the hospital early in the morning and sometimes it was late at night, but not a single day passed when they didn't root on their little fighter, imploring him to live, to breathe, to work, to overcome. Melissa insisted on believing the best— about Ethan and about God. Not once did I hear her question God; not once did I hear her complain. She was exhausted and overwhelmed and perplexed by how life felt, but still she kept on fighting. Still she kept the faith.

On Christmas Eve that year, Ethan came home from the hospital at last. But despite the fact that he'd beaten the odds, doctors were skeptical still. "Sure, he was able to go home," they'd say, "but he may not enjoy a normal life. He'll likely grow up with severe limitations. You'll have to wait and see."

Melissa brushed their qualms aside and got busy living life.

———

When it was time for me to return to LA for the Season 4 finale, I knew that I wanted Melissa there with me. She was the one who was responsible for my auditioning for the show in the first place, and I desperately wanted her to see the whole experience come full circle. Melissa had never struggled with her weight, but over the years she'd helped me struggle with mine. She'd been my friend through my gains, my losses and every plateau in between. "I knew that your weight bothered you," she would tell me later, "but I never knew you were very big."

And she didn't, largely because Melissa saw the inside of me all those years, not just the weight.

After I'd finished my time on campus and came home to work out for four months before the finale, Melissa was my constant cheerleader. "I'm so proud of you," she'd say, and mean it. She'd call her family and say, "You guys have to go see Julie! You won't *believe* how she looks!" She didn't need to work out as hard as I did, but still she'd subject herself to the rigors of Margie's class, the same Margie to whom Melissa introduced me, because she is just that good of a friend.

Melissa had been my teacher in so many aspects of life, modeling for me how to live with steadiness and wisdom and, most of all, with faith, and something in me wanted to show her a student who could actually lead for a change.

I remember walking onstage after I broke through the paper screen at the finale and seeing Melissa and Margie in the audience, jumping wildly up and down. They resembled overly enthusiastic parents at their kid's dance recital, oohing and aahing and weeping tears of joy. I don't recall much of that chaotic finale moment, but I'll keep that image of those two dear friends forever emblazoned on my mind.

<hr/>

Back on that day when Melissa sat despondently in her bathtub, she prayed a prayer to God. "I promise you that I will love you and follow you regardless of what happens to this child," she said through tears. "I will not turn my back on you and I will not allow this situation to come between us. The Lord gives and the Lord takes away. Blessed be the name of the Lord."

I think about the unimaginable pain that she was in when she whimpered out those words and I marvel at my friend's unyielding strength. On days when I think I can't go on, all I have to do is think about the framed photo hanging from the wall of a children's hospital, the one that boasts Ethan, today a happy, healthy four-year-old who wasn't supposed to live. I think about Melissa's faithfulness to God and her faithfulness to Ethan. I think about her faithfulness to our friendship that has spanned three decades and counting. "Give me Melissa's unwavering faith," I ask of God, "so that I can be that faithful too."

"GIVE ME SHIRLEY'S ACCEPTING SPIRIT"

Producers of *The Biggest Loser* made a big deal out of the fact that for the five years leading up to my experience on the show, I avoided Mike's office at all costs. I didn't attend company dinners, company picnics or company Christmas parties, all because I was terrified of what people would think. If I couldn't accept myself, how could I expect his colleagues to accept me? I steered clear so I'd never have to find out.

A woman named Shirley is one of those colleagues I avoided. After I returned from campus, I decided it was time to break the relational drought I had caused, and so I went to Mike's office one day.

Because Shirley had watched every episode of my season, she knew that my absence from the office had been intentional. But instead of giving me the cold shoulder or remaining courteous but distant, as soon as I stepped foot through the door, she came right up to me, grabbed me, hugged me, and said, "I'm so sorry you felt the way you did." She turned toward her co-workers who were looking on and said something to the effect of, "Let's get this girl in here and show her we're different than she thought!"

The thing that gets me about Shirley is that she doesn't let anything get her down. She has been deaf most of her life but doesn't use that as an excuse for self-pity. She is old enough to retire but keeps working hard. And she was overweight—at least in her own estimation—but she refused to stay that way.

Because of Shirley's hearing impairment, she engages in conversation very intentionally—and at very close range. After I chatted with several of Mike's colleagues the day that I visited his office, Shirley approached me, positioned her face within two inches of mine and began to speak slowly and with great passion. She told me that she had been so inspired by what she saw me accomplish on the show that she herself had decided to change. She faithfully watched every episode of the show by closed-captioning and told me that she had been so inspired by what she saw me accomplish that she herself decided to change. She started working out and eating properly, and in the end, she dropped a significant amount of weight. In the midst of working through her own transformation, she also prayed for me every day. "You are so beautiful," she said carefully and with teary eyes. "Because of you, I will be able to see my grandchildren grow up. I have been given a new lease on life."

Before I went on *The Biggest Loser*, it was all about me. I didn't show my face at that office because *I* was afraid, *I* was insecure and *I* was unhappy with how I looked. After I returned from campus, it was all about them. It was all about people like Shirley who are mature enough to accept themselves, which enables them to graciously accept others. Shirley told me I am the one who was an inspiration, but I know the truth about who plays that role.

"GIVE ME THE PERSISTENCE OF THE MAN IN THE PARK"

Sometimes I know the stories behind the people who are living inspiring lives, and sometimes I do not. But whenever I see them in my day-to-day life, my reaction is always the same. "You *go!*" I want to shout at the top of my lungs. "You're doing great, and you'll reach your goal in *no* time if you just see this moment through!" It's not the people with perfect figures and nary a care in the world who push me to be better myself; it's the everyman overcoming an obvious struggle who motivates me most. Which brings me to the man in the park.

For nearly two years I have trained with Margie Marshall. This means that for nearly two years I've spent five days a week at our local park. It also means that for nearly two years I have seen the same man running the same trail, wearing the very same attire.

If you're old enough to remember Olivia Newton-John's video for her song "Let's Get Physical," then you have a decent understanding of how this guy dresses. He wears a circa 1970 sweatband around his head, a baggy sleeveless shirt and polyester running shorts that are far too short for a man his age. Actually they're far too short for a man of *any* age, but that's a topic for another book.

Okay, true-confession time: Before I was married, my friends and I used to go to a karaoke club on Saturday nights, and while they opted for songs you can really rock out, like Steppenwolf's "Born to be Wild" or The B-52s' "Love Shack," I *always* chose the overly dramatic "Hopelessly Devoted to You." I'm so cool.

The man in the park has no idea who I am, mostly because whenever I try to make eye contact with him, he intently looks the other way. "I'm not a stalker, I swear," I always want to clarify. "I was just hoping to cheer you on."

He is significantly overweight and yet every day I'm there, it seems, this guy is running as hard as he can. Whether it's raining or sunny, whether it's unusually cool or ninety-eight blazing degrees, there he is, running twice around the 1.75-mile loop, sweating buckets and panting out his breath, working harder than most athletes I know.

Last week I snuck in behind him and trailed him for a mile or so, just to be downwind of his never-give-up ways. "God, give me this guy's persistence," I prayed. "May I *never* give up, just like him."

"GIVE ME MARGIE'S SELFLESS STYLE"

Margie is another source of inspiration for me because of the selflessness she exudes. She relates to me with graciousness and she relates to women half a world away with generosity that would make you weep.

Margie Marshall has a fantastic physique, but it wasn't born in a gene pool. Rail-thin fitness models who seemingly do nothing to maintain their perfection is one thing, but *real* inspiration comes from women like Margie, who has to work her tail off to achieve results. She has earned every curve she now enjoys, and she compels me to do the same. On more than a few occasions during a tough workout, Margie will look at me grimacing and wheezing my way along and say, "I know this kills. I did it yesterday." It's always just the dose of empathy that I need to stay the course.

When I first came home from campus, Margie wasn't sure how much I could handle, on the exercise front. She showed up at our first session with a laundry list of exercises that I was supposed to endure, and I remember starting at the top of that list and not stopping until we'd reached the very end. Margie didn't have much use for water breaks at the time, and so sixty minutes of working out translated into sixty *actual* minutes of working out. If I reached down to tie my shoe, for instance, she'd stop the clock so that we didn't lose even ten seconds of our agreed-upon time.

I have banished from my mind most of the memories of that first workout, but I do recall that as a way to end our time together, Margie asked me to do plyometric side-kicks all the way down the football field and then all the way back to where she was standing, stopwatch in her hand and cruel smile on her face. The next day, she called me and said, "Um, Julie? Are you okay?"

"Sure, if you consider it okay that I still can't sit down to pee," I replied.

"Yeah," Margie said. "About yesterday. I reviewed all the things that I made you do, and I think it may have been a bit too much—"

"Ya *think*?" I interrupted.

Thankfully, we never did that particular routine again.

Margie and I laugh about those early days now, but what I still take seriously is her "teachability" and grace. It's a tough thing to admit when you're wrong, but in the admission trust is forged. She is more concerned with helping me reach my goals than she is with always appearing right, and that is a real gift to me.

———∿∿∿———

D espite countless hours of training input, Margie has never charged me a dime. I've often insisted on paying her, but it's always a wrestling match to get her to take it. She reminds me that part of her "God-given role" is to help women however she can and frankly, I couldn't agree with her more. I hear her tell me each and every day how strong I am, I see her refuse to let me quit, I sense her commitment to my journey and I know in my heart that *any* woman in Margie's care is a privileged woman indeed.

Margie has such a passion for helping women reach their goals that she now donates half of her personal-training revenue—received from clients she *will* take a dime from—to organizations that help women who have been sold into slavery. The idea came to her during her afternoon run one day, which is where she gets most of her epiphanies in life. She wanted to do something significant to help those women trapped in tough lives, when suddenly the thought came to mind that she could audition for the reality TV show *The Amazing Race*. She figured she'd coerce me to be on her team and that after we won, we'd donate 70 percent of our earnings to charity. "No *way*!" I said when she called to sell me the scheme. "I've already done the reality-show gig!"

Margie went running again two days later and sensed another prompting—this time, she believes, from God. "What are you doing right now?" he seemed to ask.

"I'm running," she said out loud.

The prompting continued. "Exactly! You don't need *The Amazing Race*. You don't need *anything*, except what I've already given you."

That's so true! Margie thought. *I can make a difference through running—something that's already part of my life.*

It was the small seed that would bear great fruit.

Margie got home and got busy hatching her plan. Every forty-seven seconds, another girl or woman is sold into slavery somewhere in the world. And so in conjunction with Celebration Church of Jacksonville and an effort called the A21 Campaign[27]—so-named because of their vision to abolish injustice in the twenty-first century—Margie would establish a 4.7-mile race called "Be Her Freedom."

The inaugural run happens this fall, and proceeds will go toward the medical, legal and psychological treatment costs that are associated with rescuing, restoring and rebuilding the lives of women who have been enslaved.

A magnetic passion, a selfless spirit and an enormous drive to win—who knows what God will choose to do through a woman with Margie's heart.

"GIVE ME NOAH'S SHEER BELIEF"

Melissa's faith, Shirley's spirit of acceptance, the persistence of the man in the park, selflessness like Margie's—these are the things I ask God for, but of course I don't stop there! If there is one request I make most of God, it is for Noah's sheer *belief.*

Out of all of the people in life, it was my son Noah who never doubted that I would get picked for the show. It was Noah who never doubted that the black team would dominate. It was Noah who never doubted that I would come back much thinner than when I'd left. It was Noah who never doubted that I'd contend for the championship title.

The entire time I trained between my on-campus experience and the finale, he believed so firmly that I'd win it all that I found myself wanting to say, "You got it, Noah, whatever you say. The way that you're imagining it is *exactly* how it will be."

I sensed Noah's belief in me from the beginning and worked as hard as I could so that I wouldn't let him down. To this day he believes that I'm the strongest mom on the planet and that I'm the fastest runner to boot. He'll come home from playing at a friend's house and say that so-and-so's mother has started working out. "But she can't hold a *candle* to you," Noah always adds.

Ah, the unbiased perspective of a momma's boy. You've got to love it!

When we watch *The Biggest Loser* these days, Noah still tells me that I'm the best contestant they ever had. He helps me work out. He monitors every morsel of food I eat. And he encourages me to keep reaching for the stars, each day that I'm alive.

> I was instructed to bring cupcakes to a recent class party of Noah's, and partway through the event I decided to taste one. In front of children and parents and my son's stunned teacher, Noah immediately stood up and yelled, "Attention, everyone! My mother just ate a cupcake!"
>
> "Shut *up*, child!" I whispered under my breath, wondering who on earth raised such a tattletale.
>
> "Well, you *know* you aren't supposed to be eating cupcakes!" he said in a scolding tone as he took his seat once more.
>
> How I hate it when he's right.

Everybody needs a Noah—that person who believes in you without hesitation, without wavering, without doubt. He doesn't even bat an eye when he talks about me to his friends. "My momma did this" or "my momma did that." He is so proud of me that it makes me want to be proud of myself.

THE *REAL* INSPIRATION IS YOU

In addition to the people in my town and in my own house who inspire me every day, I'm also moved to action by the moms and dads and kids whom I hear from online. People from America and New Zealand and Great Britain and Singapore tell me how they print pictures of me from the show's site and post them on their bathroom mirror or on the fridge, and how those pictures keep them motivated to lose the next twenty pounds. They talk about how tough it is

> Evidently, the US version of *The Biggest Loser* now airs in ninety countries and the show is actually produced locally in thirty. The funniest one to me was *The Biggest Loser Hungary*. I was like, "For *real*? You're going to have *The Biggest Loser* . . . 'hungry'?"

to find time to exercise—I know!—and how much tougher it is than that to believe that they're *worth* that time.

There are posts about polycystic ovary syndrome and about blood-sugar issues and about the challenge of hitting a plateau, and with every entry, I find myself in awe that readers are sharing these things with me. Seriously, the stories that appear there just blow me away. They ask for dieting tips, they ask for a workout companion and, interestingly, they ask for prayer.

They are daughters of fathers with prostate cancer, wives of husbands who have recently been laid off, mothers of housefuls of children, sisters of workaholics and friends of those in chronic pain. And almost without exception, they're people who, just like me, are desperately "battling the bulge."

"I thank God for you!" a woman named Becki recently typed. "You have given me such inspiration!" The truth, Becki, is that *you're* the inspiration, the one who convinces me not to quit. Heather, Lisa, Theresa, Sarah, Chris, Trenda, Paula, Mary, Amy, Hannah, Kristin, Jerry and Rich—people like *you* keep people like me going. *You* make it fun to chase dreams.

———⌇⌇———

When I started my journey toward weight loss, I just wanted to lose a few pounds. Really—that was it. I remember looking toward heaven and begging God to help me. "I'm in a ditch here and *have* to lose this weight," I'd pray. "I have no idea how to regain the control I've so obviously and terrifyingly lost." I wasn't thinking about serving as an inspiration to *anyone* during those days. I just wanted to get out of my ditch.

Similarly, when I watched my friend Melissa bawl her eyes out because she feared that her baby would not live even one more hour, I'm sure her top-of-mind thought was not how that set of circumstances would one day minister to other people. She wasn't thinking about how her life would speak to the lady who had just birthed a baby who was dangerously premature. She was just trying to get through the night.

But interestingly, sometimes it's the thing you struggle with most that God chooses to use for good. I never thought that God would use my greatest challenges in life to serve as my platform to change other people's lives, but that is precisely what he has done. My weight always held me back and yet it is my weight that now sets me free.

Change isn't always fun, but when you realize that the thing you most wish you could change about your life could one day revolutionize not just your world but the worlds of countless others, somehow that change is much easier to bear. Now that I'm on the other side, I realize that real change is possible, it is *powerful* and, most importantly, it is worth every ounce of pain.

Have eyes to see the inspiration all around you. What's more, choose to be the inspiration you seek. I speak from experience when I say with great joy that you never know who will be watching.

Noah's Favorite Villain of All

FOR AS LONG as I can remember, my son Noah's heroes have always been villains. Sure, he's had Spiderman phases and Batman phases and Superman phases too. But regardless of what he was watching, he was never more captivated than when the villain appeared on the screen. The Joker, Scarecrow, the Penguin, the Green Goblin, Venom—you name the villain, I guarantee Noah loves him. Or her, as in the cases of Ursula and Harley Quinn.

I asked him recently why he loved the bad guys so much, and he said that it was because they could *always* find a way out. Try though their opposition did, they just couldn't seem to be kept down. In the know-it-all tone only an eight-year-old can nail, he reminded me that the Joker even put a microchip into the character of Robin before he was killed so that he could return as Robin and then reinvent himself from there. Who knew kids got the strategy of it all?

Now that he's old enough to weigh in on such decisions, Mike and I agreed that in the new house we just moved into, Noah should be able to decorate his room the way that he wanted. Not that there was *anything* wrong with his old room: It was done in the cutest fire-truck theme, complete with a bright red wall and furniture that was painted stark white. Adorable! And, evidently, "babyish," as I've recently been informed.

Since Noah has always loved monkeys, I found bedding and furnishings in an animal-lover theme that I just knew he'd like. "Nope," he said when he saw it. "Keep looking." After also being told that the themes of soccer and music just weren't "cool enough," I suddenly remembered why I've always said this particular kid could make a mute person scream.

〜∧∧〜

I returned from an out-of-town speaking engagement a few days ago to find that Noah had taken the room-decor task into his own hands. His latest phase, it seems, is Jillian Michaels—in her own right, a villain who also can't be kept down.

Stepping into Noah's room I saw a giant—and I mean *giant*—framed poster of my former trainer, complete with the slogan "Back in Black," and was told immediately that there's a *The Biggest Loser* banner to come.

"Why Jillian?" I asked my son.

"*Duh!*" came the response. (Every mom's favorite word, right?) "She's, like, *won* every *season*, Mom," Noah elaborated. "Also, she was allowed to kick your butt!" That one elicited a laugh from us both.

"*And* she knows Tae Kwon Do. *And* she rides a motorcycle. *And* she bosses everyone around. *And* we both like the color black."

I had the distinct feeling Noah could have kept going this way, enumerating every last awe-inspiring characteristic of the undeniably unparalleled Jillian, but I didn't stick around to find out. As I walked back into the living room a smile came upon my lips. Despite all of Noah's explanations, I knew the real reason he wanted Jillian on his wall. The woman who had ridden up on her bike and shocked an entire viewing audience had also ridden her way into my son's heart.

〜∧∧〜

For Noah's seventh birthday Mike and I took him to LA. We thought it would be fun to celebrate his special day in the city that I'd called home for four months straight. Plus, instead of toys or games, the one gift he asked for was to meet Jillian.

Kind woman that she is, Jillian agreed to join the three of us for dinner. Hollie had relocated to LA by then, and so she came along, too, and with halos perfectly in place she and I ordered salads even in the face of higher-calorie fare. When Noah couldn't decide what he wanted to eat, Jillian ordered for him. I was flabbergasted when I saw his meal arrive. "You got him deep-dish *macaroni and cheese*?" I asked Jillian.

"He's a *twig*!" she said. "Plus, there's real food in there."

Yeah, right. Just "real food" I'm not allowed to have.

After we finished our meal our server appeared with a birthday cake for Noah, with seven lighted candles on top. My son's eyes turned into saucers as he scanned the table to see who could have coordinated such a surprise. He finally got to Jillian. "It's your birthday, isn't it?" she said with a smile.

He nodded excitedly as an ear-to-ear grin took over his face.

"Just don't give any of that to your mom," Jillian added.

Talk about cruel: a giant piece of moist chocolate cake with fudgy chocolate icing, just eight inches from my grasp. So close, and yet so very, very far away.

We all left the restaurant, but before we made it to our rental car Jillian said, "Hey, Noah, come here. I want to show you something."

I never know what to expect when Jillian's involved, so I trailed Noah as he ran over to where she stood. Three seconds later I heard him say, "Oh, *cooooool!*" as Jillian hoisted him onto the back of her bike.

"You may *not* take my child for a ride," I clarified.

"Killjoy," came the reply.

Jillian let Noah take the driver's seat and pretend-ride for a good twenty minutes before we called it a night and headed back to the hotel. It was an ordinary evening that would have an extraordinary impact on my son.

In my heart of hearts I know that Noah's admiration for Jillian runs deeper than the things he's able to put words to. He knows that she took care of me, that she pushed me, that she believed in me and that she took me all the way to the end of the game. He knows that without her none of it would have been possible. And he loves her because of it.

What's more, he sees how passionately she serves *every* player she trains. These days my family has a standing appointment every Tuesday night, which happens to be when *The Biggest Loser* airs. Regardless of what else is going on in our lives, Noah won't let us miss a single episode. He cheers for various players, but mostly he cheers for his favorite villain of all. When she's happy, my son is happy, and when she gets mad, he gets mad too. It's the most charming codependency I've ever seen.

I'm not sure how much our now eight-year-old grasps about what "transformation" means, but this much I know: Noah saw his mom's insecurities on display for all the world to see. He saw her overcome them and learn to run real fast. And he's well aware that because of one motorcycle-riding bad girl dressed in black our lives are forever changed.

Appendixes

SAMPLE WORKOUTS

WHEN I RETURNED home from *The Biggest Loser* campus, I knew that I needed to find a trainer who could pick up where Jillian Michaels had left off, and thankfully, I found that and more in Margie Marshall. Margie helped me to remain focused and confident while I worked to shed those last few pounds. Not only did she motivate me physically, but she also encouraged me to grow spiritually. Margie is still my trainer today, and when I decided to add this section of sample workouts to the book, I knew she would be the perfect person to contribute.

Read through each of the workouts that follow, and then select the one that seems most doable for you today. Over time you'll want to give each of them a shot, I assure you. Margie doesn't mess around: The options that follow will rock your world!

To keep up with Margie's goings-on, I encourage you to check her out online at spidergirlfitness.com. Oh, and to sort out how many calories you're burning during each of these workouts, visit calorieking.com and click on Resources & Tools > Interactive Tools (on the drop-down menu) > Exercise Calories. With specificity I can't offer here, their estimates factor in the duration of your exercise, your gender and your current weight, height and age. Fantastic!

THE TEN-MINUTE MELT

This is a part-strength, part-cardio High-Intensity Interval Training (HIT) session that you can do with zero equipment and in ten minutes flat! Give it a go, modifying as necessary.

STOPWATCH	EXERCISE	DURATION	INSTRUCTION	MODIFICATION
:00–:30	Standard Push-ups	30 seconds	Assume a prone position on the floor and keep your feet together with the balls of your feet on the floor. Place your hands shoulder-width apart underneath your shoulders, and focus your eyes on a spot six to eight inches in front of your body's position. Lower your torso to the ground until your arms form a ninety-degree angle and then raise yourself using your arms. Breathe out as you push.	Descend into the push-up from your knees instead of from your toes.

STOPWATCH	EXERCISE	DURATION	INSTRUCTION	MODIFICATION
:30–1:00	High-Knee Run in Place	30 seconds	Stand with both feet together and place elbows in an L-shape by your side with palms facing the ground. Start running in place, getting your knees as high as possible. Touch your open-face palms if possible.	Instead of running, walk as quickly as you can, lifting your knees as high as you can.
1:00–1:30	Triceps Dips	30 seconds	Grab a chair that allows your legs to bend at ninety-degree angles when your feet are flat on the floor, and place it behind you. Curl your fingers around the edge of the seat of the chair and stretch your legs in front of you. With your elbows as close to your body as possible and your rear end as close to the chair as possible, lower your body slowly by bending your upper arms. Return to your starting position, inhaling as you move upward and exhaling as you go down. Do as many reps as you can.	Instead of stretching your legs in front of you, bend your knees to lend added support.

STOPWATCH	EXERCISE	DURATION	INSTRUCTION	MODIFICATION
1:30–2:00	Butt-Kick Jog in Place	30 seconds	Begin by standing with feet together. With arms positioned in an L-shape, start to run in place, kicking your buttocks with your heels as you go.	Walk instead of run, but still move your heels all the way to your rear end.
2:00–2:30	Squat Jumps	30 seconds	Stand with feet shoulder-width apart and your core flexed and bent slightly forward from the waist. Keep your back straight and in a neutral position. Squat down slowly, moving your buttocks toward your heels and keeping your arms in a parallel position to the floor. As you rise into a jump, reach your arms up toward the sky. Be sure to launch into your jump from your heels instead of your toes to avoid knee pain. Also, keep your knees behind your toes at all times and always tighten your core.	Instead of stretching your legs in front of you, bend your knees to lend added support.

STOPWATCH	EXERCISE	DURATION	INSTRUCTION	MODIFICATION
2:30–3:00	Mountain Climbers	30 seconds	Stand with your arms by your side and your feet together. Bend down and put your hands shoulder-width apart on the floor and your feet behind you. From this straight-arm plank position, move one knee to your chest and then as you move that leg back to straight-arm plank, move the other knee to your chest. Continue the knee-to-chest movement as quickly as possible, alternating legs each time.	Walk instead of run, but still move your heels all the way toward your rear end.

STOPWATCH	EXERCISE	DURATION	INSTRUCTION	MODIFICATION
3:00–3:30	Standard Push-ups	30 seconds	Begin in a straight-arm plank position on the floor and keep your feet together with the balls of your feet on the floor. Place your hands shoulder-width apart underneath your shoulders, and focus your eyes on a spot six to eight inches in front of your body's position. Lower your torso to the ground until your arms form a ninety-degree angle and then raise yourself using your arms. Breathe out as you push.	Descend into the push-up from your knees instead of from your toes.

STOPWATCH	EXERCISE	DURATION	INSTRUCTION	MODIFICATION
3:30–4:00	Squat Thrusts	30 seconds	Stand with your arms by your side and your feet together. Bend down and put your hands shoulder-width apart on the floor and assume a tuck position. From your tuck position, throw your feet behind you so that you wind up in a straight-arm plank. In one swift motion pull your feet back into a tuck. Continue this cycle—throwing your feet back and then reassuming a tuck—for the full thirty seconds.	From tuck position, move legs behind you one at a time instead of throwing them back simultaneously.

STOPWATCH	EXERCISE	DURATION	INSTRUCTION	MODIFICATION
4:00–4:30	Table Makers	30 seconds	Sit flat on the ground with your legs in front of you, bent at the knees and weight on your heels. Straighten your back as though you're sitting against a wall and place your hands beside you, behind each hip, fingers pointing toward your toes. Press with your hands as you raise your hips toward the ceiling and place your feet flat on the ground. Squeeze your buttocks tightly and push the soles of your feet into the ground. At the top of the exercise, your knees and shoulders should make a ninety-degree angle with your body. Without your buttocks touching the ground, descend into a dip and then swing yourself back up so that your chest, abs and hips form a table.	Simply go slower.

STOPWATCH	EXERCISE	DURATION	INSTRUCTION	MODIFICATION
4:30–5:00	Jumping Jacks	30 seconds	Start in a standing position with arms by your side and feet together. Jump to a position where your legs are spread wide and your hands are touching overhead, and then return to your starting position.	For a low-impact, no-jump move, do half-jacks instead by alternating your feet—thrust one foot to the side with bent knee, followed by the other foot to the other side. For an added arm workout, move corresponding bent elbow as though you're flapping a wing as you thrust out each foot.

To complete the Ten-Minute Melt, take three deep breaths, stretch your arms high into the air, and now (oh my word!) repeat.

THE KICK-BUTT STRESS BUSTER

This high-intensity, low-impact workout will kick every last ounce of stress out of your system. For all moves, use your knee as a fulcrum and kick through your heel instead of leading with pointed toe. Execute all kicks using one leg—thus achieving full burnout on that side—before switching to the other.

Repeat all kicks fifteen times; thirty for advanced.

Front Kick
Stand with your feet together, knees slightly bent and your arms bent at the elbow and pulled up alongside your face, with fists balled (you'll look like a boxer). Step your right foot back slightly, then kick out in front of you as high as you can, but no higher than your waist. Return to starting position. (For left-side burnout, you'll execute the same motion using your left leg.)

Side Kick
Stand with your feet hip-width distance apart, knees slightly bent, and your arms bent at the elbow and pulled up alongside your face, with fists balled. Kick your right leg to the side as high as you can, but no higher than your waist. (For left-side burnout, you'll execute using left leg.)
Note: Keep your eyes on a side-facing target when kicking to the side.

Backward Mule Kick
Stand with your feet hip-width distance apart, knees slightly bent, and your arms bent at the elbow and pulled up alongside your face, with fists balled. Leaning forward from the waist and looking behind you as you move, kick your right leg back as high as you can, but no higher than your waist. (For left-side burnout, you'll execute using left leg.)
Note: Look behind you when kicking backward.

Lunge-Back Front Kick
Begin in forward lunge position (page 211). Come out of lunge position and then using the opposite knee as a fulcrum, immediately kick

forward with the leg that is in front of you, as high as you can. Your other leg should be slightly bent at the knee.

Note: Be sure your knee stays behind your ankle when in a lunge.

Squat Side Kick

Begin in a squat position, with feet hip-width distance apart and knees slightly bent. Be sure your knees stay well behind your toes (you should be able to look down and see all of your shoelaces while in squat position. If you can't, stick out your butt further and rotate your hips backward until you can.) Ball your fists, bend your elbows, and pull your arms up alongside your face. Kick your right leg to the side as high as you can, but no higher than your waist. Return to squatting position and repeat. (For left-side burnout, execute using left leg.)

Note: Stay in your squat position throughout this entire series. Also, shift your weight to the ball of the opposing foot as you rise into your kick.

Mule Kick with High-Knee

Stand with your feet together. Bend the right leg and lift it up, so it makes a ninety-degree angle with the floor. From this starting position, take the raised right leg and kick it back behind you into an extended-leg position as you simultaneously lean your torso forward (so you are no longer standing straight up but bent slightly forward at the waist). As you return to starting position, immediately raise up the left leg into high-knee position, giving the entire rep something of a hobbyhorse motion. (For left-side burnout, execute by kicking left leg back and doing a right-side high knee.)

PLAYGROUND CARDIO

Maximize your playground time with this fun and energizing routine!

You may need to adapt the following suggestions, taking into consideration your playground's specific equipment, the number of people who are at the playground that day and the weather. (For instance, the slide-run isn't recommended when the sky is pouring rain.)

Ball-Find Suicides

Designate a "starting line" and place a bucket or shoe box for each person participating a few feet apart on that line. Give you and your child (or a friend, if your kids are occupied) five tennis balls each and sixty seconds to hide them under the slide, in the crook of a tree limb, behind a fence post, etc. Return to your designated starting point and yell "Go!" Race each other to see who can find the most balls—one ball at a time before heading back—and place them in his or her bucket the fastest.

Swing Set Incline Push-ups

Find two swings that are adjacent to each other. With one hand positioned on each seat, ease yourself down into bent-arm plank position (about five to ten minutes) until your body forms a straight line that is at a forty-five-degree angle to the ground. Using a push-up motion, straighten your arms and lift your body away from the swings, and then return to bent-arm plank. Repeat twenty times.

Slide-Runs

This move is best executed on a straight slide, not a curled one.
Using the sides of the slide for balance, run up the slide and walk yourself back down backward, completing twenty reps in a row. For added intensity, find side-by-side slides and race your child.

Park Bench Triceps Dips

Sit down on the bench and scoot all the way forward. Keeping your elbows bent and your hands placed on the bench and as close to your body as possible, ease your legs out until they are straight in front of you. Dip your rear toward the ground twenty times, keeping your back as close to the bench as possible. For added intensity, raise a leg for five reps and then switch legs for the next five reps.

Park Bench Step-Ups

Find a park bench near where your child is playing. Step up on the bench and step back down twenty times; switch to the other leg. For added intensity, when stepping up with right foot, swing left leg into a side leg raise before stepping back down. Repeat with the other side.

Monkey-Bar Negatives

Climb up to the monkey-bars launching pad. With your feet thrust out in front of you on the launching pad and with straight legs, grab the side bars with both hands. Keeping your legs straight, pull yourself toward the bars with both arms, in a chin-up motion. Allow your arms to straighten as you descend to the starting position. Repeat twenty times.

Note: Find a friend to spot you during this exercise.

Half-Step Bunny Jumps

If your playground has half-height concrete steps (like risers), position yourself on the bottom step and then jump with both feet to the next step up. Jump back down to the starting step. Repeat sequence for one minute, jumping up and back down as quickly as you can.

Note: If your area doesn't have half-height steps, simply jump rapid-fire while standing in place for one full minute.

THE TABATA ROUTINE

Invented by Dr. Izumi Tabata at the National Institute of Fitness and Sports in Tokyo, Japan, this simple, straightforward interval routine builds both stamina and strength. Each interval includes twenty seconds of exercise followed by ten seconds of rest. One routine lasts four minutes and includes eight intervals of one and *only one* specific exercise.

1. To begin, select one exercise from the list below to include in your Tabata Routine. (See glossary that follows this section for definitions of each.)

Burpees	Squat Jumps
Commando Crawls	Squat Thrusts
Jump-Ins	Standard Push-ups
Knee-Tuck Jumps	Table Makers
Military Push-ups	Triceps Dips
Rock Star Hops	Vertical Jumps
Skip Jumps	Wide-Arm Push-ups
Speed Skaters	

2. Next, follow the two-step process below, eight times in a row:
    For twenty seconds, do as many repetitions as possible.
    For ten seconds, rest.

That's it! Two simple steps. Seems easy, right? *Not!*

COMMERCIALLY YOURS

The next time you sit down to catch your favorite show, instead of fast-forwarding through the commercial breaks, *exercise* your way through them. Each commercial lasts roughly thirty seconds, and most commercial breaks include four or five commercials. Take your pick from the exercises listed here to complete during each thirty-second interval, and by the end of *American Idol* you'll have a much fitter physique!

Below, you'll find some plank exercises. Plank is one of the most effective abs exercises out there because it's impossible to cheat while doing it! Plus, you can do fewer plank-holds than traditional sit-ups and see twice the results. Who doesn't love that?

To get into plank, assume a prone position on the floor and keep your feet together with the balls of your feet on the floor. Place your hands shoulder-width apart underneath your shoulders. Tighten your abs and glutes, and don't arch or dip your back—you should be as straight as a plank. Several variations are below, to keep the exercise interesting and challenging.

Bent-Arm Plank (30 seconds)
Hold yourself in plank position, forearms resting on the floor. Remember to keep your neck in neutral position, neither tucking your chin, nor raising your chin into the air.

Straight-Arm Plank (30 seconds)
Hold yourself in plank position, arms straight and neck in neutral position.

Twisting Side-Plank (30 seconds)
Begin by lying on your right side with elbow on floor under shoulder and hips and feet stacked. Push hips up, forming straight line from head to heels. Extend left arm above shoulder, then bring left arm under body, rotating upper body to the right. Hold for one count and repeat. Switch to left side after ten reps. Alternate sides to fill the time allotted.

Isometric Up-Down Planks (30 seconds)
Begin in straight-arm plank position. Lower yourself to the bottom of a push-up, where your elbows are bent and tucked into your sides, your upper body and knees remain off the floor and your neck is in neutral position. Work to descend low enough for your nose to touch the floor. Hold for three counts and then raise yourself back to straight-arm plank. Hold for three counts and then lower once again to the bottom of a push-up. Repeat.

Standard Push-ups (30 seconds)
Begin in a straight-arm plank position with feet together and the balls of your feet on the floor. Place your hands shoulder-width apart underneath your shoulders, and focus your eyes on a spot six to eight inches in front of your body's position. Lower your torso to the ground until your arms form a ninety-degree angle and then raise yourself using your arms. Breathe out as you push. Repeat.

Forward Bicycles (30 seconds)
Begin by lying on the floor with legs outstretched in front of you and hands positioned beside each hip. Bend your knees slightly and raise your legs into the air. Begin "pedaling" forward in the air in slow, sweeping motions, keeping your abdominal muscles tight and remembering to breathe. Pumping legs in alternating fashion away from your chest, complete twenty "rotations" and then rest for ten seconds. Repeat to fill time allotted. For added intensity, keep arms raised straight above your head.

Backward Bicycles (30 seconds)
Begin by lying on the floor with legs outstretched in front of you and hands positioned beside each hip. Bend your knees slightly and raise your legs into the air. Begin "pedaling" backward in the air in slow, sweeping motions, keeping your abdominal muscles tight and remembering to breathe. Pumping legs in alternating fashion toward your chest, complete twenty "rotations" and then rest for ten seconds. Repeat to fill time allotted. For added intensity, keep arms raised straight above your head.

Forward Lunges (30 seconds)
Begin by standing with feet shoulder-width apart and hands on hips. Step forward with one leg, landing heel-first in front of you. Your knee should be at a ninety-degree angle. Hold for one count, and then pushing off of your heel, return to starting position. Alternate legs to fill time allotted.
Note: Remember to keep hands on hips and be sure your knee stays behind your toes as you lunge.

Backward Lunges (30 seconds)
Begin by standing with feet shoulder-width apart and hands on hips. Step backward with one leg, landing toe-first behind you. The opposite knee should be at a ninety-degree angle. Hold for one count, and then pushing off of your toe, return to starting position. Alternate legs to fill time allotted.
Note: Remember to keep hands on hips and be sure your knee stays behind your toes on leg that is bent.

Chair Pose (30 seconds)
Starting with feet together, bend over and place your hands on the floor. In one fluid motion, raise your arms straight in front of you toward the ceiling, making sure that your biceps are beside your ears and sit down on an imaginary chair. Your knees should not go beyond your toes. Keep your neck and back straight like a launching pad and your thighs parallel to the floor. Hold for the allotted time.

THE 60-SECOND SUICIDE

This thirty-minute high-intensity, high-impact monster will hit every major muscle group, as well as provide a massive cardio burn. It helps to have a friend with a stopwatch calling out each cue on a minute-by-minute basis. Complete it at your own risk!

If you're up for a real killer of a workout, give this one a try—a favorite go-to exercise of athletes of all kinds. Buy an inexpensive stopwatch, and time yourself—do thirty seconds of the first exercise, and thirty seconds of the second, as follows.

See glossary that follows this section for descriptions of these exercises.

Minute 1:	Slow Jog	Slow Jog
Minute 2:	Jumping Jacks*	Push-ups*
Minute 3:	Run	Run
Minute 4:	Knee-tuck Jumps	Vertical Jumps
Minute 5:	Run	Run
Minute 6:	Straight-Arm Plank Holds	Side-to-Side Lunge
Minute 7:	Run	Run
Minute 8:	Front Kick (Right)	Up-down Planks
Minute 9:	Run	Run
Minute 10:	Front Kick (Left)	Scissor Lunge
Minute 11:	Slow Jog	Slow Jog
Minute 12:	One Leg Hop (Right)	Squat Jumps*
Minute 13:	Run	Run
Minute 14:	One Leg Hop (Left)	Superman Holds (legs together)
Minute 15:	Run	Run
Minute 16:	Triceps Push-ups	Walking Lunge
Minute 17:	Run	Run
Minute 18:	Crab Forward	Crab Backward
Minute 19:	Run	Run
Minute 20:	Butt-Kick Jog in Place*	Mountain Climbers*
Minute 21:	Slow Jog	Slow Jog
Minute 22:	Helicopter Right	Helicopter Left
Minute 23:	Run	Run

Minute 24:	Right-side Kick	Left-side Kick
Minute 25:	Run	Run
Minute 26:	High Knees	High Knees
Minute 27:	Burpees	Jumping Jacks*
Minute 28:	Run	Run
Minute 29:	Straight-Arm Plank	Side-to-Side Lunge
Minute 30:	Slow Jog	Slow Jog

See chart beginning on page 196 for modified version of this exercise.

Be sure you're exercising at the proper level, based on your target heart rate. As a rule of thumb your target heart rate is 220 minus your age. The American Heart Association suggests that "when starting an exercise program, aim at the lowest part of your target zone (50 percent) during the first few weeks. Gradually build up to the higher part of your target zone (75 percent). After six months or more of regular workouts, you may be able to exercise comfortably at up to 85 percent of your maximum heart rate." A great way to keep tabs on how your pumper is pumping is by purchasing a wristwatch-style heart rate monitor.[28]

EVERYGIRL EXERCISES

If you're a busy stay-at-home mom like me, then you know that daily exercise can sometimes seem an impossible feat. On those days when life tries to get in the way of a good workout, I turn my normal chores into a stress-busting, muscle-building routine. Let the following suggestions fuel your creativity as you think through a few "everygirl exercises" of your own.

Speed Clean

Set the microwave timer for five minutes and clean your bathroom as fast as you can, making sure you break a sweat while doing it. For an added challenge, set the timer for another five minutes as you speed-vacuum the carpets and speed-sweep the floors. Crank up the tunes if you need a boost to your heart rate.

Phone-Pace

Don't sit while you talk on the phone; instead, pace back and forth in your living room or kitchen.

Dishpan Lifts

While standing at your sink washing dishes, do leg lifts to the side for fifty counts and then to the back for fifty counts. Switch legs. For a real challenge, work your way up to two hundred counts to the side and two hundred counts to the back on each leg. Your leg muscles will be exhausted, but your dishes will be ultraclean!

Brushed-Teeth Raises

In the time it takes to brush your teeth, you can do fifty bent-knee leg raises to the back per leg. To execute, stand tall with both feet together. Using the countertop to balance yourself, stand on one leg and pull the opposite foot perpendicularly toward the standing leg's ankle. Keeping your weight on your standing leg, lift the opposite foot behind you until you feel your glute muscle contract. Return to starting position. That's one rep. If you're a thorough toothbrusher, you should be able to complete about fifty reps per leg in the time it takes you to tend to this chore. Your teeth—and your butt—will look better as a result.

Laundry Squats

While folding clothes, separate clean clothes into piles—one pile for underwear, one for socks, one for towels, etc. Place one pile in front of you on the couch or an ottoman and assume a squat position, making sure that your knees stay behind your toes. Fold the entire pile of clothes while in your squat and then stand up and rest your legs for thirty seconds. Repeat with the next pile until all of your laundry is folded.

Commuter Squeezes

If you find yourself sitting behind the wheel of a car all day long, turn those commutes into a glute-burner. As you drive, squeeze your buttocks together and hold for one count before releasing the muscles. Repeat to exhaustion, which might mean five hundred or even one thousand contractions. Sure, you won't be able to get out of your car to get the mail upon returning home, but that's what kids are for, right?

Note: If your responsibilities cause you to sit in front of a computer instead of a steering wheel all day, these exercises are equally effective when executed from a desk chair.

Terminal Sits

The next time you find yourself waiting in an airport terminal for the flight that seems terminally delayed, find a blank wall and have a seat. With ankles and knees together, lower yourself along the wall until your knees are at a ninety-degree angle. Work to stay in that position for a full minute before standing up and resting. Repeat until your legs shake. For an added challenge, lift one leg off the floor for ten seconds while in your wall squat and then switch legs.

Line Lunges

Lunge in place while in line at the grocery store. People will eye you suspiciously, but rest assured, they're just jealous that you have the confidence to risk looking like a fool and the determination to exercise even when errands vie for your time.

GLOSSARY OF EXERCISES

<u>Burpee</u> Begin in a squat position with your hands on the floor in front of you. Kick your feet back, while simultaneously lowering yourself into a push-up. Immediately return your feet to the squat position, while simultaneously pushing up with your arms. Leap up as high as possible, hands toward the ceiling and then return to the squat position.

<u>Commando Crawl</u> Start in bent-arm plank position, with forearms resting on the floor. Using your elbows, your inner thighs and your kneecaps, "walk" yourself forward as quickly as you can. Remember to keep your butt as low as possible as you move.

<u>Crab Backward</u> Sit flat on the ground with your legs in front of you, bent at the knees and weight on your heels. Place your hands behind each hip, fingers pointing toward your toes. Lift yourself off the ground with the strength of your arms so that your butt is hovering over the ground. Lift your left leg and extend it so that you are balanced on your right leg and your hands. From this "crab" position, move yourself backward by alternating your legs and arms. Remember to look over your shoulder so that you don't run into anything!

<u>Crab Forward</u> Sit flat on the ground with your legs in front of you, bent at the knees and weight on your heels. Place your hands behind each hip, fingers pointing toward your toes. Lift yourself off the ground with the strength of your arms so that your butt is hovering over the ground. Lift your left leg and extend it so that you are balanced on your right leg and your hands. From this "crab" position, move yourself forward by alternating your legs and arms.

<u>Helicopter Left</u> Lie on your back with your legs extended straight up into the ceiling at a ninety-degree angle (so that you resemble a sideways L). Tuck your hands just under your lower back to protect it. Circle your legs gently to the left about ten to fifteen degrees, using your oblique (side stomach) muscles, before returning to starting position. Be sure not to pick up your right hip during the rotations.

<u>Helicopter Right</u> Lie on your back with your legs extended straight up into the ceiling at a ninety-degree angle (so that you resemble a sideways L). Tuck your hands just under your lower back to protect it. Circle your legs gently to the right about ten to fifteen degrees, using your oblique (side stomach) muscles, before returning to starting position. Be sure not to pick up your left hip during the rotations.

<u>High Knees</u> Stand with both feet together and place elbows in an L-shape by your side with palms facing the ground. Start running in place, getting your knees as high as possible. Touch your open-face palms with your knees as you go, if possible.

<u>Jump-In</u> Begin by sitting on the ground with your legs outstretched in front of you. Place your hands beside your hips, flat on the ground. Raise your butt off of the floor, which will place you in a reverse-straight-arm plank position. With swift motions, pull your knees up toward your chest and your feet as close to your butt as possible, and then thrust your legs back to a straight position. Repeat.

<u>Knee-Tuck Jump</u> Begin in standing position with feet together and arms at a ninety-degree angle by your side. In one fluid movement, and without adjusting your arms, jump into the air while bringing both knees up to your hands.
Note: Remember to jump from your toes and to land on your toes to avoid knee strain.

<u>Military Push-up</u> Begin in straight-arm plank position. Position your hands so that they are directly beneath your chest. Lower yourself into a push-up, making sure that your elbows brush the sides of your body as you descend. Raise back up to straight-arm plank position and repeat.

<u>Moving Mountain Climbers</u> Stand with your arms by your side and your feet together. Bend down and put your hands shoulder-width apart on the floor and your feet behind you so that your legs are extended, the balls of your feet are on the ground, and you are parallel to the floor. This position is called straight-arm plank. From this position, move one knee to your chest and then as you move that leg back to straight-arm plank,

move the other knee to your chest in something of a running-in-place motion. As you do this, simultaneously walk yourself forward with your hands for an added cardio burst. Continue the knee-to-chest movement as quickly as possible, alternating legs each time.

Rock Star Hop Begin in standing position with feet together and arms by your side. In one fluid motion, jump into the air, raise your arms above your head and kick your butt with both heels. Land on your toes and repeat.

Scissor Lunges Begin in a lunge position, your right knee bent and in front of you, your left leg extended behind you. Be careful to keep the knee directly over your heel (don't extend knee past your toes). From this position, jump up and switch legs so that your left leg is in front of you and your right leg is behind you in a lunge. Continue alternating lunges in this quick way, paying careful attention to your form.

Side-to-Side Lunge Stand with feet together and hands at your side. Step your right leg away from your left and squat down on the right leg. Your left leg should be extended. Return to starting position and repeat on the other side.

Skip Jump Begin in standing position with feet together and arms by your side. In one fluid motion, begin skipping forward, exaggerating the skip by raising the lifted knee and lifted arm as high as possible. Work to increase your vertical height with each skip.

Speed Skater Begin in standing position with feet shoulder-width apart. Using a lateral movement, jump from side to side, landing on one leg and swinging forward the opposite arm. Keep your body low to the ground and knees bent the entire time. Work to increase the distance of your lateral jump each time.

Squat Jump Begin in standing position with feet shoulder-width apart and arms hanging by your side. Bend down into squat position, making sure your toes stay in front of your knees. As you rise from the squat, jump into the air as high as possible. Return to squat and repeat.

<u>Squat Thrust</u> Begin in standing position with feet together and arms by your side. Bend down and put your hands shoulder-width apart on the floor and assume a tuck position. From your tuck position, throw your feet behind you so that you wind up in a straight-arm plank. In one swift motion pull your feet back into a tuck. Repeat.

<u>Standard Push-up</u> Begin in a straight-arm plank position with feet together and the balls of your feet on the floor. Place your hands shoulder-width apart underneath your shoulders, and focus your eyes on a spot six to eight inches in front of your body's position. Lower your torso to the ground until your arms form a ninety-degree angle and then raise yourself using your arms. Breathe out as you push. Repeat.

<u>Straight-Arm Plank Holds</u> Hold yourself in plank position for as long as you can with arms straight and neck in neutral position.

<u>Superman Hold</u> Lie face down on the ground. Squeeze your inner thighs together so that your legs are touching. From this prone position, lift your legs and arms at the same time, so that you look like Superman in flight. Hold for ten seconds before taking a two-second break. Then repeat. This is a great way to strengthen your back muscles!

<u>Table Maker</u> Sit flat on the ground with your legs in front of you, bent at the knees and with your weight on your heels. Straighten your back as though you're sitting against a wall and place your hands beside you, behind each hip, fingers pointing toward your toes. Press with your hands as you simultaneously raise your hips toward the ceiling and place your feet flat on the ground. Squeeze your buttocks tightly and push the soles of your feet into the ground. At the top of the exercise, your knees and shoulders should make a ninety-degree angle with your body. Without your buttocks touching the ground, descend into a dip and then swing yourself back up so that your chest, abs and hips form a table. Repeat.

<u>Triceps Dip</u> Begin by sitting on a chair with your legs bent at a ninety-degree angle. Scoot all the way forward on the seat. Keeping your elbows bent and your hands as close to your body as possible, ease your legs out until they are straight in front of you. Dip your rear toward the floor

twenty times, keeping your back as close to the chair as possible. For added intensity, raise one leg straight out in front of you with foot flexed and hold in the air for five reps, then switch legs for the next five reps.

<u>Triceps Push-ups</u> Start in straight-arm plank position, as though you are about to do a standard push-up. Instead of keeping elbows out to the side, bring elbows toward your rib cage so that as you descend into the push-up they will graze the sides of your body. Also, before you begin your push-up descent, be sure to rotate the inside of your elbows (not the bony part) so that they are facing forward instead of facing each other.

<u>Up-Down Plank</u> Start in straight-arm plank position, arms straight and neck in neutral position. Move down to bent-arm plank position, forearms resting on the floor. Repeat, alternating straight-arm and bent-arm plank. (If this move is too challenging with both arms moving simultaneously, modify by moving one arm at a time so that you move in a right-left-right-left progression from straight-arm to bent-arm plank and back again.)

<u>Vertical Jump</u> Begin in a standing position with feet together and hands by your side. In one fluid motion, jump into the air, reaching for the ceiling with straight arms thrust above your head. Land on your toes and repeat.

<u>Walking Lunges</u> Begin by standing with feet shoulder-width apart and hands on hips. Step forward with one leg, landing heel-first in front of you. Your knee should be at a ninety-degree angle and stay well behind your toes. Hold for one count and then step forward with the other leg so that it's now at a ninety-degree angle. Continue walking forward with alternating lunges.

<u>Wide-Arm Push-up</u> Begin in a straight-arm plank position with feet together and the balls of your feet on the floor. Place your hands on the floor, about 50 percent wider apart than shoulder-width, and focus your eyes on a spot six to eight inches in front of your body's position. Lower your torso to the ground until your arms form a ninety-degree angle and then raise yourself using your arms. Breathe out as you push. Repeat.

I KNEW OF "Chef Jessica" long before she knew of me. She has a local radio program on 88.1FM (WCRJ) in Jacksonville, and my mother is her self-proclaimed biggest fan. Every once in awhile, I'd tune in to hear Chef Jessica talk about easy kid-friendly dinner ideas or less sinful ways to enjoy chocolate indulgences, and each time I'd think, "This girl and I could *so* be friends."

Fast-forward to my *The Biggest Loser* experience. Jessica had no idea who I was because she doesn't watch TV. But shortly after my return to Jacksonville, a church in the area asked both of us to come speak at a women's event—I was asked to give the motivational talk, and Jessica was to follow up with a few healthy recipes. Mere minutes into that event, I had a brand-new friend.

Chef Jessica is actually Jessica Bright, wife to Chris and mom to two amazing kids. She has a very fancy title—something like "Master Food and Nutrition Educator"—but to me, she's simply "Jess."

I hope you love her suggestions on the pages that follow as much as I do. Many of her dishes have become staples in the Hadden household—especially the pita pizzas and the protein pancakes. Yum.

Chef Jessica continues to deliver a weekly radio program, as well as frequent local-TV spots and cooking classes for home-school co-ops and community organizations. If you'd like to learn more about her current endeavors, visit cookingbright.com.

Bon appétit!

HONEY FRUIT WITH YOGURT

Serves one

Ingredients
½ cup plain Greek-style yogurt
¼ cup fresh blueberries, washed
   (substitute strawberries or raspberries, if desired)
Honey to taste

Greek yogurt is much thicker than most other yogurts on the market, and despite having no added sugar, it tastes just as good. Because of its increased popularity in recent years, it can be found in many grocery stores. This recipe makes a fantastic breakfast, snack or dessert option. Just go easy on that honey.

Directions
Put yogurt in a bowl, top with berries and then drizzle with honey. Enjoy!

Per-Serving Nutritional Information[29]
161 calories
0.2g total fat (0g saturated fat)
0mg cholesterol
58mg sodium
25.8g total carbohydrates (1.6g fiber; 24.2g sugar)
13.7g protein

NOAH'S PROTEIN PANCAKES

Serves two

Ingredients
¼ cup low-fat cottage cheese
2 egg whites
¼ cup old-fashioned oats
Dash of cinnamon
2 tablespoons unsweetened applesauce

This easy recipe is a hit with Noah, as you probably guessed from the title. If you want more variety, try adding a packet of flavored oatmeal or mix in a few chunks of fresh fruit, such as bananas, strawberries or blueberries. Also, leftover batter (if there is any!) keeps well in the refrigerator to cook later.

Directions
Heat a nonstick pan to medium heat. Combine all ingredients in the blender and blend until smooth, or mix with a hand mixer—either way, be sure you blend/mix until all cottage-cheese curds are dissolved into the mixture. Drop by tablespoons onto heated pan. When bubbles appear, flip the cakes over. Cook until golden on both sides. Serve topped with fresh sliced fruit and/or a dollop of low-fat vanilla yogurt.

Per-Serving Nutritional Information
101 calories
1.4g total fat (0.6g saturated fat)
2.5mg cholesterol
285mg sodium
16.8g total carbohydrates (2.2g fiber; 3.7g sugar)
11.3g protein

MOCHA BREAKFAST SMOOTHIES

Serves one

Ingredients
1 cup skim milk (or fat-free
  half-and-half)
1 teaspoon vanilla extract
1 tablespoon cocoa powder
1 tablespoon instant coffee powder
Stevia to taste
¼ cup low-fat vanilla yogurt
Dash of cinnamon (optional)
1 cup ice

There are plenty of high-fat, high-calorie coffee-flavored drinks you can buy to start your day with decadence. But by making your own morning-time beverage at home and using healthier ingredients, you not only save money but also calories.

Stevia is a noncaloric herb that is deliciously sweet. It has been around for hundreds of years, but it didn't rise in popularity in this country until the Food and Drug Administration recently declared it an approved "dietary supplement." None of the chemicals of artificial sweeteners, none of the calories of sugar and all of the taste you could want. Mmm!

Directions
Mix everything together in your blender until smooth. For variety change the type of extract (try almond or mint, for example).

Per-Serving Nutritional Information
170 calories
2.1g total fat (0.8g saturated fat)
8mg cholesterol
186mg sodium
27.7g total carbohydrates (1.8g fiber; 24.9g sugar)
13.5g protein

THE RANCH'S YOGURT SMOOTHIES

Serves one

Ingredients
1 cup plain low-fat yogurt
1 cup frozen berries (such as blueberries and strawberries)
1 fresh banana
Honey to taste, if desired

Smoothies are a fun, fast and easy way to start the day right. Frozen prepared fruit is available in the freezer case at the grocery store or you can plan ahead by purchasing seasonal fruit in bulk and freezing your own. By adding yogurt, you also get closer to your daily calcium needs. Bonus!

Directions
Combine everything in the blender and pulse until consistently smooth. Add a little water (or 100 percent fruit juice) if necessary to blend.

Per-Serving Nutritional Information (when made with blueberries and 1 tablespoon honey)
296 calories
5.1g total fat (2.6g saturated fat)
15mg cholesterol
174mg sodium
70g total carbohydrates (6.1g fiber; 56.3g sugar)
14.4g protein

HEAVENLY HUMMUS

Serves four

Ingredients
1 14.5-ounce can garbanzo beans
   (also called chick peas), drained
   and rinsed
¼ cup tahini (sesame butter)
2 tablespoons lemon juice
2 cloves garlic, pressed
1 tablespoon extra-virgin olive oil[30]
3 green onions (scallions), minced
Sea salt, to taste
Fresh ground black pepper, to taste

Hummus is a wonderful food to munch on as long as you choose the right things to dip in it. Instead of using high-fat packaged chips or pita crisps, try fresh vegetables. You can even make your own chips by spritzing whole-wheat pitas or tortillas with olive oil, spreading them on a baking sheet, sprinkling them with sea salt and baking at 300 degrees until crisp. (Thanks for that tip, Chef Jessica!)

Directions
Combine everything in a food processor and blend until smooth. For an extra kick, add a dash of cayenne pepper.

Per-Serving Nutritional Information
178.2 calories
6.2g total fat (2.4g saturated fat)
0mg cholesterol
313mg sodium
26.2g total carbohydrates (5g fiber; 0.3g sugar)
6.6g protein

HOLY GUACAMOLE!

Serves four

Ingredients
2 ripe avocados
1 tablespoon fresh-squeezed lime juice
¼ teaspoon garlic salt
¼ teaspoon cumin
2 tablespoons fresh minced cilantro

Although avocados are high in fat, this particular fat is beneficial to your diet. And aren't we guacamole lovers grateful!

Try this guacamole on homemade pita chips. See page 226 for the recipe.

Directions
Peel, seed and mash avocados with the lime juice. Add remaining ingredients and mix thoroughly. Add more garlic salt if needed.

Per-Serving Nutritional Information
121.9 calories
10.9g total fat (1.6g saturated fat)
0mg cholesterol
122.5mg sodium
7g total carbohydrates (6.8g fiber; .6g sugar)
1.6g protein

TOMATO SALSA

Serves four

Ingredients
2 cups fresh chopped tomatoes
1 tablespoon freshly squeezed lime
    juice
Pinch of sugar
Pinch of kosher salt
1 jalapeño pepper, finely minced (leave
    seeds in for hotter flavor; substitute
    with sweet bell pepper for milder
    flavor)
¼ cup green onion, finely minced
2 tablespoons fresh cilantro, finely chopped
1 clove garlic, pressed

I have always loved salsa, mostly because it involves dipping. While I used to enjoy it with fried tortilla chips, which are absolutely terrible for you, these days I eat it with warm, toasted homemade pita chips (see page 226 for recipe) or as a dressing for my salad. These are two of my favorite salsa recipes. Enjoy!

Directions
Drain excess juice from tomatoes and place in a medium-size bowl.
Add remaining ingredients, stir well and serve.

Note: The flavor will improve as it sits, so prepare an hour in advance of when you plan to enjoy it.

Per-Serving Nutritional Information
22.2 calories
0.2g total fat (0.05g saturated fat)
0mg cholesterol
97.7mg sodium
6.1g total carbohydrates (1.4g fiber; 3.8g sugar)
1g protein

MANGO SALSA

Serves four

Ingredients
1 ripe mango, peeled and seeded, or 2 cups fresh peaches, peeled and
     seeded
4 medium plum tomatoes (or 2 large regular tomatoes)
½ red bell pepper, finely minced
Juice of 1 lime
2 scallions (green onions)
½ cup fresh cilantro
1 tablespoon honey
Salt and pepper, to taste
1 jalapeño, seeded and minced, if preparing for adults

Directions
Combine all ingredients in your food processor, pulse until desired
consistency and serve.

Per-Serving Nutritional Information [for mango salsa without jalapeño]
40 calories
0.2g total fat (0.02g saturated fat)
0mg cholesterol
68mg sodium
16.6g total carbohydrates (1.7g fiber; 13.6g sugar)
0.8g protein

"MMM, GOOD" RANCH DRESSING

Serves fourteen

Ingredients
1 cup low-fat mayonnaise
½ cup low-fat buttermilk
1 teaspoon fresh squeezed lemon
　　juice
2 cloves garlic, pressed
¼ teaspoon sea salt
2 tablespoons fresh parsley, minced
¼ cup green onions (scallions),
　　minced
½ teaspoon dry dill
Fresh ground black pepper to taste

I love ranch dressing, and I mean *love* it. I'd prefer a smaller portion of the tastier real thing than a boatload of the flavorless "diet" version, and trust me, this recipe really delivers the goods! By using light or low-fat mayo and low-fat buttermilk, you significantly cut back on both the fat and calories that are normally found in salad dressings. Also, in addition to dressing salads, it's fantastic on baked potatoes or as a dip for rolled-up, low-sodium, nitrate-free deli turkey or cut-up veggies.

Directions
Pour mayonnaise, buttermilk and lemon juice into blender. Add remaining ingredients and blend briefly. Can be stored in enclosed container in refrigerator for up to one week.

Per-Serving Nutritional Information
212.8 calories
19.4g total fat (3.3g saturated fat)
22.5mg cholesterol
449.5mg sodium
9.1g total carbohydrates (0.3g fiber;
　　5.6g sugar)
2.8g protein

This recipe also makes an excellent jalapeño ranch dressing. Add half-chopped jalapeño before blending (remove the seeds if you don't want it to be hot). Yum!

DELICIOUS LENTIL SOUP

Serves eight

Ingredients
1 pound dried lentils
1 tablespoon extra virgin olive oil
1 red bell pepper, chopped
1 large sweet onion, chopped
4 cloves garlic, minced
3 carrots, chopped
3 celery ribs, chopped
3 bay leaves
3 sprigs fresh thyme
2 sprigs fresh rosemary
½ cup red wine
1 bag fresh spinach, chopped
½ cup fresh parsley, minced
Fresh squeezed juice of 1 lemon
1 teaspoon honey
1 cup quinoa, rinsed
6 cups water

Lentil soup warms you from the inside out. Even better than the comfort of it is the nutritional value it brings. Lentils are a fantastic source of fiber and a good source of protein, and the addition of the vegetables helps this soup to be packed with plenty of vitamins, minerals and flavor.

Directions
Sort and rinse lentils. Sauté onion, pepper and garlic in olive oil until onion is translucent. Add celery, carrots, lentils, six cups water, bay leaves, thyme, rosemary and wine. Cover, bring to a boil and simmer about forty-five minutes. Stir in spinach, parsley, lemon juice and honey. Stir in quinoa and cook until done, about fifteen minutes. Add salt and fresh ground pepper to taste.

Per-Serving Nutritional Information
174 calories
2.9g total fat (0.3g saturated fat)
0mg cholesterol
84mg sodium
28.3g total carbohydrates (8.3g fiber; 5.5g sugar)
9.1g protein

JULIE'S SKINNY-SOUTHERN-GIRL OKRA

Serves four

Okra is a good source of vitamins C and A and is also known for its iron and calcium content. It's low in calories, a good source of dietary fiber and is fat-free. Plus, it's referred to as "Lady Fingers"— with a name like that, it must be good.[31]

I come from the South, which means I was fed fried okra as soon as I was old enough to chew. You can imagine my dismay when I was told that my favorite side dish wasn't allowed at *The Biggest Loser* campus. Really, now, did they even know what they were missing? Although my teammates initially turned up their noses at this adjusted recipe, after one bite they were converted. I think you will be too.

Ingredients
4 cups fresh (not frozen) okra, trimmed
    and cut into ½-inch pieces
Olive oil cooking spray to coat pan
Sea salt and pepper to taste

A great alternative is to line up the okra in a row, run a skewer through the top and the bottom of each piece, and cook them on the grill until slightly brown and tender.

Directions
Heat a nonstick skillet over medium heat. Spray with cooking oil, add okra and sauté, turning frequently, until okra is slightly brown and crispy, about fifteen minutes. Season with salt and pepper to taste.

Per-Serving Nutritional Information
31 calories
0.1g total fat (0g saturated fat)
0mg cholesterol
8mg sodium
7g total carbohydrates (3.2g fiber; 1.2g sugar)
2g protein

GOOD-AS-GOURMET VEGGIES

Serves four

You just think you can't make a dinner out of vegetables. Give it a try! You'll be shocked by how satisfied you feel—guaranteed!

Ingredients
1 bunch of asparagus, rinsed and
    trimmed
1 head of broccoli, rinsed and cut into
    spears
2 bell peppers, stem and seeds removed, cut into quarters
Low-sodium seasoning of choice, to taste
Extra-virgin olive oil

Directions
Heat oven to 450 degrees. Prepare vegetables and toss them in a little of the olive oil. Sprinkle with the seasoning, place them on a roasting pan and bake until slightly tender, about twenty-five minutes.

Other great options to roast (or grill):
Zucchini, summer (yellow) squash, sweet onions, shallots, scallions, button mushrooms, portabella mushrooms, cauliflower and eggplant.

Per-Serving Nutritional Information
221 calories
2.3g total fat (0.4g saturated fat)
0mg cholesterol
142mg sodium
44.6g total carbohydrates (18.3g fiber; 16g sugar)
17.4g protein

SWEET POTATO FRIES

Serves four

Ingredients
4 cups sweet potato, peeled and cut
    to ½-inch by 3-inch strips
1 large sweet onion, diced
1 tablespoon fresh thyme minced or
    1 teaspoon dry thyme
Olive oil cooking spray
Sea salt and freshly ground black
    pepper to taste

Chef Jessica tells me that because sweet potatoes are simply *packed* with beta carotene, they're a much more nutritious option than their less-colorful counterparts. I have no idea if she's right. All I know is that these fries are so yummy, you'll wind up eating all four servings yourself. I don't recommend this, of course. I just call it like I see it.

If you prefer a sweeter option, omit the onion, salt, pepper and thyme, and substitute cinnamon and a sweetener like stevia to taste.

Directions
Preheat oven to 425 degrees. Combine potatoes, onion and thyme in a large bowl. Spritz with some of the olive oil and toss. Spread evenly on a baking sheet that has been sprayed with olive oil, and season with salt and pepper. Cook until potatoes are browned to your liking, thirty to forty-five minutes.

Per-Serving Nutritional Information
180 calories
0.4g total fat (0.1g saturated fat)
0mg cholesterol
72mg sodium
41.4g total carbohydrates (6.6g fiber; 16.8g sugar)
4g protein

ROCKIN' QUINOA

Serves four

Whether you're into an all-things-vegan lifestyle or you prefer a more traditional approach, quinoa is a fantastic source of protein. What's more, it's packed with dietary fiber and necessary minerals like phosphorus, magnesium and iron. Oh, and quinoa is gluten-free, which is great news for those who wrestle with finding tasty options to meet a restricted diet. Enjoy!

Ingredients
2 cups water
1 cup quinoa
¼ teaspoon salt
1 small sweet onion, diced
½ cup golden raisins
2 teaspoons cumin
2 tablespoons white wine vinegar
1 clove fresh garlic, pressed
1 cup (packed) minced fresh parsley
2 medium tomatoes, diced
Sea salt and freshly ground black
    pepper to taste

In addition to fried okra, grits are a southern culinary tradition that dies hard. Especially grits with a huge hunk of soft butter on top. Obviously, Jillian wasn't going to be a fan of the meal, so I caved to the dreaded *keen-wah*. But here's the thing: It was actually pretty good. In fact, quinoa, which I now know how to pronounce all by myself, has become one of my favorite comfort foods—you know, when there are no grits to be found.

Here's Chef Jessica's note on the following recipe: "While it is growing, quinoa is protected by its saponin, which covers the exterior of the grain and gives the grain an unpleasant taste. After harvesting, the saponin is removed, but the quinoa still needs to be rinsed well before cooking to make certain that none of the bitterness remains." Isn't she so smart?

Directions
Rinse quinoa in a fine sieve. In a medium saucepan bring two cups of water to boil. Add quinoa, ¼ teaspoon salt, onion, raisins, cumin and vinegar, and mix well. Place lid on pot and simmer for ten minutes. Quinoa will be translucent when done. Remove from heat, fluff with a fork and stir in garlic, parsley and tomatoes. Add salt and pepper to

taste. Serve warm or chilled.

Per-Serving Nutritional Information
239 calories
2.9g total fat (0.3g saturated fat)
0mg cholesterol
23.5mg sodium
49g total carbohydrates (4.8g fiber; 13.2g sugar)
6.9g protein

PASTA IN HIDING

Serves four

Ingredients
1 spaghetti squash (about 2 pounds)
Extra-virgin olive oil cooking spray
Sea salt and pepper to taste
Fresh chopped parsley and fresh basil for
    garnish

It is just plain wonderful when you can find a vegetable that tastes like a carb but, in fact, is not. Spaghetti squash is one of those amazing options and makes a wonderful substitute for pasta.

Directions
Choose a pot that is large enough to hold the squash. Measure enough water to immerse the squash and then heat the water to boiling. Carefully add the squash. Boil until the skin of the squash is easily pierced and the squash is tender. Remove from water, cut in half, scrape out seeds and then shred with a fork. Serve as you would pasta or spray with a little of the olive oil, season with salt, pepper and fresh herbs.

Per-Serving Nutritional Information
61 calories
0.6g total fat (0.2g saturated fat)
0mg cholesterol
41mg sodium
14.7g total carbohydrates (3g fiber; 6g sugar)
1.5g protein

PITA PIZZAS

Serves two

Ingredients
1 whole-wheat pita
Nonstick baking spray
3 tablespoons tomato sauce
½ teaspoon sriracha Asian chili sauce
    (optional)
¼ teaspoon honey
½ cup low-fat grated Italian cheese blend
Turkey pepperoni, if desired
2 tablespoons fresh, chopped basil
Crushed chili pepper (optional)

The first time Chef Jessica cooked for my family, she made us do all the work. Some friend, right? Admittedly, she prepped all of the ingredients, which meant that Mike, Noah and I were more "assemblers" than chefs. Still, the result was the most incredible pizza substitute I'd ever seen. Or tasted. And you know what a pizza freak I am.

Directions
Preheat oven to 400 degrees. Separate the top from the bottom of the pita to create two equal circles. Place both circles on a baking sheet sprayed with nonstick baking spray (smooth side down). Combine the tomato sauce, sriracha and honey for a spicy sweet sauce. Spread the tomato mixture on the pitas and top with the Italian cheese blend and pepperoni. Place in oven and bake for ten minutes, or until cheese is melted and crust is toasted. Top with fresh basil and chili pepper if desired.

Per-Serving Nutritional Information (with sriracha, half-cup turkey pepperoni and chili pepper)
132 calories
3.9g total fat (1.8g saturated fat)
25mg cholesterol
633.5mg sodium
15g total carbohydrates (1.7g fiber; 2.3g sugar)
8.7g protein

LESS-SINFUL NOT-HOT CHOCOLATE FONDUE

Serves one

Ingredients
1 tablespoon unsweetened cocoa
   powder, preferably one of the
   "Dutch-processed" varieties
1 teaspoon instant coffee
1 teaspoon vanilla extract
2 tablespoons plain low-fat yogurt
Sweetener of choice, to taste
   (I use slightly less than one packet
   of stevia.)

Sometimes life calls for chocolate. Am I right? When you find yourself in the cookie aisle with a massive hankering for some rich, gooey, decadent treat, step away from the fudge-dipped double-stuff Oreos, head home to your kitchen and make this fondue instead. Especially delicious with juicy, sweet strawberries. Mmm!

Directions
Mix together cocoa, coffee and sweetener. Mix in the vanilla to form a paste. Mix in one tablespoon of yogurt and stir thoroughly. Add in final tablespoon of yogurt, stir thoroughly and serve with fresh fruit.

Per-Serving Nutritional Information
62 calories
1.6g total fat (1g saturated fat)
3mg cholesterol
40mg sodium
7.8g total carbohydrates (1.8g fiber; 4.6g sugar)
4.1g protein

FAQs

WHETHER I'M SPEAKING to a group of stay-at-home moms, a hospital's medical staff or a complete stranger in aisle seven of the grocery store, people with whom I come in contact seem to share the same handful of questions. Here are the answers to the questions I get, in some form or fashion, nearly everywhere I go.

1. Is Jillian Michaels REALLY as mean as she comes across on TV?

   Meaner! But only in the gym.

2. Is it realistic to tell morbidly obese people that they can lose half their body weight in such a short period of time?

   Yes. *If* the weight-loss is handled correctly. When the basic principles of diet and exercise are honored, meaning the person is eating the right amount of calories and working out in a way that suits his or her unique physical ability, it is *absolutely* possible to experience dramatic change in a short period of time.

3. Would you ever consider having surgery to remove your loose skin?

   Sure—especially if it were free! Actually, these days I choose to view my loose skin as my battle scar for a well-won war. But I never say never.

4. What was the hardest thing you did while on the set of *The Biggest Loser*?

   The hardest thing for me was simply getting up every day, knowing that I was going to have to do the very same thing I had done the day before. It was hard to stay motivated for four months straight, when every sunrise brought with it the realization that I was going to have to deny myself chocolate cake for another twenty-four hours and die another death in the gym.

5. What was the single most important thing you learned while on *The Biggest Loser*?

   The single most important thing I learned as a result of being on show is that I am worthy of living the life that I believe I was created to live.

6. What was your "defining moment?" When did you know that you were ready to make a change?

   I think I was standing in front of a mirror at home. I can't really remember. What I do remember is thinking, "You are thirty-five years old. You either make a *big* change now, or you basically agree to live the rest of your life fat."

7. Has your relationship with your husband improved since you've lost weight?

   Losing my weight caused me to feel altogether differently about myself. And when you feel differently about yourself you feel differently about everyone else around you. I'm so thankful for Mike—for his love for me when I was overweight and for his love for me now.

8. How did it feel to come within just eight pounds of being named the first female biggest loser?

   It felt great to see how far I was able to go . . . and yet terrible at the same time. Let's be real: *Nobody* likes to be the first runner-up.

9. Was there anyone you had avoided for years that you especially wanted to see after your transformation was complete?

   Yes! I have an acquaintance with whom I have been in competition my entire adult life. I don't think she was aware of this fact, but I definitely viewed her as my competition. Ironically, as soon as I got home from the show, she reached out to me, invited me to lunch, and celebrated my accomplishment with me. What a perfect model of grace.

10. Do you still count your calories?

    Oh yes. I don't necessarily write them all down, but I'm an absolute calorie freak. Really. It drives my friends nuts. I can tell you how many calories are in almost any food, or at least guess within twenty or thirty of being right. For instance, did you know that instead of suffering through a skinny grande latte you can order a tall full-strength, full-flavored mocha for only thirty calories more? Handy tips like this help me stick to my daily total . . . without sacrificing taste.

11. What is an average workout like for you?

Painful! And, more specifically, it involves sixty to ninety minutes of cardio (70 percent), and resistance training (30 percent), *at least* five days a week.

12. Could you have accomplished your weight-loss goal without having been on the show?

In retrospect I could have. I just don't think I *would* have. It would have been a far longer, harder process, but in the end I know that the real need I had was changing my mindset, not changing my weight. And that work was mine alone to do.

13. Did you mind forfeiting your privacy while shooting the show? Weren't there cameras everywhere?

I'm not a very private person to begin with, so for me the individual interviews were a blast and the adrenaline rush of knowing that cameras were constantly rolling actually helped me to push myself harder than I would have if I'd been all by myself. Still, eventually it got old, knowing that every blessed word I said was going to be typed up and saved somewhere.

14. How hard was it to leave your husband and son while you were on the show?

Oh man. I cried on the plane to LA. I cried the whole time I was in LA. Cry, cry, cry. When the last image you have of your son is of him kissing a photograph of you because his little heart is being ripped out by your departure . . . well, that's a special kind of torture. And don't get me started about missing Mike.

15. Would you do it all again?

I would. Knowing what I know now, I would. I will have a different life from here on out, and I wouldn't trade that for the world.

16. Do you think you are beautiful now?

    Some days.

17. Do you still see yourself as fat?

    Some days.

18. Was there a particular passage of Scripture that ministered to you while you were on the show?

    Absolutely. Jeremiah 29:11 was a gift to me every week I was away. "I know the plans I have for you, declares the Lord," it says, "plans to prosper you and not to harm you, plans to give you hope and a future." The verse in Psalms that says, "I praise you because I am fearfully and wonderfully made"—that one was powerful for me. And of course the Psalm about God's thoughts toward me outnumbering even the grains of sand. I stood on those truths every day.

19. How did you really feel about your other castmates?

    I loved them during the show, and I love them now. The casting staff did a great job with our season because, while we all had our individual idiosyncrasies, we meshed together incredibly well. There is not a single castmate from Season 4 that I could bump into and *not* hug their necks. They are great, great people.

20. How much of what we see on "reality TV" is real?

    All of it. Well, at least the first take of all of it.

21. Were you fairly depicted on TV, or did the show's producers edit you to fit a particular role?

    I was fairly depicted, as is every player on *every* season. The show's executive producer once told us that if we saw our season air and thought we came across looking like a mean-spirited person, it's because we *are* mean-spirited. "We can't make that stuff up," he said. For example, I was initially cast as the "ex-pageant queen," but that's not at all how I come across. Very quickly the production staff shifted gears to begin referring to me as the "stay-at-home mom who wanted to make her husband proud."

22. Did you "water load?"

    Are you kidding me? I *wish* I had! No, I absolutely did not water load. Who knows, if I'd caved on that front, maybe I would have won.

23. As the smallest contestant, do you find it amazing that you ended up achieving one of the largest percentages of weight loss?

    Yeah, I do! Like Jillian said, my success proved that the question is not, "Why me?," but rather, "Why *not* me?"

24. Do you believe that the at-home contestants truly can compete with those who stay on *The Biggest Loser* campus and make it into the finals?

    Hello, did you see Jim's success? He was a contestant on my season who got booted in week five and then came back to the finale with an incredible weight-loss percentage. He is a husband, a dad and a cop who coaches lacrosse and yet still found time to work out for four hours a day. He *can't* be human. But he is proof that you can do whatever you determine to do, if you remain committed to your own cause.

25. How much of the show is "the game" and how much is people really wanting to lose weight and change their lives?

    I would say that the first 80 percent of the show revolves around people wanting to change their lives, and the last 20 percent revolves around gamesmanship. Nobody gets to campus thinking, "I'm gonna win this thing!" I know people say that for the cameras, but they don't truly believe that it can happen. They're not even sure they'll live through week one, so the thought of actually *winning*? It just doesn't cross their minds. (Ask me how I know.) It's not until later in the game, when you're left standing, that you think, "Holy cow! I could seriously take home the title!"

26. What was your true motivation for wanting to be on *The Biggest Loser?*

    There are so many reasons, but if I were to sum it up I'd say my motivation was to live in a body that I had dreamed about but had never truly seen.

27. How many people auditioned for your season of the show?

   You'd have to Google it, but from what I heard, more than 250,000 people submitted videos for casting-staff consideration. I think now it's up to half a million or more each season, which wouldn't surprise me, given the show's popularity.

28. What do you mean when you say that, "Jillian Michaels changed your life forever"?

   Just meeting Jillian provided proof that a woman can be anything she chooses to be. Without even saying a word, Jillian represented everything that I wanted in life but did not have—health, confidence, strength and resilience. There are a *million* ways she has changed my life, and I'll be forever grateful for that.

29. Many women suffer from the condition of polycystic ovary syndrome (PCOS) like you do. How much did that condition affect your ability to lose weight? Can it be overcome?

   Weight-loss is harder and slower for those with PCOS, but it's still possible. Because of that condition, I am insulin resistant, so literally my body was fighting against me while I worked to lose my weight. But I am living proof that even with a condition like PCOS, a woman can reach her goals.

30. What does your daily diet look like now?

   I actually eat breakfast now, so that's a start. Typically for breakfast I have turkey bacon or egg whites with cilantro, a slice of Ezekiel bread and a cup of coffee, which I never used to drink before *The Biggest Loser*. For lunch I'll have a salad or a pita sandwich, and dinner usually consists of a grilled chicken breast and veggies. A handful of almonds or a piece of fruit make a great midday snack. It ain't rocket science . . .

31. Did you have trouble acclimating to "real life" after the show?

   Yes—that's the short answer. For more detail, see chapter 8, *This Is Me Now.*

32. How much did your participation in *The Biggest Loser* affect your ability to adopt a child so quickly?

The only effect from being on the show was that Mike and I had the discretionary funds to adopt in the first place—a huge, huge blessing for us.

33. How is your parenting approach different now from how you parented before the show?

I no longer sweat the small stuff. As I type this, it's two o'clock in the afternoon, and empty milk cartons from breakfast still litter the kitchen counter; four loads of clean laundry still sit, unfolded, at my feet; and in the last ten minutes my son Jaxon has pulled out every single Tupperware container from the pantry and every plastic utensil from underneath the sink. If this were an audio book you'd hear him banging the doorstop that he somehow unscrewed from the baseboard against the lid to a stainless-steel pan, which is making the loveliest *clang-clang-clang* sound. It's a combined effect that would have sent me over the edge before *The Biggest Loser.* But it's interesting what a few months away from your family can do. I now appreciate every single moment for what it is—another place in time when I can be with the ones I love most.

34. In what ways has your relationship with God changed?

Before the show I knew a lot *about* God. Now I sense that I know *him.*

35. One of the promos identified you as "A wife who wants to make her husband proud . . ." Do you think you make your husband proud now? Was he not proud of you when you were obese?

Mike has always been proud of me, but now I'm actually proud of me too. And a woman who has healthy self-esteem makes for a man who can barely contain his pride.

36. What was it like the first time you walked into Mike's office after hiding from there for five years?

If I had to choose one adjective to describe how I felt when I finally stepped back into Mike's office, it would be this: EMBARRASSED.

I had projected onto those people my own insecurities, and when I reentered their lives I felt ashamed. They were so gracious and lovely. "We're so sorry that you thought we wouldn't welcome you!" they said. How embarrassing. I had outed them on national TV and had been proven patently wrong.

37. Did your weight loss influence your husband's weight?

Yes. Once he remembered that during *every* season of the show producers let contestants come home to see their families, he had a genuine "Oh no!" moment. He dropped nearly thirty pounds before my home visit, but he did it in all the wrong ways and for all the wrong reasons. These days he's not quite as obsessive about healthful eating as am I, but he's come around pretty well. (He still detests Ezekiel bread, saying "it tastes like cardboard," while I, on the other hand, would eat dehydrated bugs if Jillian called and told me I should.)

38. What do you do for recreation now?

Sleep. No, I'm just kidding. While I hated being outside before the show, I can't get through a day *without* being outside now. It represents to me a world I'd never known. My boys and I play in the park, we race, we jump rope—whatever it takes to enjoy fresh air and sunshine.

39. You seem so natural speaking about this life-changing experience. Do you love talking about it?

I do. In fact, although my family members will roll their eyes every time, I can tell the same stories over and over again. The other night Mike and I were at dinner at his mom's house. She had invited some friends over, who happened to be big-time *The Biggest Loser* fans. The husband pelted me with questions until his wife said, "Honey, leave her alone! She's probably exhausted from all these questions," but I loved every minute of it!

40. Do people recognize you when you go out in public?

Yes. It's fun. And annoying. And yet still somehow fun.

41. Did you enjoy your time living in LA?

I did! I was always the kid who wanted summer camp to last just one more week. I didn't go away for college or anything, so there is a spirit of adventure in me that has never really been satisfied. Out of all of the Season 4 contestants I'm probably the one who feels most strongly about having a monthly reunion. "Come on, guys!" I cheer, "don'tcha miss me yet?"

42. What are you the most thankful for?

I'm most thankful for second chances.

43. Who, or what, inspires you?

(I know I'm supposed to be concentrating intently on this meaningful, in-depth question, but it's more than a little difficult with my own miniature Ringo Starr playing his pots and pans in the background!) Okay. Who or what inspires me. Let's see . . .

Actually, the people who inspire me most are the ones who are able to do what I myself never seemed able to do—namely, lose weight and live their best life without the help of a four-month getaway, a personal trainer, a nutritional education and a group of people surrounding them who would hold them accountable to their goals. *Those* people make me proud. They make me want to work even harder to keep walking this road that I'm on.

44. What is your favorite exercise?

I don't know that I can answer that with any credibility whatsoever. I'm devoted to this lifestyle, but to use the term "favorite" and the term "exercise" in the same sentence? Fishy.

Now, if someone could come up with a way to make the atrocious "mountain climbers" (see page 199) somehow involve a piece of chocolate cake at the end, *that* would be a good exercise.

45. Who is your favorite *The Biggest Loser* contestant and why?
No shocker here: Season 2's Suzy Preston. I actually know her now, and she is *still* my favorite.

46. Did you think you'd win your season?

    Heck, yeah! Well, okay, to be fair, I didn't think I'd win at the beginning. But after I survived the first few beatings from my beloved Jillian, yes, even I believed I could win.

47. What are the foods you're still tempted to eat?

    I'm from the South, where things like hush puppies and corn muffins abound. And man, are they good. My biggest food temptations are still pizza and chocolate cake—well, *anything* chocolate, as it turns out.

48. What can you do now that you used to not be able to do?

    You name it! I can outrun an eight-year-old. I can hula-hoop. I can carry in the groceries without stopping to take a break. I can exercise for ninety minutes without needing a four-hour nap afterward. I can do everything I need to do in a day without utterly falling apart. Wow. That last one could bring me to tears.

    I can sleep *soundly* at night. What a gift.

49. Would you ever consider writing a book?

    Hmm . . . I guess the answer's yes.

NOTES

1. Proverbs 31:30–31, MSG.
2. Genesis 1:26, John 10:10 and John 15:11.
3. www.goodreads.com/author/quotes/3503.Maya_Angelou?page=3.
4. www.quotesdaddy.com/quote/263494/william-shakespeare/to-climb-steep-hills-requires-slow-pace-at-first.
5. Esther 4:16.
6. One of the coolest aspects of being on *The Biggest Loser* was that we were given great resources to help us achieve our goals. In addition to Jillian's books, I remember being given a copy of Devin Alexander's *The Biggest Loser Cookbook*, as well as a small-form *The Biggest Loser Complete Calorie Counter*. Helpful reads still to this day.
7. Matthew 17:20.
8. Ephesians 3:20.
9. Casting Crowns, "Stained Glass Masquerade" from *Lifesong* album. Reunion Records, 2005.
10. Luke 19:40.
11. "Gloria" by Watermark. © Rocketown Music, Sweater Weather Music, Word Music LLC.
12. Ibid.
13. Julia Indichova, *Inconceivable*. Broadway Books, 1997, page 57.
14. "On the Right Path." As printed in *Living Choices* magazine, a publication of Women's Resource Center of Jacksonville, Volume 1, Issue 1, January 2009, page 8.
15. Ibid.
16. Ibid.
17. Julie Hadden, "All I Needed to Know about Life I Learned from My One-Year-Old." Originally published at www.guideposts.com, 14 January 2009.
18. "The Real Me," written by Something Distant; produced by Lu Rubino.
19. Max Lucado, *You Are Special*. Crossway Books, 1997, page 19.
20. Ibid, page 23.
21. Ibid, page 25.
22. Julie Hadden, "Worth the Weight." *Guideposts* magazine, January 2009, page 45.
23. Beijing 2008 Humanity Archives, http://en.beijing2008.cn/29/16/article212011629.shtml. Home > Road to 2008 > Education > Humanity > John Stephen Akhwari.

24. Marianne Williamson, from *A Return to Love: Reflections on the Principles of a Course in Miracles*. HarperCollins, 1992.
25. Ephesians 1:11–12, MSG. Emphasis added.
26. Luke 15:24.
27. For more information on how you can help abolish human trafficking, visit www.thea21campaign.org.
28. See http://americanheart.org/presenter.jhtml?identifier=4735.
29. Nutritional values that are provided with each recipe are estimates and can vary depending on brands you choose. All information provided by Calorie King (calorieking.com).
30. Instead of using cooking spray in recipes that call for it, fill an ordinary plastic spray-bottle with extra-virgin olive oil and spritz that instead.
31. Taken from information found at www.foodreference.com/html/artokra.html.

CONTACTING JULIE

For more information on Julie Hadden or to contact her directly, please visit her at juliehadden.com.

(Continued from page IV)

Acknowledgments

All Scripture quotations, unless otherwise noted, are taken from *The Holy Bible, New International Version*. Copyright © 1973, 1978, 1984 International Bible Society. Used by permission of Zondervan Bible Publishers.

Scripture quotation on page 31 is taken from *The Message*. Copyright © 1993, 1994, 1995, 1996, 2000, 2001, 2002 by Eugene H. Peterson.

Lyrics on page x are from "From the Inside Out." Words and music by Joel Houston. Copyright © 2005 Joel Houston and Hillsong Publishing (admin. in the United States and Canada by Integrity Worship Music/ASCAP) c/o Integrity Media, Inc., 1000 Cody Road, Mobile, AL 36695. All rights reserved. International copyright secured. Used by permission.

Lyrics on pages 89–90 are from "Believe." Words and music by Kara DioGuardi and Marti Frederikson. Copyright © 2008 Bug Music Inc. (BMI). All rights reserved. Used by permission.

Lyrics on pages 98–99 are from "Made Me Glad." Words and music by Miriam Webster. Copyright © 2001 Miriam Webster and Hillsong Publishing (admin. in the United States and Canada by Integrity Worship Music/ASCAP) c/o Integrity Media, Inc., 1000 Cody Road, Mobile, AL 36695. All rights reserved. International copyright secured. Used by permission.

Lyrics on page 107 are from "Stained Glass Masquerade" written by Mark Hall and Nichole Nordeman. Copyright © 2005 Birdwing Music (ASCAP) Club Zoo Music (BMI) SWECS Music (BMI) Birdboy Songs (ASCAP) My Refuge Music (BMI) (adm. by EMI CMG Publishing). All rights reserved. Used by permission.

Lyrics on pages 108–109 are from "Gloria" Christy Nockels/Nathan Nockels. © 1997 Sweater Weather Music (Admin. by Word Music, LLC), Rocketown Music, LLC (Admin. by Word Music, LLC), Word Music, LLC. All rights reserved. Used by permission.

Lyrics on page 109 are from "He'll Find a Way" written by Donna Douglas. Copyright © 1987 C.A. Music (div. of C.A. Records, Inc.). All rights reserved. ASCAP. Used by permission.

Lyrics on page 154 are from "The Real Me." Copyright © 2008 Something Distant Music. Used by permission.